T0125971

Butterflies OF GEORGIA

FIELD GUIDE

by Jaret C. Daniels

Adventure Publications, Inc.
Cambridge, MN

WATCHING BUTTERFLIES IN GEORGIA

People are rapidly discovering the joy of butterfly gardening and watching. Both are simple, fun and rewarding ways to explore the natural world and bring the beauty of nature closer. Few other forms of wildlife are more attractive or as easy to observe as butterflies. Butterflies occur just about everywhere. They can be found from suburban gardens and urban parks to rural meadows and remote natural areas. Regardless of where you may live, there are a variety of butterflies to be seen. *Butterflies of Georgia Field Guide* is for those who wish to identify and learn more about the many different butterflies found in Georgia.

There are more than 725 species of butterflies in North America north of Mexico. While the majority of these are regular breeding residents, others show up from time to time as rare tropical strays. In Georgia, over 160 different butterflies have been recorded. Within that mix, there are widespread representatives that occur commonly over a large portion of the continent and others that are rare or limited to only a few localized areas. Although such numbers pale in comparison to many tropical countries, Georgia boasts a rich and diverse butterfly fauna. To aid in that exploration, this field guide covers all resident, visitor and stray species recorded within the state.

The breathtaking scenic beauty and many diverse natural environments of Georgia make it a premier vacation destination as well as a great place to observe and enjoy butterflies. But neither the state's lush mountain forests nor the sun-drenched coastline account for the abundant butterfly life. Georgia's rich fauna is directly related to elevation, climate and geography. Totaling over 59,000 square miles, it is the 24th largest state in the U.S. and contains three main physiographic regions. Knifing into the northwestern portion of the state are the Appalachian Mountains. This mountainous region, which includes Brasstown Bald, the state's highest peak at 4,784 feet, is dominated by mixed Mesophytic (moderately moist) forest, the most diverse plant community in the Southeast. Here, four well-defined seasons exist. Although cooled somewhat by changes in elevation, summers tend to be warm. Winters are cool with occasional accumulations of snow and extended periods of subfreezing temperatures. As a result, a variety of more typical northern species such as the Great Spangled Fritillary, Green Comma and Hickory Hairstreak can be found.

Further to the south is the Piedmont. This central region, also known as the Piedmont Plateau, is characterized by gently rolling foothills with an assortment of rivers, lakes, old fields, agricultural land and woodlands that comprise a diverse assortment of natural communities. Here, four distinct seasons are still the rule. Shielded by the western mountains from cold interior air and tempered by the warm Atlantic to the east, year-round temperatures are generally more moderate.

Continuing southward toward the sea is the Atlantic Coastal Plain. This primarily flat region occupies much of the southern half of the state and includes a unique assortment of natural communities from longleaf pine savanna and bottomland swamp forest to saltwater marshes and maritime forest. Blessed with abundant sunshine and low elevation, and warmed by the nearby waters of the Atlantic and Gulf of Mexico, the climate is considered subtropical. Here summers tend to be long, hot and humid. In contrast, winters are short and very mild with only brief periods of freezing temperatures. As a result, many more tropical representatives such as the Zebra Longwing, Ceraunus Blue and Brazilian Skipper annually extend their ranges northward into the region to establish temporary breeding colonies.

For butterfly enthusiasts, Georgia has much to offer. From the mountainous northwestern corner to the coastal southeastern tip, you can pass through a rich assortment of natural communities and encounter a diverse butterfly fauna that includes species typical of northern forests or even tropical Florida. What more could you ask!

WHAT ARE BUTTERFLIES?

Butterflies are insects. Along with moths, they comprise the Order Lepidoptera, a combination of Greek words meaning scale-winged, and can be differentiated from all other insects on that basis. Their four wings, as well as body, are typically almost entirely covered with numerous tiny scales. Overlapping like shingles on a roof, they make up the color and pattern of a butterfly's wings. Although generally wide and flat, some scales may be modified in shape, depending on the species and body location.

Butterflies and moths are closely related and often difficult to quickly tell apart. Nonetheless, there are some basic differences that are easy to identify even in the field. Generally, butterflies fly during the day, have large colorful wings that are held vertically together over the back when at rest, and bear distinctly clubbed antennae. In contrast, most moths are nocturnal. They are usually overall drabber in color and may often resemble dirty, hairy butterflies. At rest, they tend to hold their wings to the sides, and have feathery or threadlike antennae.

The following illustration points out the basic parts of a butterfly.

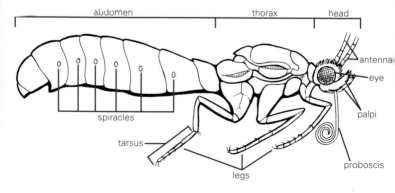

BUTTERFLY BASICS

Adult butterflies share several common characteristics, including six jointed legs, two compound eyes, two antennae, a hard exoskeleton and three main body segments: the head, thorax and abdomen.

Head

The head has two large compound eyes, two long clubbed antennae, a proboscis and two labial palpi. The rounded compound eyes are composed of hundreds of tiny individually lensed eyes. Together, they render a single, somewhat pixelated color image. Adult butterflies have good vision and are able to distinguish light in both the visible and ultraviolet range. Above the eyes are two long and slender antennae that are clubbed at the tip. They bear various sensory structures that help with orientation and smell. At the front of the head, below the eyes, are two protruding, hairy, brush-like structures called labial palpi. They serve to house and protect the proboscis, or tongue. The proboscis is a long, flexible, straw-like structure used for drinking fluids. It can be tightly coiled below the head or extended when feeding. The length of a butterfly's proboscis determines the types of flowers and other foods from which it may feed.

Thorax

Directly behind the head is the thorax. It is a large muscular portion divided into three segments that bear six legs and four wings. Each leg is jointed and contains five separate sections, the last of which is the tarsus (pl. tarsi) or foot, which bears a tiny, hooked claw at the end. In addition to enabling the butterfly to securely grasp leaves, branches or other objects, the tarsi have sensory structures that are used to taste. Adult females scratch a leaf surface with their front tarsi to release the leaf's chemicals and taste whether they have found the correct host plant. Above the legs are two pairs of wings. Made up of two thin membranes supported by rigid veins, the generally large, colorful wings are covered with millions of tiny scales that overlap like shingles on a roof. The wings serve a variety of critical functions, including flight, thermoregulation, sex recognition, camouflage, mimicry and predator deflection.

Abdomen

The last section of a butterfly's body is the long, slender abdomen. It is comprised of ten segments and contains the reproductive, digestive and excretory systems along with a series of small lateral holes, called spiracles, for air exchange. The reproductive organs or genitalia are located at the end of the abdomen. Male butterflies have two modified structures called claspers that are used to grasp the female during copulation. Females possess a genital opening for mating and a second opening for egg laying. While these structures are often difficult to see in certain species, females generally have a much larger, "fatter-looking" abdomen because they carry a large complement of eggs.

THE BUTTERFLY LIFE CYCLE

All butterflies pass through a life cycle consisting of four developmental stages: egg, larva, pupa and adult. Regardless of adult size, they begin life as a small egg. A female butterfly may lay her eggs singly, in small clusters or in large groupings on or near the appropriate host plant. Once an egg hatches, the tiny larva begins feeding almost immediately. Butterfly larvae are herbivores—with the exception of Harvester larvae, which eat aphids—and they essentially live to eat. As a result, they can grow at an astonishing rate. All insects including butterflies have an external skeleton. In order to grow, a developing caterpillar (or larva) must shed its skin, or molt, several times during its life. Each time the larva does, it discards its old, tight skin to make room for the new, roomier and often different-looking skin underneath. These different stages in a caterpillar's growth are called instars. Once fully grown, the larva stops eating and seeks a safe place to pupate. It usually attaches itself to a branch, twig or other surface with silk and molts for the last time to reveal the pupa (or chrysalis). Inside, the larval structures are broken down and reorganized into the form of an adult butterfly. At the appropriate time, the pupa splits open and a beautiful new butterfly emerges. The adult hangs quietly and begins to expand its crumpled wings by slowly forcing blood through the veins. After a few hours, its wings are fully hardened and the butterfly is ready to fly.

BUTTERFLY FAMILIES

Butterflies can be divided into five major families: Hesperiidae, Lycaenidae, Nymphalidae, Papilionidae and Pieridae. The members of each family have certain basic characteristics and behaviors that can be particularly useful for identification. Keep in mind that the features listed are only generalities, not hard and fast rules, and that there may be individual exceptions.

Hesperiidae: Skippers

Skippers are small- to medium-sized butterflies with robust, hairy bodies and relatively compact wings. They are generally brown, orange or white and their antennae bear short, distinct hooks at the tip. Adults have a quick and erratic flight, usually low to the ground. There are three main subfamilies: banded skippers, giant-skippers and spread-wing skippers.

Banded skippers (Subfamily Hesperiinae) are small brown or orange butterflies with somewhat pointed forewings. Many have dark markings or distinct black forewing stigmas. They readily visit flowers and hold their wings together over the back while feeding. Adults often perch or rest in a characteristic posture with forewings held partially open and hindwings separated and lowered further.

As their name suggests, **giant-skippers** (Subfamily Megathyminae) dwarf most other members of the family. They are medium-sized brown butterflies with yellow markings and thick, robust bodies. The adults have a fast and rapid flight. Males establish territories and generally perch on low vegetation. Adults do not visit flowers.

Spread-wing skippers (Subfamily Pyrginae) are generally dark, dull-colored butterflies with wide wings. Most have small, light spots on the forewings. Some species have hindwing tails. The adults often feed, rest and perch with their wings outstretched. They readily visit flowers.

Lycaenidae: Gossamer Wings

This diverse family includes coppers, harvesters, blues, hairstreaks and metalmarks. The adults are small and often brilliantly colored but easily overlooked. Within the family is the Georgia's smallest butterfly, the Eastern Pygmy-Blue. Throughout the state, blues and hairstreaks predominate, with harvesters, metalmarks and coppers represented by only one species each.

Coppers (Subfamily Lycaeninae) are small, sexually dimorphic butterflies. As their name suggests, the upper wing surfaces of most species are ornately colored with metallic reddish orange or purple. Many eastern species are associated with moist habitats including bogs, wet meadows and marshes. Populations are often quite localized but may be numerous when encountered. Adults typically scurry close to the ground with a quick flight and frequently visit available flowers or perch on low-growing vegetation with their wings held partially open.

The **harvester** (Subfamily Miletinae) is the only North American member of this unique, primarily Old World, subfamily. It is our only butterfly with carnivorous larvae. Instead of feeding on plants, the larvae devour woolly aphids. The adults do not visit flowers, but sip honeydew, a sugary secretion produced by their host aphids.

Aptly named, **blues** (Subfamily Polyommatinae) are generally bright blue on the wings above. The sexes differ and females may be brown or dark gray. The wings beneath are typically whitish gray with dark markings and distinct hindwing eyespots. The eyes are wrapped around the base of the antennae. The palpi are reduced and close to the head. Adults have a moderately quick and erratic flight, usually low to the ground. At rest, they hold their wings together over the back. Males frequently puddle at damp ground. Most blues are fond of open, disturbed sites with weedy vegetation.

Metalmarks (Subfamily Riodininae) are characterized by metallic flecks of color or even overall metallic-looking wings. They have eyes entirely separate from the antennal bases, and the palpi are quite prominent. Metalmarks reach tremendous diversity of colors and patterns in the tropics. By contrast, most U.S. species are small rust, gray or brownish butterflies. They characteristically perch with their colorful wings outstretched and may often land on the underside of leaves, especially when disturbed. Adults have a low, scurrying flight. Several species are of conservation concern.

Hairstreaks (Subfamily Theclinae) tend to be larger than blues. The wings below are often intricately patterned and bear colorful eyespots adjacent to one or two small, distinct, hair-like tails on each hindwing. The adults have a quick, erratic flight and can be a challenge to follow. They regularly visit flowers and hold their wings together over the back while feeding and at rest. Additionally, they have a unique behavior of moving their hindwings up and down when perched. The sexes regularly differ. Hairstreaks can be found in a wide range of habitats. Many species have a single spring generation.

Nymphalidae: Brush-Foots

Brush-foots are the largest and most diverse family of butterflies. In all members, the first pair of legs is significantly reduced and modified into small brush-like structures, giving the family its name and the appearance of only having four legs.

Emperors (Subfamily Apaturinae) are medium-sized and brownish with short, stubby bodies and a robust thorax. Their wings typically have dark markings and small dark eyespots. The adults are strong and rapid fliers. Males establish territories and perch on tree trunks or overhanging branches. At rest, they hold their wings together over the back. They feed on dung, carrion, rotting fruit or tree sap and do not visit flowers. Emperors inhabit rich woodlands and rarely venture far into open areas. They are nervous butterflies and difficult to closely approach.

Leafwings (Subfamily Charaxinae) are medium-sized butterflies with irregular wing margins. They are bright tawny orange above, but mottled gray to brown below and resemble a dead leaf when resting with their wings closed. The adults have a strong, rapid and erratic flight. They are nervous butterflies and difficult to closely approach. Males establish territories and perch on tree trunks or overhanging branches. Individuals also often land on the ground. They feed on dung, carrion, rotting fruit or tree sap and do not visit flowers.

Milkweed butterflies (Subfamily Danainae) are large butterflies with boldly marked black and orange wings. Their flight is strong and swift with periods of gliding. Adults are strongly attracted to flowers and feed with their wings folded tightly over the back. Males have noticeable black scent patches in the middle of each hindwing. This subfamily includes the Monarch, which undergoes massive long-distance migrations.

Longwing butterflies (Subfamily Heliconiinae) are colorful, medium-sized butterflies. They have narrow, elongated wings, slender bodies, long antennae and large eyes. Their flight tends to be slow and fluttering. The adults readily visit flowers and nectar with their wings open. Most tend to be long-lived. Within the group are fritillaries. They are medium-sized orange and black butterflies of open, sunny habitats. Those in the genus *Speyeria* have boldly patterned ventral hindwings with conspicuous metallic silver spots.

Snouts (Subfamily Libytheinae) are medium-sized, generally drab brown butterflies representing about ten species worldwide with only one found in the U.S. They have extremely elongated labial palpi and cryptically colored ventral hindwings. They rest with their wings tightly closed and resemble dead leaves.

Admirals (Subfamily Limenitidinae) are medium- to large-sized butterflies with broad, colorful wings. The adults fly with a series of quick wing beats followed by a brief period of gliding. They are typically associated with immature, secondary-growth woodlands or semi-open shrubby sites. Males perch on sunlit leaves or branches and make periodic exploratory flights. They will feed at flowers as well as rotting fruit, dung, carrion and tree sap.

True brush-foots (Subfamily Nymphalinae) are colorful, small- to medium-sized butterflies with no overall common wing shape. Most have stubby, compact bodies and a robust thorax. The adults have a strong, quick flight, usually low to the ground. Most are nervous and often difficult to approach. At rest, they hold their wings together over the back. Many are attracted to flowers while others feed on dung, carrion, rotting fruit or tree sap.

Satyrs and *wood nymphs* (Subfamily Satyrinae) are small- to medium-sized drab brown butterflies. Their wings are marked with dark stripes and prominent eyespots. The adults have a slow, somewhat bobbing flight usually low to the ground. They inhabit shady woodlands and adjacent open, grassy areas. The adults rarely visit flowers. They are instead attracted to dung, carrion, rotting fruit or tree sap. At rest, they hold their wings together over the back and are generally easy to closely approach. They regularly land on the ground.

Papilionidae: Swallowtails

Swallowtails are easily recognized by their large size and noticeably long hindwing tails. Within Georgia, only the Polydamas Swallowtail lacks tails. They are generally dark with bold markings. The adults have a swift and powerful flight, usually several meters off the ground, and regularly visit flowers. Most swallowtails continuously flutter their wings while feeding. Males often puddle at damp ground. They generally are found in and along woodland areas and adjacent open sites.

Pieridae: Sulphurs and Whites

Members of the family are small- to medium-sized butterflies. As their name suggests, the adults are typically some shade of white or yellow. Many have dark markings. Most species are sexually dimorphic and seasonally variable. The adults have a moderately quick and erratic flight, usually low to the ground. They are fond of flowers and hold their wings together over the back while feeding. Males often puddle at damp ground. *Sulphurs* (Subfamily Coliadinae) and *whites* (Subfamily Pierinae) are common butterflies of open, disturbed sites where their weedy larval host plants abound.

OBSERVING BUTTERFLIES IN THE FIELD

While butterflies are entertaining and beautiful to watch, correctly identifying them can often be a challenge. But it's generally not as difficult as it might seem. With a little practice and some basic guidelines, you can quickly learn to peg that unknown butterfly.

One of the first and most obvious things to note when you spot a butterfly is its size. You will discover that butterflies generally come in one of three basic dimensions: small, medium and large. This system may sound ridiculously arbitrary at first, but when you begin to regularly observe several different butterflies together in the field, these categories quickly start to make sense. For a starting point, follow this simple strategy: the next time you see a Monarch butterfly, pay close attention to its size. You may wish to use your hand as a reference. Most Monarchs have a wingspan close to the length of your palm (about four inches) as measured from the base of your fingers to the start of your wrist. This is considered a large butterfly. From here it's basically a matter of fractions. A medium-sized butterfly by comparison would have a wingspan of generally about half that size (about two inches). Finally, a butterfly would be considered small if it had a wingspan one quarter that of a Monarch (around one inch).

Next, pay close attention to color and pattern of the wings. This field guide is organized by color, and you can quickly navigate to the appropriate section. First, start by noting the overall ground color. Is it, for example, primarily black, yellow, orange or white? Then try to identify any major pattern elements such as distinct stripes, bands or spots. Depending on the behavior of the butterfly in the wild, keep in mind that the most visible portion of a butterfly may either be the upper surface of the wings (dorsal surface) or the underside (ventral surface). If you have a particularly cooperative subject, you may be able to closely observe both sides. Finally, carefully note the color and position of any major markings. For example, if the butterfly has a wide yellow band on the forewing, is it positioned in the middle of the wing or along the outer edge? Lepidopterists have a detailed vocabulary for wing pattern positions. The following illustrations of general wing features and wing areas should help you become familiar with some terminology.

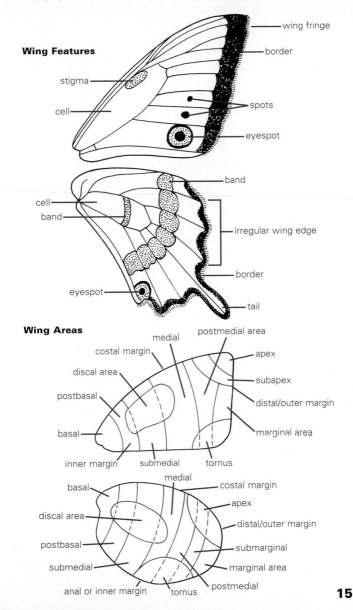

Wing Features

wing fringe
border
stigma
cell
spots
eyespot

band
cell
band
irregular wing edge
border
eyespot
tail

Wing Areas

postmedial area
medial
costal margin
apex
discal area
subapex
postbasal
distal/outer margin
basal
marginal area
inner margin
submedial
tornus

basal
medial
costal margin
apex
discal area
distal/outer margin
postbasal
submarginal
submedial
marginal area
anal or inner margin
tornus
postmedial

Next, note the shape of the butterfly's wings, particularly the forewings. Are they generally long and narrow, rounded, broad, pointed or angled? Butterflies such as the Gulf Fritillary and Zebra Longwing have noticeably elongated wings. Others, like the Carolina Satyr and Eastern Tailed-Blue, have short, generally rounded wings. Next, do the wings have any unique features? Many swallowtails and hairstreaks have distinct hindwing tails, while Question Marks and Eastern Commas have visibly irregular wing margins. Clues like this can help you quickly narrow the butterfly down to a particular family or distinguish it from a similarly colored species.

The way a butterfly flies may also be useful for identification. While it is generally difficult to easily pick up particular features or color patterns when a butterfly is moving, its flight pattern can often be very distinctive. Carefully follow the butterfly as it flies and watch how it behaves in the air. Is it soaring above your head or scurrying rapidly along the ground? Is it moving fast and erratically, or fluttering slowly about? Monarchs, for instance, have a very unique flight pattern. They flap their wings quickly several times, glide for bit, and then quickly flap their wings again. Other butterflies, such as most wood nymphs and satyrs, have a characteristic low, bobbing flight.

Sometimes you can gain important clues about a butterfly by the way it behaves when feeding. Next time you see a butterfly feeding, watch its wings. Does it hold them tightly closed, spread them wide open, or flutter them? Most swallowtails continuously flutter their wings. This behavior is a quick and reliable diagnostic that can be seen from a fair distance.

Note the habitat in which the butterfly occurs. Is it darting between branches along a shady and moist woodland path? Perched on the top of a grass blade in a saltwater marsh? Bobbing among low grasses in a wet prairie? Fluttering from one flower to the next in a fallow agricultural field? Many butterflies have strong habitat preferences. Some are restricted to a single particular habitat while others may occur in a wide range of habitats.

Sometimes even the date can offer a useful hint. Many hairstreaks are univoltine, meaning they produce just one generation. As a result, the adults occur only during a narrow window of time each spring. Similarly, several butterflies overwinter as adults. They may be active at times when few other species are around.

Butterfly observation and identification are skills, and it takes time and practice to master them. To speed up the learning curve, you may also wish to join a local butterfly gardening or watching club or society. The members can help give advice, accompany you in the field, or share directions to great butterfly watching spots.

DETERMINING A BUTTERFLY'S COLOR

To help make butterfly field identification fun and easy, this guide is organized by color, allowing you to quickly navigate to the appropriate section. In addition, smaller butterflies are always toward the beginning of each section, and the largest are toward the back. Butterflies are not static subjects, so determining their color can be a bit tricky. Several factors such as age, seasonal variation and complex wing and color patterns may affect your perception of a butterfly's color.

Age

Adult age can influence a butterfly's color. While butterflies don't get wrinkles or gray hairs, they do continue to lose wing scales during their life. This type of normal wing wear combined with more significant wing damage can cause once vibrant colors or iridescence to fade and pattern elements to become less distinct. As a result, the bright tawny orange wings of a freshly emerged Great Spangled Fritillary may appear dull orange or almost yellowish in an old, worn individual.

Seasonal Variation

Time of year can play a role as well. Some butterflies produce distinct seasonal forms that may vary significantly in color and to a lesser extent in wing shape or overall size. For the Sleepy Orange, the change is dramatic. Individuals produced during the summer are bright butter yellow on the wings below. Winter-forms, by contrast, have dark rust-colored ventral hindwings perfect for blending into a predominantly brown fall and winter landscape. For species that display extensive seasonal variation, the differences are discussed and every attempt is made to include an image of both forms. Since you'll probably be looking for butterflies in the warmer months, pictures of winter-forms are insets and not main images.

Complex Wing and Color Patterns

For many butterflies, wing color and pattern can vary tremendously between the dorsal and ventral surface. The wings of a Great Purple Hairstreak are brilliant iridescent blue above and dull black below. The bright dorsal coloration is readily visible during flight but concealed at rest when the hairstreak holds its wings firmly closed. As a result, the butterfly may appear either blue or black depending on your perspective and the butterfly's activity.

Most hairstreaks (subfamily Theclinae) and sulphurs (subfamily Coliadinae) typically feed and rest with their wings closed. As a result, very few photographs of the dorsal wing surface of free-flying butterflies in these groups exist. Similarly, most blues (subfamily Polyommatinae) perch and feed with their wings closed or hold them only partially open when basking. Many of these same butterflies are also two-toned (blue on the dorsal surface, but whitish to grubby gray below; or orange on the dorsal surface, but much yellower below). But because a large number of these butterflies are so small, chances are that you'll notice them first when they fly and reveal their brighter dorsal coloration. Two-toned butterflies such as these have been placed in the color section that reflects the brighter coloration that you're most likely to notice first.

For example, if you're looking in the white section for a small butterfly with lots of bands and spots on the ventral surface, but can't find it, try the blue section. You might be looking at a perched Spring Azure, which is bright blue above but a rather nondescript brownish gray white below.

Color can vary slightly even among butterflies of the same

species. If you see a butterfly that appears to be tawny colored, but you can't find it in the orange section, try the brown section. You might be looking at a Tawny Emperor, which can be perceived as orange or brown, depending on the individual.

Finally, females are generally more drab than males of the same species. They can have less iridescent color, fewer or darker markings, and can appear overall darker or paler. For some species, such as the Diana Fritillary and Eastern Tailed-Blue, the females and males look very different and are pictured in separate color sections.

COLOR SECTION TROUBLESHOOTING

With all the variables that can impact the perception of a butterfly's color, identifying these creatures may seem daunting. Taking the time to check a color section or two is worth being able to positively identify a mystery butterfly.

Can't find it in...   Try looking in...

Black   Brown
In certain conditions, some of the dark brown butterflies, especially swallowtails and skippers, might appear black

Blue   Blue or Black
Blues (subfamily Polyommatinae) often rest or feed with their wings closed, so the blue dorsal coloration is visible primarily during flight or when the individual is basking. Check the illustration and description for field marks. Some black butterflies have varying amounts of iridescent blue scales; they may look blue in certain conditions.

Brown   Orange
Many butterflies described as tawny can be perceived as either brown or orange.

Gray   Brown
Many of the Hairstreaks (subfamily Theclinae) have light colored ventral wings that can vary in the amount of gray or brown they show.

Green   White
Some of the female Sulphurs (subfamily Coliadinae) have a common white form that may appear to be greenish.

Orange   Brown

Many of the skippers are brown but have bright orange field marks. Other butterflies are tawny colored, so could be perceived as either brown or orange.

White   Blue

Blues (subfamily Polyommatinae) perch with their wings closed, so appear to be white butterflies.

Yellow   Orange

Some of the Sulphurs (subfamily Coliadinae) have bright orange dorsal wings.

BUTTERFLY GARDENING

One of the easiest ways to observe local butterflies is to plant a butterfly garden. Even a small area can attract a great variety of species directly to your yard. For best results, include both adult nectar sources and larval host plants. Most adult butterflies are generalists and will visit a broad range of colorful flowers in search of nectar. Developing larvae, on the other hand, typically have very discriminating tastes and often rely on only a few very specific plant species for food. For assistance with starting a butterfly garden, seek the guidance of local nursery professionals. They can help you determine which plants will grow well in your area. This field guide provides a list of larval host plants for each species, as well as a listing of good nectar plants. These lists begin on page 396.

BUTTERFLY Q & A:
What's the difference between a butterfly and a moth?

While there is no one simple answer to this question, butterflies and moths generally differ based on their overall habits and structure. Butterflies are typically active during the day (diurnal), while moths predominantly fly at night (nocturnal). Butterflies possess slender antennae that are clubbed at the end. Those of moths vary from long narrow filaments to broad fern-like structures. At rest, butterflies tend to hold their wings together vertically over the back. Moths rest with their wings extended flat out to the sides or folded alongside the body. Butterflies generally have long, smooth and slender bodies. The bodies of moths are often robust and hairy. Finally, most butterflies are typically brightly colored, while most moths tend to be dark and somewhat drab.

What can butterflies see?

Butterflies are believed to have very good vision and to see a single color image. Compared to humans, they have an expanded range of sensitivity and are able to distinguish wavelengths of light into the ultraviolet range.

Do butterflies look the same year-round?

Many butterflies produce distinct seasonal forms that differ markedly in color, size, reproductive activity and behavior. Good examples within Georgia include the Common Buckeye, Barred Sulphur and Sleepy Orange. The seasonal forms are determined by the environmental cues (temperature, rainfall, day length) that immature stages experience during development. Warm summer temperatures and long days forecast conditions that are highly favorable for continued development and reproduction. Summer-form individuals are generally lighter in color, short-lived, and reproductively active. As fall approaches, cooler temperatures and shortening day lengths mean future conditions may be unfavorable for continued development and reproduction. Winter-form adults display increased pattern elements, are generally darker, larger, longer lived, and survive the winter months in a state of reproductive diapause.

Do caterpillars have eyes?

Yes, caterpillars or larvae generally have six pairs of simple eyes called ocelli. They are able to distinguish basic changes in light intensity but are believed to be incapable of forming an image.

How do caterpillars defend themselves?

Caterpillars or larvae are generally plump, slow moving creatures that represent an inviting meal for many predators. To protect themselves, caterpillars employ a variety of different strategies. Many, like the Zebra Longwing or Pipevine Swallowtail, sequester specific chemicals from their host plants that render them highly distasteful or toxic. These caterpillars are generally brightly colored to advertise their unpalatability. Others rely on deception or camouflage to avoid being eaten. Palamedes Swallowtail larvae have large, conspicuous false eyes on an enlarged thorax that help them resemble a small snake or lizard. By contrast, larvae of the Georgia Satyr are solid green and extremely well camouflaged against the green leaves of their host. Some larvae conceal their whereabouts by constructing shelters. American Painted Lady larvae weave leaves and flowerheads together with silk and rest safely inside when not actively feeding. Still others have formidable spines and hairs or produce irritating or foul-smelling chemicals to deter persistent predators.

Do butterfly caterpillars make silk?

Yes, butterfly larvae produce silk. While they don't typically spin an elaborate cocoon around their pupa like moths, they use silk for a variety of purposes, including the construction of shelters, anchoring or attaching their chrysalides, and to gain secure footing on leaves and branches.

What happens when a butterfly's scales rub off?

Contrary to the old wives' tale, if you touch a butterfly's

wing and remove scales in the process it is still capable of flying. In fact, a butterfly typically continuously loses scales during its life from normal wing wear. Scales serve a variety of purposes, from thermoregulation and camouflage to pheromone dispersal and species or sex recognition, but are not critical for flight. Once gone, the scales are permanently lost and will not grow back.

Why do butterflies gather at mud puddles?

Adult butterflies are often attracted to damp or moist ground and may congregate at such areas in large numbers. In most cases, these groupings, or "puddle clubs," are made up entirely of males. They drink from the moisture to gain water and salts (sodium ions) that happen to come into solution. This behavior helps males replenish the sodium ions lost when they pass a packet of sperm and accessory gland secretions to the female during copulation. The transferred nutrients have been shown to play a significant role in egg production and, thus, female reproductive output.

How long do butterflies live?

In general, most butterflies are extremely short-lived and survive in the wild for an average of about two weeks. There are, of course, numerous exceptions to this rule. The Zebra Longwing is a perfect example. Adults may survive for 4–6 months. Still others, particularly species that migrate long distances and/or overwinter as adults, are capable of surviving for extended periods of time.

Where do butterflies go at night?
Where do they go during a rainstorm?

In the evening or during periods of inclement weather, most butterflies seek shelter under the leaves of growing plants or among vegetation.

Do all butterflies visit flowers?

All butterflies are fluid feeders. While a large percentage of them rely on sugar-rich nectar as the primary energy source for flight, reproduction and general maintenance, many species also feed on, or exclusively utilize, the liquids and dissolved nutrients produced by other food resources such as dung, carrion, rotting fruit or vegetation, sap and bird droppings.

Do butterflies grow?

No. An adult butterfly is fully grown upon emergence from its chrysalis.

How do caterpillars grow?

A caterpillar's job in life is to eat and grow. But larvae, like all other insects, have an external skeleton. Therefore, in order to increase in size, they must shed their skin, or molt, several times during development. Essentially, their skin is like a trash bag. It is packed full of food until there is no more room. Once full, it is discarded for a larger, baggier one underneath and the process continues.

What eats butterflies?

Butterflies face an uphill battle for survival. Out of every one hundred eggs produced by a female butterfly, approximately only one percent survive to become an adult. And as an adult, the odds don't get much better. Various birds, small mammals, lizards, frogs, toads, spiders and other insects all prey on butterflies.

What's the difference between a chrysalis and a cocoon?

Once fully grown, both moth and butterfly caterpillars molt a final time to form a pupa. Most moths surround their pupae with a constructed silken case called a cocoon. By contrast, a butterfly pupa, frequently termed a chrysalis, is generally naked. In most cases, butterfly chrysalides are attached to a leaf, twig or other surface with silk. In some instances, they may be unattached or surrounded by a loose silken cocoon.

Are all butterfly scales the same?

No. The scales on a butterfly's wings and body come in a variety of different sizes and shapes. Some may be extremely elongated and resemble hairs while others are highly modified for the release of pheromones during courtship. Those responsible for making up wing color and pattern are generally wide and flat. They are attached at the base and overlap like shingles on a roof. The colors we see are the result of either pigments contained in the scales or the diffraction of light caused by scale structure. Iridescent colors such as blue, green, purple and silver usually result from scale structure. While pigmented scales are the norm, many species have a combination of both types on their wings.

BUTTERFLY QUICK-COMPARE

Common Sootywing pg. 43	**Great Purple Hairstreak** pg. 45	**Texan Crescent** pg. 47
Red Admiral pg. 49	**Baltimore Checkerspot** pg. 51	**Zebra Longwing** pg. 53
Red-spotted Purple pg. 55	**Zebra Swallowtail** pg. 57	**Black Swallowtail** pg. 59
Pipevine Swallowtail pg. 61	**Mourning Cloak** pg. 63	**Diana Fritillary** pg. 65

Spicebush Swallowtail
pg. 67

Eastern Tiger Swallowtail
pg. 69

Palamedes Swallowtail
pg. 71

Polydamas Swallowtail
pg. 73

Cassius Blue
pg. 75

Ceraunus Blue
pg. 77

Eastern Tailed-Blue
pg. 79

Spring Azure
pg. 81

Summer Azure
pg. 83

Silvery Blue
pg. 85

Appalachian Azure
pg. 87

White M Hairstreak
pg. 89

Great Purple Hairstreak
pg. 91

Eastern Pygmy-Blue
pg. 93

Eastern Tailed-Blue
pg. 95

Dusky Roadside-Skipper
pg. 97

Brown Elfin
pg. 99

Frosted Elfin
pg. 101

Baracoa Skipper
pg. 103

Swarthy Skipper
pg. 105

Tawny-edged Skipper
pg. 107

Eastern Pine Elfin
pg. 109

Henry's Elfin
pg. 111

Pepper and Salt Skipper
pg. 113

Eufala Skipper pg. 115	Coral Hairstreak pg. 117	Banded Hairstreak pg. 119
Edwards' Hairstreak pg. 121	Hickory Hairstreak pg. 123	King's Hairstreak pg. 125
Crossline Skipper pg. 127	Peck's Skipper pg. 129	Whirlabout pg. 131
Southern Hairstreak pg. 133	Striped Hairstreak pg. 135	Common Roadside-Skipper pg. 137

Hayhurst's Scallopwing
pg. 139

Salt Marsh Skipper
pg. 141

Zabulon Skipper
pg. 143

Northern Broken-Dash
pg. 145

Southern Broken-Dash
pg. 147

Little Glassywing
pg. 149

Sachem
pg. 151

Carolina Satyr
pg. 153

Bell's Roadside-Skipper
pg. 155

Carolina Roadside-Skipper
pg. 157

Clouded Skipper
pg. 159

Cobweb Skipper
pg. 161

Dun Skipper pg. 163	**Reversed Roadside-Skipper** pg. 165	**Dreamy Duskywing** pg. 167
Twin-spot Skipper pg. 169	**Two-spotted Skipper** pg. 171	**Lace-winged Roadside-Skipper** pg. 173
Mottled Duskywing pg. 175	**Confused Cloudywing** pg. 177	**Southern Cloudywing** pg. 179
Northern Cloudywing pg. 181	**Gemmed Satyr** pg. 183	**Horace's Duskywing** pg. 185

Wild Indigo Duskywing pg. 187	Dotted Skipper pg. 189	Hobomok Skipper pg. 191
Sleepy Duskywing pg. 193	Yehl Skipper pg. 195	Dusted Skipper pg. 197
Hoary Edge pg. 199	Georgia Satyr pg. 201	Dorantes Skipper pg. 203
Leonard's Skipper pg. 205	Ocola Skipper pg. 207	Little Wood Satyr pg. 209

Juvenal's Duskywing
pg. 211

Zarucco Duskywing
pg. 213

American Snout
pg. 215

Golden-banded Skipper
pg. 217

Long-tailed Skipper
pg. 219

Palmetto Skipper
pg. 221

Viola's Wood Satyr
pg. 223

Brazilian Skipper
pg. 225

Appalachian Brown
pg. 227

Silver-spotted Skipper
pg. 229

Common Buckeye
pg. 231

Cofaqui Giant-Skipper
pg. 233

33

Northern Pearly Eye
pg. 235

Hackberry Butterfly
pg. 237

Common Wood Nymph
pg. 239

Tawny Emperor
pg. 241

Southern Pearly Eye
pg. 243

Yucca Giant-Skipper
pg. 245

Creole Pearly Eye
pg. 247

Giant Swallowtail
pg. 249

Red-banded Hairstreak
pg. 251

Dusky Azure
pg. 253

Gray Hairstreak
pg. 255

Early Hairstreak
pg. 257

Hessel's Hairstreak
pg. 259

Juniper Hairstreak
pg. 261

Southern Skipperling
pg. 263

Little Metalmark
pg. 265

Least Skipper
pg. 267

European Skipper
pg. 269

Phaon Crescent
pg. 271

Fiery Skipper
pg. 273

Whirlabout
pg. 275

American Copper
pg. 277

Harvester
pg. 279

Delaware Skipper
pg. 281

Zabulon Skipper
pg. 283

Gorgone Checkerspot
pg. 285

Sachem
pg. 287

Arogos Skipper
pg. 289

Indian Skipper
pg. 291

Meske's Skipper
pg. 293

Pearl Crescent
pg. 295

Aaron's Skipper
pg. 297

Hobomok Skipper
pg. 299

Tawny Crescent
pg. 301

Yehl Skipper
pg. 303

Dion Skipper
pg. 305

Berry's Skipper
pg. 307

Byssus Skipper
pg. 309

Duke's Skipper
pg. 311

Sleepy Orange
pg. 313

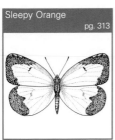

Silvery Checkerspot
pg. 315

Broad-winged Skipper
pg. 317

Palmetto Skipper
pg. 319

Rare Skipper
pg. 321

Palatka Skipper
pg. 323

Variegated Fritillary
pg. 325

Orange Sulphur
pg. 327

Painted Lady
pg. 329

37

American Painted Lady
pg. 331

Green Comma
pg. 333

Eastern Comma
pg. 335

Gray Comma
pg. 337

Goatweed Butterfly
pg. 339

Question Mark
pg. 341

Gulf Fritillary
pg. 343

Viceroy
pg. 345

Aphrodite Fritillary
pg. 347

Queen
pg. 349

Great Spangled Fritillary
pg. 351

Monarch
pg. 353

Diana Fritillary pg. 355	Common/White Checkered-Skipper pg. 357	Tropical Checkered-Skipper pg. 359
Barred Sulphur pg. 361	West Virginia White pg. 363	Falcate Orangetip pg. 365
Checkered White pg. 367	Cabbage White pg. 369	Great Southern White pg. 371
White Peacock pg. 373	Clouded Sulphur pg. 375	Zebra Swallowtail pg. 377

Dainty Sulphur
pg. 379

Little Sulphur
pg. 381

Barred Sulphur
pg. 3

Southern Dogface
pg. 385

Clouded Sulphur
pg. 387

Cloudless Sulphur
pg. 3

Statira Sulphur
pg. 391

Orange-barred Sulphur
pg. 393

Eastern Tiger Swallowta
pg. 3

Common Name
Scientific Name

color section indicators →

Family/Subfamily: tells which family and subfamily the butterfly belongs to (see p. 9–13 for descriptions)

Wingspan: gives minimum and maximum wing spans, from one forewing tip to the other

Above: description of upper, or dorsal, surface of wings

Below: description of lower, or ventral, surface of wings

Sexes: describes differences in appearance between male and female

Egg: description of eggs and where they are deposited

Larva: description of the butterfly's larva, or caterpillar

Larval Host Plants: lists plants that eggs and larva are likely to be found on

Habitat: describes where you're likely to find the butterflies

Broods: lists number of broods, or generations, hatched in a span of one year

Abundance: when the butterflies are flying, this tells you how often you're likely to encounter them

Compare: describes differences among similar-looking species

range map shows where in Georgia this butterfly is present

phenogram: shows population flux throughout the year

Resident: predictably present
Visitor: occasionally present
Stray: rarely present

Resident Visitor Stray

| Jan. | Feb. | Mar. | Apr. | May | June | July | Aug. | Sept. | Oct. | Nov. | Dec. |

Dorsal (above)

Ventral (below)

silhouette behind Comments section shows actual average size of butterfly

illustration shows field marks and features to look for

41

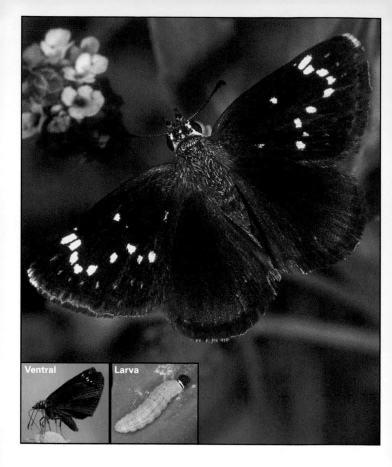

Ventral

Larva

Comments: The Common Sootywing indeed looks as if it fell into a pail of ashes. This solid brownish black coloring and the small white spots on the wings quickly distinguish it from other duskywings and cloudywings. The Common Sootywing is avidly drawn to available flowers. Adults have a low, erratic flight and scurry around quickly, stopping occasionally to rest on nearby vegetation or bare soil with their wings spread. The larvae construct individual shelters on the host by folding over part of a leaf with silk.

Common Sootywing
Pholisora catullus

Family/Subfamily: Skippers (Hesperiidae)/
Spread-wing Skippers (Pyrginae)

Wingspan: 0.90–1.25" (2.3–3.2 cm)

Above: shiny dark brown to black with a variable number
of small white spots on the forewing and a few on top
of the head

Below: as above but paler brown

Sexes: similar, although female often has larger white
forewing spots

Egg: reddish pink, laid singly on upperside of host leaves

Larva: pale gray-green with a narrow dorsal stripe, pale
green lateral stripes, a black collar and black head;
body is covered with numerous tiny yellow-white dots,
each bearing a short hair

Larval Host Plants: Lamb's Quarters, Mexican Tea,
Spiny Amaranth

Habitat: open, disturbed sites including roadsides, old
fields, utility easements and fallow agricultural land

Broods: two or more generations

Abundance: occasional

Compare: Northern Cloudywing (pg. 181) is lighter
brown with small, glassy forewing spots, a light wing
fringe and two central dark bands across the ventral
hindwings.

Resident

Jan. Feb. Mar. Apr. May June July Aug. Sept. Oct. Nov. Dec.

male

Dorsal (above)
small white spots
otherwise black

white spots on head

occasionally has a row
of small white spots
on hindwing

Ventral (below)

43

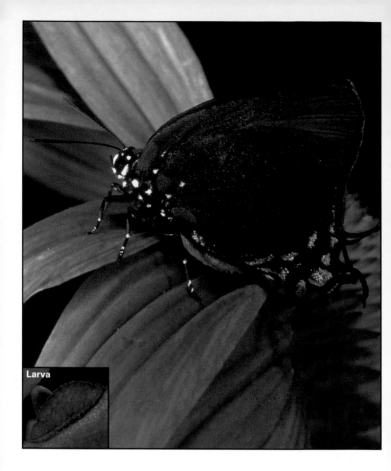

Larva

Comments: The Great Purple Hairstreak significantly dwarfs most other members of its family. The upper wing surfaces of this stunning hairstreak are actually bright metallic blue, not purple. Primarily a butterfly of forested areas, it usually dwells high in the canopy close to its mistletoe host. Adults readily venture down to available flowers where they can be more closely observed. Quickly identified by its orange abdomen, the butterfly's bold ventral coloration warns potential predators that it is distasteful. It typically rests and feeds with its wings closed, so its blue color is seen primarily in flight or while basking.

Great Purple Hairstreak
Atlides halesus

Family/Subfamily: Gossamer Wings (Lycaenidae)/ Hairstreaks (Theclinae)

Wingspan: 1.0–1.7" (2.5–4.3 cm)

Above: male is bright metallic purple-blue with black margins and dark forewing stigma; female is dull black with metallic blue scaling limited to wing bases; two hindwing tails

Below: dull brownish black with metallic green and blue spots near tails and red spots at wing bases; underside of abdomen reddish orange; head and thorax have white spots

Sexes: dissimilar; female is duller with less blue and more rounded wings

Egg: green, laid singly on host leaves

Larva: green with numerous short hairs

Larval Host Plants: Mistletoe

Habitat: woodland edges, adjacent open areas, gardens and parks

Broods: multiple generations

Abundance: occasional

Compare: White M Hairstreak (pg. 89) is smaller with a narrow white M on the underside of the hindwing near the tails and prominent red spot.

Resident

| Jan. | Feb. | Mar. | Apr. | May | June | July | Aug. | Sept. | Oct. | Nov. | Dec. |

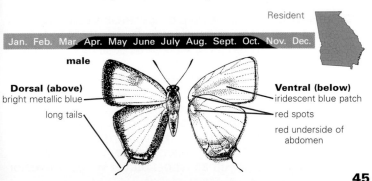

male

Dorsal (above)
bright metallic blue

long tails

Ventral (below)
iridescent blue patch

red spots

red underside of abdomen

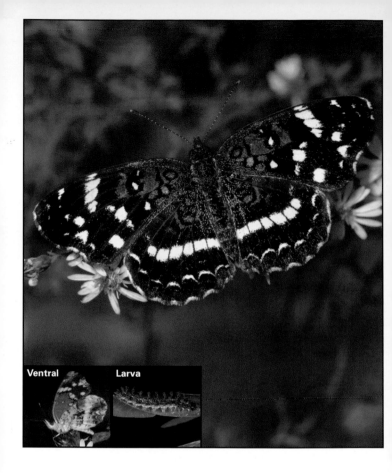

Ventral Larva

Comments: This distinctive dark crescent can be confused with no other small butterfly. Restricted to southern and costal portions of Georgia, it frequents watercourses and adjacent open areas where its wetland hosts can be found. Adults scurry low to the ground with a gliding and somewhat erratic flight. They frequently stop to perch on low vegetation or to nectar at available flowers, holding their ornately patterned wings outstretched. The eastern subspecies *P. texana seminole* has brighter reddish orange basal coloration and larger cream spots on the wings above.

Texan Crescent
Phyciodes texana

Family/Subfamily: Brush-foots (Nymphalidae)/
True Brush-foots (Nymphalinae)

Wingspan: 1.3–1.8" (3.3–4.6 cm)

Above: black with cream white spots and reddish orange basal markings; forewing margin is noticeably concave

Below: hindwing is mottled dark and light brown with a distinct cream band through the center

Sexes: similar

Egg: pale green, laid in clusters on the underside of host leaves

Larva: dark brownish black with white dashes, a cream yellow lateral band with orange-based yellow ochre spines, and a black head; dorsal spines black

Larval Host Plants: various acanthus family plants including Carolina Wild Petunia, Branched Foldwing and snake-herb

Habitat: stream and river corridors and open, disturbed sites

Broods: multiple generations

Abundance: rare to occasional

Compare: unique

Resident

Jan. Feb. Mar. Apr. May June July Aug. Sept. Oct. Nov. Dec.

Dorsal (above)
concave margin
reddish orange marks
cream spot bands

Ventral (below)
orange basally
cream band

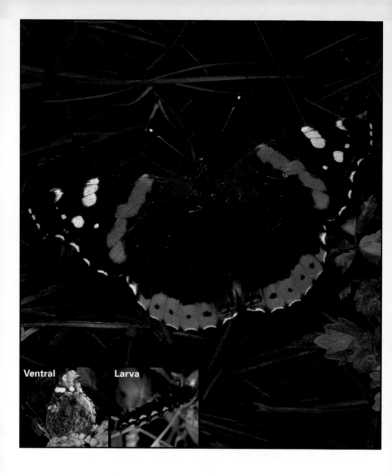

Ventral

Larva

Comments: The Red Admiral is a medium-sized dark butterfly that is quickly distinguished from any other species by its distinctive reddish orange forewing band. Particularly common in spring, the butterfly will readily explore suburban gardens. Adults have a quick, erratic flight and are often quite wary. Males frequently perch on low vegetation or on the ground in sunlit locations. Adults occasionally nectar at flowers, but more frequently visit sap flows, dung or fermenting fruit. The larvae construct individual shelters on the host by folding together one or more leaves with silk.

Red Admiral
Vanessa atalanta

Family/Subfamily: Brush-foots (Nymphalidae)/ True Brush-foots (Nymphalinae)

Wingspan: 1.75–2.50" (4.4–6.4 cm)

Above: dark brownish black with reddish orange hind-wing border and distinct, reddish orange median forewing band; forewing has small white spots near apex

Below: forewing as above with blue scaling and paler markings; hindwing ornately mottled with dark brown, blue and cream in bark-like pattern

Sexes: similar

Egg: small green eggs laid singly on host leaves

Larva: variable; pinkish gray to charcoal with lateral row of cream crescent-shaped spots and numerous branched spines

Larval Host Plants: False Nettle, Pellitory and nettles

Habitat: moist woodlands, forest edges, roadside ditches, along canals and ponds, wetlands and gardens

Broods: two or more generations

Abundance: occasional to common; locally abundant

Compare: unique

Resident Visitor

Jan. Feb. Mar. Apr. May June July Aug. Sept. Oct. Nov. Dec.

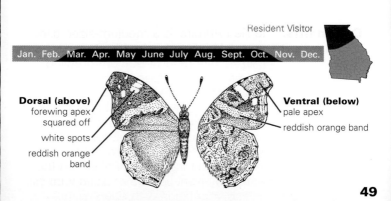

Dorsal (above)
forewing apex squared off
white spots
reddish orange band

Ventral (below)
pale apex
reddish orange band

49

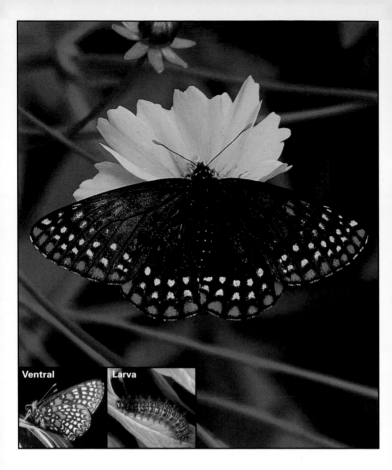

Ventral

Larva

Comments: The outrageously colored Baltimore is truly a must-see butterfly! Unfortunately it is generally scarce and localized in northern Georgia. Turtlehead is the primary host on which females lay eggs. Upon hatching, the larvae construct a communal silken web on the plant and feed gregariously inside. By the end of summer, they stop feeding, construct a new web near the base of the plant and overwinter. They become active in spring and wander to secondary hosts to complete development. It has a quick, low flight of rapid wingbeats followed by brief periods of gliding. Both sexes perch on low vegetation with open wings.

Baltimore Checkerspot
Euphydryas phaeton

Family/Subfamily: Brush-foots (Nymphalidae)/
True Brush-foots (Nymphalinae)

Wingspan: 1.75–2.50" (4.4–6.6 cm)

Above: black with reddish orange spots along the outer
wing margins and several rows of cream white spots

Below: marked as above with several large reddish
orange basal spots on both wings

Sexes: similar

Egg: yellow, soon turning reddish, laid in large clusters of
several hundred on the underside of host leaves

Larva: tawny orange with black transverse stripe and
several rows of black, branched spines; front and rear
end segments are black

Larval Host Plants: Turtlehead is the primary host;
secondary hosts include a wider range of plants such
as false foxglove, Narrowleaf Plantain, Canadian
Lousewort, and Southern Arrowwood

Habitat: wet meadows, bogs, stream margins, marshes

Broods: single generation

Abundance: rare to occasional, often highly localized

Compare: unique

Resident

Jan. Feb. Mar. Apr. May June July Aug. Sept. Oct. Nov. Dec.

Dorsal (above)
reddish orange
marginal spots

several rows of
pale spots on
both wings

Ventral (below)
reddish orange
crescents

reddish orange spots

51

Ventral

Larva

Comments: Aptly named, the Zebra Longwing is quickly identified by its distinctive elongated, yellow-white striped wings. Although a year-round resident in south Florida, it is only a temporary seasonal colonist of Georgia, and tends to be most abundant following mild winters. It can be a regular garden visitor. Adults have slow, graceful flight. Unlike most butterflies, the adults are extremely long-lived and may survive for several months. As evening approaches, they often form resting aggregations on Spanish moss or on overhanging branches. The same communal roost may be used for many nights.

Zebra Longwing
Heliconius charitonius

Family/Subfamily: Brush-foots (Nymphalidae)/ Longwing Butterflies (Heliconiinae)

Wingspan: 2.9–3.5" (7.4–8.9 cm)

Above: elongated black wings with pale yellow stripes; long, slender abdomen and antennae

Below: as above with small red basal spots

Sexes: similar

Egg: yellow, laid in small groups on new growth and tendrils of host; host is typically shaded or semi-shaded

Larva: white with small black spots and numerous long black spines

Larval Host Plants: Various Passion-Flowers including Maypop, Corky-Stemmed Passion-Flower, Yellow Passion-Flower and Incense Passion-Flower

Habitat: woodlands, forest edges and adjacent open, disturbed areas such as gardens

Broods: multiple generations

Abundance: rare to common

Compare: unique

Visitor

Jan. Feb. Mar. Apr. May June July Aug. Sept. Oct. Nov. Dec.

Dorsal (above)
black with yellow stripes

long antennae

long abdomen

Ventral (below)
elongated wings

small red spots on wing base

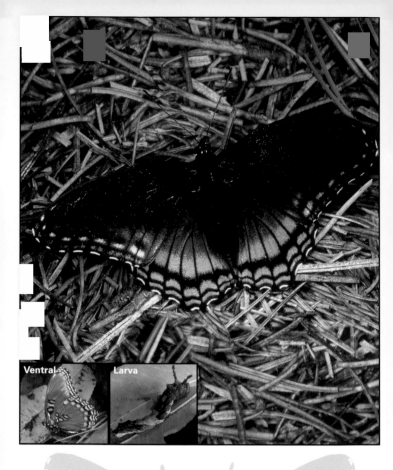

Ventral

Larva

Comments: The Red-Spotted Purple is one of several Georgia butterflies that mimic the toxic Pipevine Swallowtail to gain protection from predators such as birds. It is a common butterfly of immature wood-lands, but is rarely encountered in large numbers. Adults have a strong, gliding flight and are often quite wary. Males perch on sunlit leaves along trails or for-est margins and make periodic exploratory flights. Adults occasionally visit flowers but often prefer rot-ting fruit, dung, carrion or tree sap.

Red-Spotted Purple
Limenitis arthemis astyanax

Family/Subfamily: Brush-foots (Nymphalidae)/ Admirals and Relatives (Limenitidinae)

Wingspan: 3.0–3.5" (7.6–8.9 cm)

Above: dark velvety bluish black with iridescent blue scaling on hindwing and small orange and white spots near forewing apex

Below: brownish black with an iridescent blue sheen and basal red-orange spots; hindwings have a row of red-orange spots toward the outer margin

Sexes: similar

Egg: gray-green, laid singly on the tips of host leaves

Larva: mottled green, brown and cream with two long, knobby horns on thorax; resembles a bird dropping

Larval Host Plants: Black Cherry, Wild Cherry and willow

Habitat: open woodlands, forest edges and adjacent open areas

Broods: multiple generations

Abundance: occasional to common

Compare: Pipevine Swallowtail (pg. 61) has hindwing tail and a low, rapid flight; continually flutters wings when nectaring.

Resident

Jan. Feb. Mar. Apr. May June July Aug. Sept. Oct. Nov. Dec.

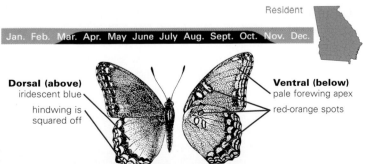

Dorsal (above)
iridescent blue
hindwing is squared off

Ventral (below)
pale forewing apex
red-orange spots

55

Ventral | Larva

Comments: Easily our most elegant species, the long-tailed black-and-white striped Zebra Swallowtail can be confused with no other resident Eastern butterfly. Adults have a low, rapid flight and adeptly maneuver through the understory or among shrubby vegetation. Seldom found far from stands of its larval host, it is unlikely to be encountered in highly developed areas although may occasionally wander into nearby home gardens. The swallowtail has a proportionately short proboscis and is thus unable to nectar at many long, tubular flowers. It instead prefers composites, and is regularly attracted to white flowers.

Zebra Swallowtail
Eurytides marcellus

Family/Subfamily: Swallowtails (Papilionidae)/
Swallowtails (Papilioninae)

Wingspan: 2.5–4.0" (6.4–10.2 cm)

Above: white with black stripes and long, slender tails;
hindwings bear a bright red patch above the eyespot;
spring-forms are smaller, lighter and have shorter tails

Below: as above, but with a red stripe through hindwing

Sexes: similar

Egg: light green, laid singly on host leaves or budding
branches

Larva: several color forms; may be green, green with
light blue and yellow stripes or charcoal with white and
yellow stripes

Larval Host Plants: Pawpaw

Habitat: rich woodlands, stream corridors, swamp margins, forest edges and old fields

Broods: multiple generations

Abundance: occasional to common

Compare: unique

Resident

Jan. Feb. Mar. Apr. May June July Aug. Sept. Oct. Nov. Dec.

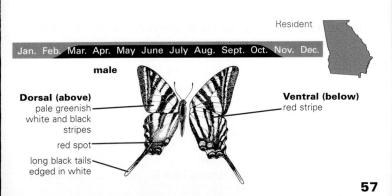

male

Dorsal (above)
pale greenish
white and black
stripes

red spot

long black tails
edged in white

Ventral (below)
red stripe

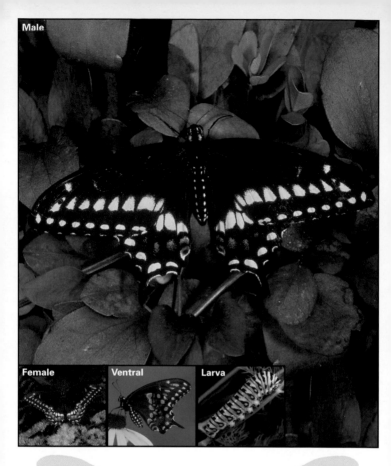

Male

Female | Ventral | Larva

Comments: The Black Swallowtail is one of our most commonly encountered garden butterflies. Its plump, green larvae, often referred to as parsley worms, feed on many cultivated herbs and may occasionally become minor nuisance pests. It is equally at home along farm roads or in rural meadows as suburban yards and urban parks. Males have a strong, rapid flight and frequently perch on low vegetation. Both sexes are exceedingly fond of flowers and readily stop to nectar. It is one of six eastern butterflies that mimic the toxic Pipevine Swallowtail to gain protection from predators.

Black Swallowtail
Papilio polyxenes

Family/Subfamily: Swallowtails (Papilionidae)/ Swallowtails (Papilioninae)

Wingspan: 2.5–4.2" (6.4–10.7 cm)

Above: male is black with a broad, postmedian yellow band and a row of marginal yellow spots; female is mostly black with increased blue hindwing scaling and marginal yellow spots, the yellow postmedian band is reduced; both sexes have a red hindwing eyespot with a central black pupil, and a yellow-spotted abdomen

Below: hindwing has orange-tinted yellow spot bands

Sexes: dissimilar; female has reduced yellow postmedian band and increased blue hindwing scaling above

Egg: yellow, laid singly on host leaves

Larva: green with black bands and yellow-orange spots

Larval Host Plants: wild and cultivated members of the Carrot Family including dill, fennel and parsley

Habitat: old fields, roadsides, pastures, freshwater marshes, suburban gardens, agricultural land

Broods: multiple generations

Abundance: occasional to abundant

Compare: Spicebush Swallowtail (pg. 67) is larger, has green-blue spots and lacks black-centered hindwing eyespot. Pipevine Swallowtail (pg. 61) is mostly black and lacks yellow marking.

Resident

Jan. Feb. Mar. Apr. May June July Aug. Sept. Oct. Nov. Dec.

male

Dorsal (above)
yellow bands
blue scaling
black "pupil" in center of spot
tail

Ventral (below)
yellow-orange bands
faint yellow-orange cell spot

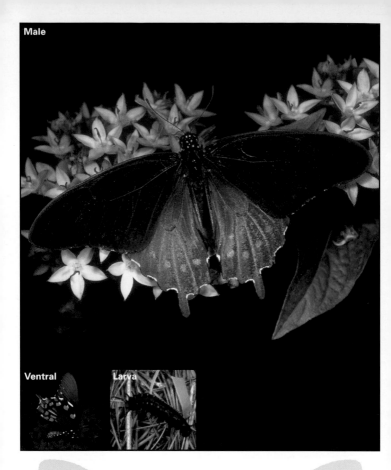

Male

Ventral

Larva

Comments: A relatively small member of the family, the Pipevine Swallowtail has a strong, rapid flight. It is unlikely to be encountered in urban areas. Adults are fond of colorful flowers and continuously flutter their wings while feeding. Nonetheless, they rarely linger at any one blossom for long, tending to be rather wary and nervous of close approach. The velvety black larvae sequester various toxins from their host. These chemicals render them and the resulting adults highly distasteful to many predators. As a result, several other butterfly species mimic the color pattern of the Pipevine Swallowtail in order to gain protection.

Pipevine Swallowtail
Battus philenor

Family/Subfamily: Swallowtails (Papilionidae)/ Swallowtails (Papilioninae)

Wingspan: 2.75–4.00" (7.0–10.2 cm)

Above: overall black; male has iridescent greenish blue hindwings; female has a single row of white marginal spots

Below: hindwings are iridescent blue with a row of prominent orange spots

Sexes: dissimilar; female is duller black with a more prominent row of white spots

Egg: brownish orange, laid singly or in small clusters

Larva: velvety black with orange spots and numerous fleshy tubercles

Larval Host Plants: various pipevines including Wooly Pipevine, Dutchman's Pipe and Virginia Snakeroot

Habitat: fields, pastures, roadsides, woodlands, stream corridors, suburban gardens

Broods: multiple generations

Abundance: occasional to common

Compare: Spicebush Swallowtail (pg. 67) is larger with prominent crescent-shaped marginal spots. Red-Spotted Purple (pg. 55) lacks hindwing tails. Female Black Swallowtail (pg. 59) is larger with an orange hindwing eyespot.

Resident Visitor

Jan. Feb. Mar. Apr. May June July Aug. Sept. Oct. Nov. Dec.

male

Dorsal (above)
black forewings
iridescent green-blue
row of pale spots

Ventral (below)
large orange spots
iridescent blue

61

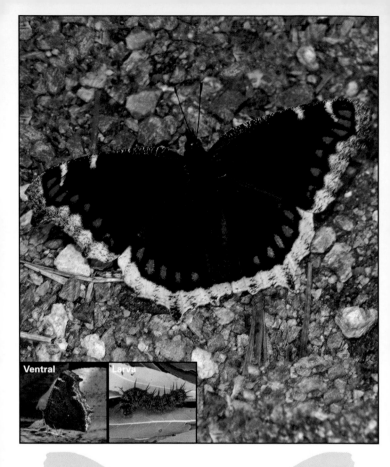

Ventral

Larva

Comments: This rich beauty of a butterfly is often the first harbinger of spring. Overwintering adults occasionally become active on warm winter days and are seen flying even when snow remains on the ground in northern regions. Adults emerge in early summer, aestivate until fall, then become active again to feed and build up fat reserves before seeking protected sites to hibernate—making it one of our longest-lived butterflies. It is typically encountered as solitary individuals. Adults do not visit flowers but are frequently seen at rotting fruit or sap flows.

Mourning Cloak
Nymphalis antiopa

Family/Subfamily: Brush-foots (Nymphalidae)/ True Brush-foots (Nymphalinae)

Wingspan: 3.0–4.0" (7.6–10.2 cm)

Above: velvety black, often appearing iridescent, with broad irregular yellow border and a row of bright purple blue spots; forewing apex is extended and squared off; hindwing bears a single short, stubby tail

Below: silky black with pale wing border, heavily striated and bark-like in appearance

Sexes: similar

Egg: light brown, laid in clusters on host leaves or twigs

Larva: black with a dorsal row of crimson patches, fine white speckling and several rows of black, branched spines

Larval Host Plants: birch, willow, aspen, elm and hackberry

Habitat: deciduous forests, clearings, riparian woodlands, woodland roads, forest edges, wetland and watercourse margins, and adjacent open areas including suburban yards, parks and golf courses

Broods: single generation

Abundance: uncommon to common

Compare: unique

Resident Visitor

| Jan. | Feb. | Mar. | Apr. | May | June | July | Aug. | Sept. | Oct. | Nov. | Dec. |

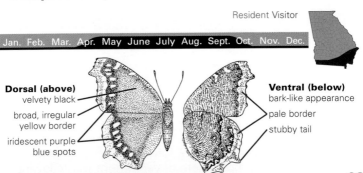

Dorsal (above)
velvety black
broad, irregular yellow border
iridescent purple blue spots

Ventral (below)
bark-like appearance
pale border
stubby tail

63

Female

Male pg. 355

Male

Larva

Comments: The Diana Fritillary is a showstopper! Strikingly sexually dimorphic, the blue and black female mimics the toxic Pipevine Swallowtail to presumably gain protection from predators. Although often spotty and localized, it can be fairly numerous when encountered. Adults have a strong, directed flight but readily stop to nectar at colorful wildflowers, being particularly fond of milkweeds, Joe-pye Weed and thistles. As with other fritillaries, males typically emerge several weeks before females. Young larvae overwinter and complete development the following spring.

Diana Fritillary
Speyeria diana

Family/Subfamily: Brush-foots (Nymphalidae)/
Longwing Butterflies (Heliconiinae)

Wingspan: 3.5–4.4" (8.9–11.2 cm)

Above: male is dark unmarked blackish brown with
bright orange on the outer third; female is black basally
with white and iridescent blue spots on outer half

Below: forewing is orange with heavy black markings
toward base; male hindwing is brownish orange with
two rows of small narrow silver dashes; female hindwing is chocolate brown

Sexes: dissimilar; female is black basally with white and
iridescent blue spots on outer half; ventral hindwing is
chocolate brown

Egg: tiny cream eggs laid singly and somewhat haphazardly near host leaves

Larva: velvety black with several rows of reddish orange
based black spines

Larval Host Plants: various woodland violets

Habitat: rich, moist deciduous mountain woodlands,
stream corridors, forested roads, clearings and adjacent open areas

Broods: single generation

Abundance: rare to locally common

Compare: unique

Resident

Jan. Feb. Mar. Apr. May June July Aug. Sept. Oct. Nov. Dec.

male

Dorsal (above)
black
orange

(female primarily black
and blue)

Ventral (below)
black markings toward
base

lacks prominent silvery
hindwing spots
characteristic of
other fritillaries

65

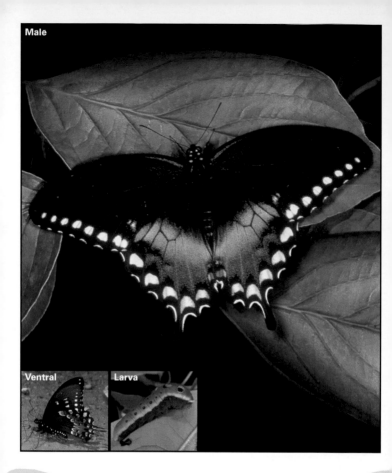

Male

Ventral

Larva

Comments: The lovely Spicebush Swallowtail is one of five Georgia butterflies that mimic the unpalatable Pipevine Swallowtail to gain protection from predators. Adults are strong, agile fliers but rarely stray far from their preferred woodland habitat and larval hosts and are unlikely to be found in highly urban areas. A true lover of flowers, they readily nectar at available wild-flowers and may be occasional garden visitors. They continuously flutter their wings while feeding. The brightly colored larvae make individual shelters on the host by curling up both edges of a leaf with silk. They rest motionless inside when not actively feeding.

Spicebush Swallowtail
Papilio troilus

Family/Subfamily: Swallowtails (Papilionidae)/ Swallowtails (Papilioninae)

Wingspan: 3.5–5.0" (8.9–12.7 cm)

Above: black with a row of large, pale greenish blue spots along the margin; hindwings have greenish blue scaling and a single, orange eyespot

Below: black with postmedian band of blue scaling bordered by row of yellow-orange spots on each side; abdomen black with longitudinal rows of light spots

Sexes: similar, female has duller hindwing scaling

Egg: cream, laid singly on the underside of host leaves

Larva: green above, reddish below with enlarged thorax, two false eyespots and several longitudinal rows of blue spots

Larval Host Plants: Sassafras, Red Bay and Spicebush

Habitat: woodlands, forest edges, wooded swamps, pastures, old fields and suburban gardens

Broods: multiple generations

Abundance: occasional

Compare: Pipevine Swallowtail (pg. 61), female Black Swallowtail (pg. 59) and dark-form female Eastern Tiger Swallowtail (pg. 69) all lack marginal greenish blue spots.

Resident

Jan. Feb. Mar. Apr. May June July Aug. Sept. Oct. Nov. Dec.

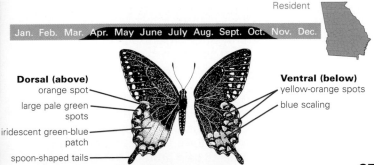

Dorsal (above)
orange spot
large pale green spots
iridescent green-blue patch
spoon-shaped tails

Ventral (below)
yellow-orange spots
blue scaling

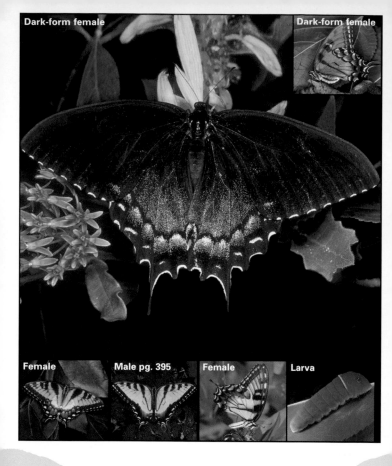

Dark-form female

Dark-form female

Female

Male pg. 395

Female

Larva

Comments: Easily recognized by its bold, black stripes and bright yellow wings, the Eastern Tiger Swallowtail is the state butterfly of Georgia. Adults have a strong, agile flight and often soar high in the treetops. Although fond of woodlands and waterways, it is equally at home in more urban areas. It is a common garden visitor favoring red, pink and purple flowers. Unlike many other swallowtails, it seldom flutters its wings while feeding. It instead rests on the blossom with wings open. Dark-form females mimic the toxic Pipevine Swallowtail to gain protection from predators. Females exhibit numerous intermediate-colored forms.

Eastern Tiger Swallowtail
Papilio glaucus

Family/Subfamily: Swallowtails (Papilionidae)/ Swallowtails (Papilioninae)

Wingspan: 3.5–5.5" (8.9–14.0 cm)

Above: yellow with black forewing stripes and broad black wing margins; single row of yellow spots along outer edge of each wing

Below: yellow with black stripes and black wing margins; hindwing margins have increased blue scaling and a single submarginal row of yellow-orange, crescent-shaped spots; abdomen yellow with black stripes

Sexes: dissimilar; male always yellow but females have two color forms; yellow female has increased blue scaling in black hindwing border; dark-form female is mostly black with extensive blue hindwing markings

Egg: green, laid singly on upper surface of host leaves

Larva: green; enlarged thorax and two small false eyespots

Larval Host Plants: Black Cherry, Wild Cherry, ash and Tulip Tree

Habitat: mixed forests, wooded swamps, forest edges, suburban gardens, old fields

Broods: multiple generations

Abundance: occasional to common

Compare: Pipevine Swallowtail (pg. 61) is much smaller. Spicebush Swallowtail (pg. 67) has greenish-blue spots on hindwing margin.

Resident

Jan. Feb. Mar. Apr. May June July Aug. Sept. Oct. Nov. Dec.

male

Dorsal (above)
yellow with black stripes

wide black border

yellow spots

long tail

Ventral (below)
yellow-orange spots

blue scaling

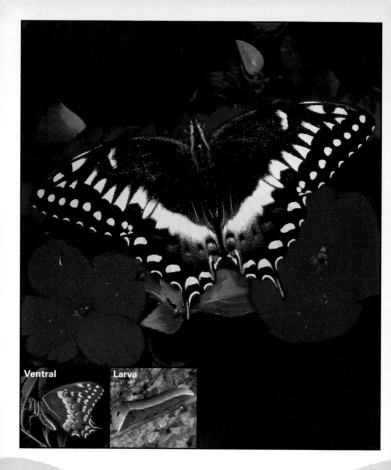

Ventral

Larva

Comments: Restricted to the Deep South, the Palamedes Swallowtail is a common butterfly of Georgia's moist woodlands and evergreen swamps. It readily ventures into adjacent areas in search of nectar and may be commonly encountered in suburban gardens or along roadsides. Adults have a strong, directed flight and avidly nectar at available flowers with their wings continuously fluttering. Males often congregate at moist ground to imbibe diluted minerals and salts. The cartoonish larvae have an enlarged thorax with a prominent pair of false eyespots that resemble the head of a small lizard or snake.

Palamedes Swallowtail
Papilio palamedes

Family/Subfamily: Swallowtails (Papilionidae)/ Swallowtails (Papilioninae)

Wingspan: 3.5–5.5" (8.9–14.0 cm)

Above: black with a broad, postmedian yellow band and a row of marginal yellow spots

Below: hindwing has a band of blue scaling bordered by median and submarginal rows of yellow-orange spots; narrow yellow line near wing base runs parallel to the abdomen, no other black colored swallowtail in the Carolinas has this marking

Sexes: similar

Egg: cream, laid singly on leaves; prefers new growth

Larva: green above, reddish below with enlarged thorax and two false eyespots

Larval Host Plants: Red Bay

Habitat: wooded swamps, hammocks, forest edges, suburban gardens, moist woodlands and evergreen swamps

Broods: multiple generations

Abundance: occasional to abundant

Compare: Black Swallowtail (pg. 59) is smaller and has a black-centered orange hindwing eyespot. Giant Swallowtail (pg. 249) has crossing yellow dorsal bands.

Resident Stray

Jan. Feb. Mar. Apr. May June July Aug. Sept. Oct. Nov. Dec.

Dorsal (above)
wide yellow band

yellow tail edged
in black with
pale yellow
cream ray

Ventral (below)
narrow yellow stripe

orange crescents

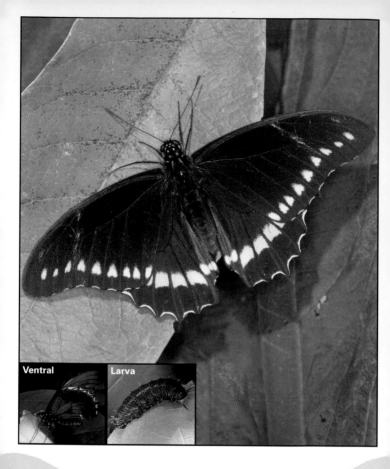

Ventral

Larva

Comments: The Polydamas Swallowtail lacks the characteristic hindwing tails common to most other North American members of the family. This trait, combined with its broad yellow wing bands, makes the species easy to identify. It is a fast and powerful flier with a preference for suburban gardens, open woodlands and weedy, overgrown sites. Adults are good colonizers and readily disperse long distances in search of suitable hosts. Nonetheless, it is primarily a tropical butterfly seldom found north of the Florida border.

Polydamas Swallowtail
Battus polydamas

Family/Subfamily: Swallowtails (Papilionidae)/ Swallowtails (Papilioninae)

Wingspan: 4.0–5.0" (10.2–12.7 cm)

Above: black with a prominent yellow band along the outer margin of wings; lacks tails

Below: hindwings have marginal row of narrow red spots; thorax and abdomen black with red spots

Sexes: similar

Egg: amber-brown, laid in small clusters on new growth of the host

Larva: robust, chocolate-brown with numerous short orange, fleshy tubercles

Larval Host Plants: various native and ornamental pipevine species

Habitat: fields, gardens, woodland edges, suburban parks, disturbed sites

Broods: multiple generations

Abundance: rare

Compare: Black Swallowtail (pg. 59) is smaller with two yellow spot bands above and hindwing tails.

Stray

Jan. Feb. Mar. Apr. May June July Aug. Sept. Oct. Nov. Dec.

Dorsal (above)
black wings
yellow band
no tails

Ventral (below)
red spots
scalloped margin

73

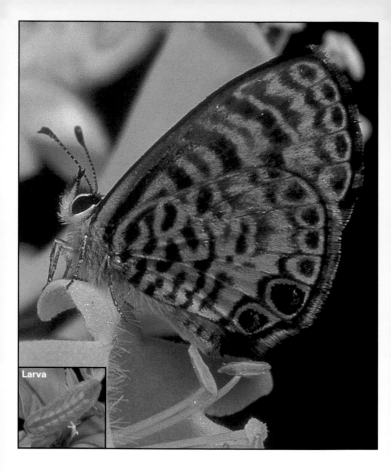

Larva

Comments: The dainty Cassius Blue is a rare find in Georgia. While it may occasionally disperse northward across the border from Florida, many of these isolated records appear to be the result of the immature stages "piggybacking" on shipments of Plumbago or Leadwort, now a widely used popular landscape plant. I have found small, thriving colonies at several commercial nurseries in Georgia and South Carolina, all of which receive regular shipments from the sunshine state. It typically rests and feeds with its wings closed; blue color is seen primarily in flight or while basking.

Cassius Blue
Leptotes cassius

Family/Subfamily: Gossamer Wings (Lycaenidae)/ Blues (Polyommatinae)

Wingspan: 0.75–1.00" (1.9–2.5 cm)

Above: blue with thin black border and white wing fringe; female is light blue with broad gray borders; hindwing bears one dark marginal spot

Below: whitish with numerous gray bands and spots; hindwing has two orange-rimmed black and metallic blue eyespots

Sexes: dissimilar; female is brownish blue with pale whitish blue basal scaling

Egg: greenish blue, laid singly on flower buds, flowers or immature fruit of host

Larva: variable; green to green with pinkish red markings

Larval Host Plants: numerous plants including Wild Tamarind, Leadwort, Blackbead and milk peas

Habitat: open, disturbed sites including roadsides, vacant or weedy fields, coastal dunes, forest edges and gardens

Broods: multiple generations

Abundance: rare

Compare: Ceraunus Blue (pg. 77) is more uniform gray beneath with white-rimmed black spots near wing base and lacks banded appearance.

Stray

Jan. Feb. Mar. Apr. May June July Aug. Sept. Oct. Nov. Dec.

male

Dorsal (above)
purple blue wings
white fringe
faint dark spot

Ventral (below)
numerous dark bands and spots

white open areas

orange-rimmed black and metallic blue eyespots

75

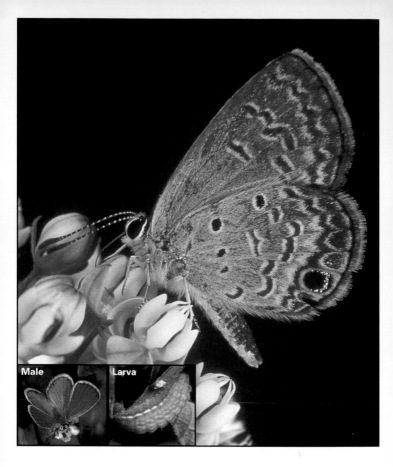

Male

Larva

Comments: Although generally common throughout much of Florida, the Ceraunus Blue is an uncommon vagrant or temporary colonist northward into southern Georgia. The small, relatively dull-colored adults scurry erratically close to the ground among low-growing vegetation and may be easily overlooked. Both sexes are fond of flowers and readily pause to nectar at available blossoms. Males periodically congregate at damp ground. This butterfly typically rests and feeds with its wings closed, so its blue color is seen primarily in flight or when the butterfly is basking in the sun.

Ceraunus Blue
Hemiargus ceraunus

Family/Subfamily: Gossamer Wings (Lycaenidae)/
Blues (Polyommatinae)

Wingspan: 0.75–1.00" (1.9–2.5 cm)

Above: male is bright lavender blue with a narrow black
border and white wing fringe; single black dot along
hindwing margin

Below: light gray with numerous dark markings and
spots; hindwing has a prominent orange-rimmed black
spot with metallic blue scaling

Sexes: dissimilar; female is brown with blue scaling at
wing bases

Egg: greenish blue, laid singly on flower buds of host

Larva: highly variable; green with a red lateral stripe to
highly patterned pinkish red

Larval Host Plants: numerous Fabaceous plants
including Hairy Indigo, Creeping Indigo, Partridge Pea
and milk peas

Habitat: open, disturbed sites including roadsides, vacant
fields, utility easements and fallow agricultural land

Broods: multiple generations

Abundance: rare to uncommon

Compare: Cassius Blue (pg. 75) is generally larger, and
is chalky white beneath with numerous dark bands.

Stray

Jan. Feb. Mar. Apr. May June July Aug. Sept. Oct. Nov. Dec.

male

Dorsal (above)
narrow black border
lavender blue wings
white fringe
small black spot

Ventral (below)
gray bars and spots
outlined in white

black spots outlined
in white

single black spot
outlined in orange

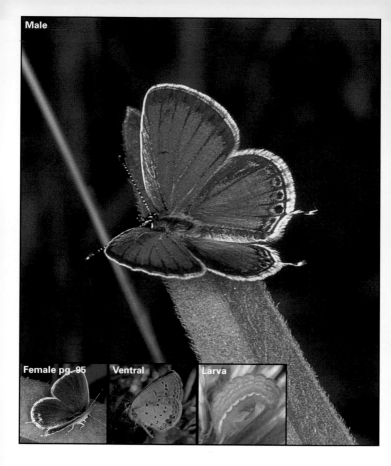

Male

Female pg. 95 | Ventral | Larva

Comments: The Eastern Tailed-Blue is widespread and common throughout most of the eastern United States. Named for its distinctive hindwing tail, it is the only blue in Georgia with this characteristic hairstreak-like feature. Do not rely solely on the presence of tails for identification, as they are fragile and may be lost with normal wing wear. Adults have a weak, dancing flight. They are fond of flowers and are easily attracted to gardens. Males often gather in small puddle clubs at damp sand or gravel. It typically rests and feeds with its wings closed, so its blue color is seen primarily in flight or when the butterfly is basking in the sun.

Eastern Tailed-Blue
Everes comyntas

Family/Subfamily: Gossamer Wings (Lycaenidae)/
Blues (Polyommatinae)

Wingspan: 0.75–1.00" (1.9–2.5 cm)

Above: male is blue with brown border; female is
brownish gray; both sexes have one or two small
orange and black hindwing spots above single tail

Below: silvery gray with numerous dark spots and
bands; hindwing has two small orange-capped black
spots above tail

Sexes: dissimilar; female is primarily brownish gray

Egg: pale green, laid singly on flowers or young leaves of
host

Larva: variable, typically green with dark dorsal stripe and
light lateral stripes

Larval Host Plants: various herbaceous Fabaceae
including clovers, bush clovers and beggarweeds

Habitat: open, disturbed sites including roadsides,
vacant lots and old fields

Broods: multiple generations

Abundance: occasional to common

Compare: Summer Azure (pg. 83) lacks hindwing tails.
Gray Hairstreak (pg. 255) has distinct black-and-white
(occasionally orange) ventral hindwing stripe.

Resident

Jan. Feb. Mar. Apr. May June July Aug. Sept. Oct. Nov. Dec.

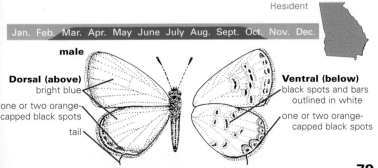

male

Dorsal (above)
bright blue

one or two orange-
capped black spots

tail

Ventral (below)
black spots and bars
outlined in white

one or two orange-
capped black spots

79

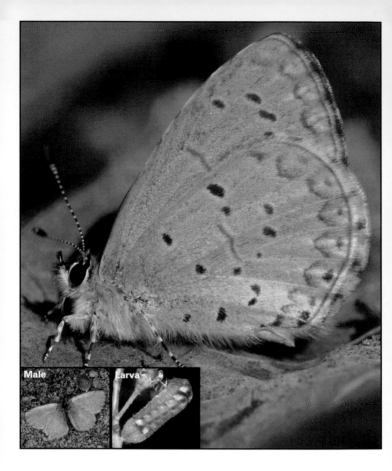

Male

Larva

Comments: Encountered earlier than most other species, the Spring Azure is by far the most conspicuous early-season blue in Georgia, often seen even before many of the colorful spring flowering trees and shrubs are in full bloom. It may frequently wander into nearby suburban yards and gardens. Adults have a moderately slow flight and erratically scurry from ground level to canopy height moving just over the surface of the vegetation. They are extremely fond of flowers and often congregate in at damp ground. It typically rests and feeds with its wings closed; blue color is seen primarily in flight or while basking.

Spring Azure
Celastrina ladon

Family/Subfamily: Gossamer Wings (Lycaenidae)/
Blues (Polyommatinae)

Wingspan: 0.75–1.25" (2.0–3.2 cm)

Above: male is pale blue with narrow, faint dark
forewing border; lacks white scaling on wings

Below: somewhat variable; dusky gray with black spots
and dark scaling along hindwing margin and often a
dark patch in the center of the hindwing

Sexes: dissimilar; female has a broader, more extensive
dark forewing border above

Egg: whitish green; laid singly on flower buds of host

Larva: variable; green to pinkish green to whitish with
dark dorsal stripe and cream bands

Larval Host Plants: flowers of various trees and
shrubs including Black Cherry, blueberry, Flowering
Dogwood, viburnum and holly

Habitat: open, deciduous woodlands, forest edges and
trails, roadsides, brushy fields, utility easements,
wooded swamps and gardens

Broods: single generation

Abundance: occasional to common

Compare: All other azures are silver gray on the wings
below with reduced dark markings.

Resident

Jan. Feb. Mar. Apr. May June July Aug. Sept. Oct. Nov. Dec.

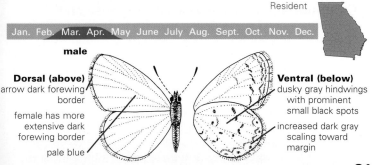

male

Dorsal (above)
arrow dark forewing
border

female has more
extensive dark
forewing border

pale blue

Ventral (below)
dusky gray hindwings
with prominent
small black spots

increased dark gray
scaling toward
margin

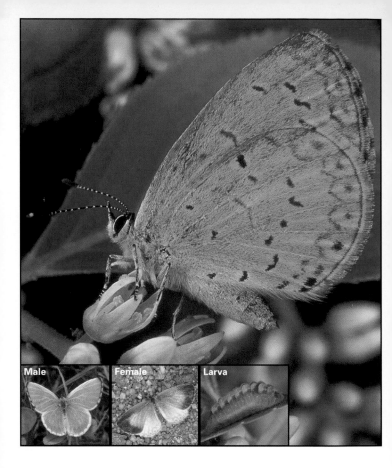

Male

Female

Larva

Comments: Now viewed as a distinct species, the Summer Azure was previously considered a lighter second generation form of the Spring Azure. Adults of this small dusty blue butterfly are found in and along woodlands but readily venture out into nearby open areas in search of nectar and frequently wander into suburban gardens. They have a moderately slow dancing flight. Unlike most other blues, they are often encountered fluttering high among the branches of trees and shrubs. Males often congregate at damp ground. It typically rests and feeds with its wings closed; blue color is seen in flight or while basking.

Summer Azure
Celastrina neglecta

Family/Subfamily: Gossamer Wings (Lycaenidae)/ Blues (Polyommatinae)

Wingspan: 0.80–1.25" (2.0–3.2 cm)

Above: male is light blue with narrow, faint dark forewing border and increased white scaling on hindwing

Below: chalky white with small dark spots and bands

Sexes: dissimilar, female has increased white scaling above and wide, dark forewing borders

Egg: whitish green, laid singly on flower buds of host

Larva: variable; green to pinkish green with dark dorsal stripe and cream bands

Larval Host Plants: flowers of various trees and shrubs including New Jersey Tea, Wing-stem, hollies and sumac

Habitat: open, deciduous woodlands, forest edges, roadsides, old fields and utility easements and gardens

Broods: several generations

Abundance: occasional to common

Compare: Spring Azure (pg. 81) is duskier gray and more heavily marked below; lacks dorsal white scaling. Appalachian Azure (pg. 87) is slightly larger and best separated by its host association.

Resident

Jan.	Feb.	Mar.	Apr.	May	June	July	Aug.	Sept.	Oct.	Nov.	Dec.

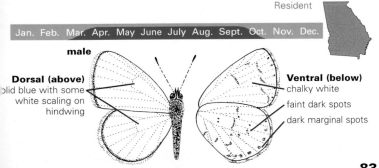

male

Dorsal (above)
solid blue with some white scaling on hindwing

Ventral (below)
chalky white
faint dark spots
dark marginal spots

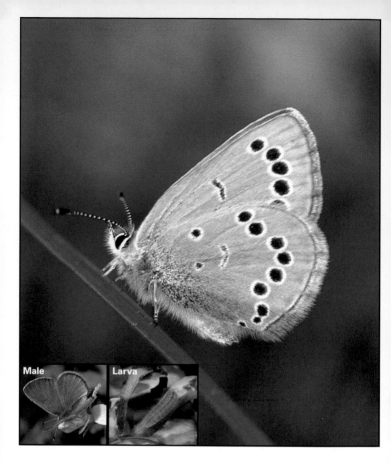

Male

Larva

Comments: The Silvery Blue is one of our most beautiful spring butterflies. It is typically encountered alongside several of the early-season azures. Extending southward through the Appalachians into northern Georgia, the Silvery Blue typically occurs in low density, isolated colonies and is seldom found far from stands of its larval hosts. Adults have a low, quick and often directed flight but frequently stop to nectar at small spring flowers and are particularly fond of their host blossoms. Males often gather at mud puddles to imbibe moisture. It typically rests and feeds with its wings closed; blue color is seen in flight or while basking.

Silvery Blue
Glaucopsyche lygdamus

Family/Subfamily: Gossamer Wings (Lycaenidae)/ Blues (Polyommatinae)

Wingspan: 1.00–1.25" (2.5–3.2 cm)

Above: male is uniform bright metallic silvery blue with narrow black wing borders and a white fringe

Below: light brownish gray with a prominent row of white-rimmed round black spots across the wings

Sexes: dissimilar; female is charcoal gray with dusky metallic blue overscaling and broad dark wing borders

Egg: pale blue-green, laid singly young shoots, new leaves or flower buds of host

Larva: gray green with a dark green dorsal stripe and white, oblique dashes; turns reddish prior to pupation

Larval Host Plants: Carolina Vetch, Veiny Pea and other legumes

Habitat: moist openings or clearings in deciduous woodlands, utility corridors, forested roads and brushy fields

Broods: single generation

Abundance: occasional

Compare: unique

Resident

Jan. Feb. Mar. Apr. May June July Aug. Sept. Oct. Nov. Dec.

male

Dorsal (above)
bright blue
narrow black border
female is grayer

Ventral (below)
dull gray
row of round white-rimmed black spots

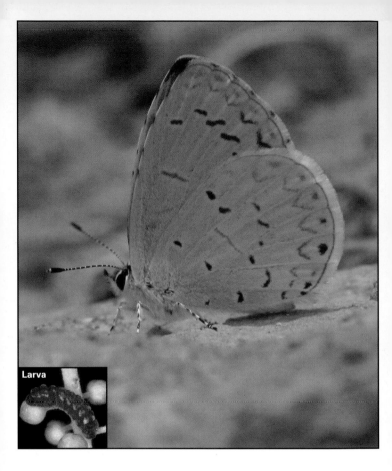

Larva

Comments: The Appalachian Azure is our largest resident blue. It is restricted to the moist, deciduous mountain forests of northern Georgia. Its single spring generation is seldom on the wing for more than a few short weeks. It appears to be temporally isolated from other azures, flying after the peak of the Spring Azure and just before the emergence of the Summer Azure. It is generally rather uncommon, occurring in small, isolated and low-density colonies in close proximity to its sole larval host. Males often gather in numbers at mud puddles along stream banks or unpaved woodland roads. Blue color shows in flight or while basking.

Appalachian Azure
Celastrina neglectamajor

Family/Subfamily: Gossamer Wings (Lycaenidae)/ Blues (Polyommatinae)

Wingspan: 1.1–1.4" (2.8–3.6 cm)

Above: male is uniform light blue with a narrow dark forewing border; lacks extensive white scaling

Below: chalky white with very pale, small dark spots; hindwing has faint zigzag band along margin enclosing an incomplete row of one to three prominent dark spots

Sexes: dissimilar; female has broad dark wing borders

Egg: pale green, laid singly (although often several on each plant) on flower buds of host

Larva: variable; yellow green to reddish brown with an often incomplete dark dorsal band and faint or absent oblique cream dashes

Larval Host Plants: flowers of Black Cohosh

Habitat: moist, cool shaded woodlands, forest trails, woodland roads and stream corridors

Broods: single generation

Abundance: uncommon and local

Compare: Summer Azure (pg. 83) is smaller and has increased white scaling on dorsal hindwing, but may not reliably be separated in the field.

Resident

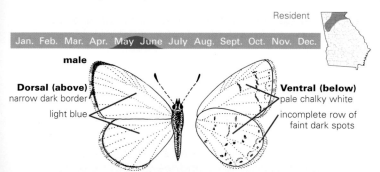

Jan. Feb. Mar. Apr. May June July Aug. Sept. Oct. Nov. Dec.

male

Dorsal (above)
narrow dark border

light blue

Ventral (below)
pale chalky white

incomplete row of faint dark spots

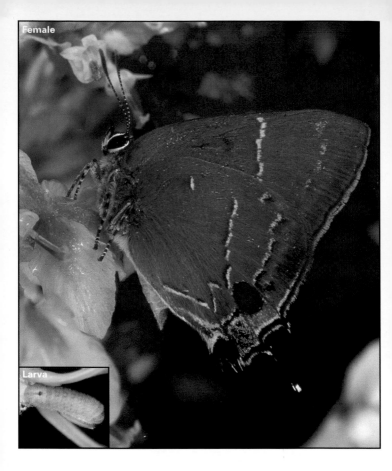

Female

Larva

Comments: The White M Hairstreak is named for the narrow white band on the underside of the hindwing that forms the letter M or W, depending on your perspective. The true beauty of this species can be seen mainly during flight, when the bright iridescent blue scaling of the upper wing surfaces flashes in the sunlight. It is a comparatively large member of its family. Adults readily explore open areas adjacent to their woodland habitats for available flowers. Adults have a quick, erratic flight and can be difficult to follow. This butterfly typically rests and feeds with its wings closed.

White M Hairstreak
Parrhasius m-album

Family/Subfamily: Gossamer Wings (Lycaenidae)/
Hairstreaks (Theclinae)

Wingspan: 1.0–1.5" (2.5–3.8 cm)

Above: male is bright iridescent blue with broad, black
margins and two hindwing tails; female is dull black
with blue scaling limited to wing bases

Below: brownish gray; hindwing has a single red eyespot
above tail, white spot along leading margin, and a narrow white line forming a distinct M in middle of wing

Sexes: dissimilar; female duller with blue basal scaling

Egg: whitish, laid singly on twigs or buds of host

Larva: variable, dark green to mauve

Larval Host Plants: various oaks including Live Oak
and White Oak

Habitat: forest edges and clearings, woodland trails, oak
hammocks, scrub and adjacent open areas

Broods: multiple generations

Abundance: occasional to common

Compare: Great Purple Hairstreak (pg. 91) is larger and
lacks white M and red spot on ventral hindwing.
Southern Hairstreak (pg. 133) is brown above.

Resident

Jan. Feb. Mar. Apr. May June July Aug. Sept. Oct. Nov. Dec.

male

Dorsal (above)
iridescent blue
wide black borders

Ventral (below)
white spot
white M
red spot
blue patch

89

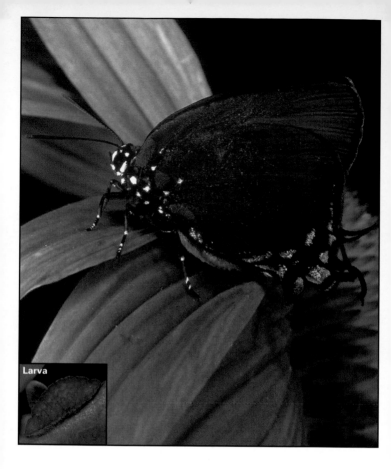

Larva

Comments: The Great Purple Hairstreak significantly
dwarfs most other members of its family. The upper
wing surfaces of this stunning hairstreak are actually
bright metallic blue, not purple. Primarily a butterfly of
forested areas, it usually dwells high in the canopy
close to its mistletoe host. Adults readily venture
down to available flowers where they can be more
closely observed. Quickly identified by its orange
abdomen, the butterfly's bold ventral coloration warns
potential predators that it is distasteful. It typically
rests and feeds with its wings closed, so its blue color
is seen primarily in flight or while basking.

Great Purple Hairstreak
Atlides halesus

Family/Subfamily: Gossamer Wings (Lycaenidae)/
Hairstreaks (Theclinae)

Wingspan: 1.0–1.7" (2.5–4.3 cm)

Above: male is bright metallic purple-blue with black
margins and dark forewing stigma; female is dull black
with metallic blue scaling limited to wing bases; two
hindwing tails

Below: dull brownish black with metallic green and blue
spots near tails and red spots at wing bases; underside of abdomen reddish orange; head and thorax have
white spots

Sexes: dissimilar; female is duller with less blue and
more rounded wings

Egg: green, laid singly on host leaves

Larva: green with numerous short hairs

Larval Host Plants: Mistletoe

Habitat: woodland edges, adjacent open areas, gardens
and parks

Broods: multiple generations

Abundance: occasional

Compare: White M Hairstreak (pg. 89) is smaller with a
narrow white M on the underside of the hindwing near
the tails and prominent red spot.

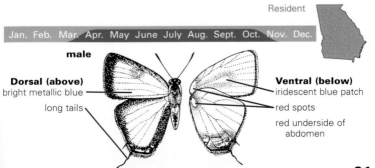

Resident

Jan. Feb. Mar. Apr. May June July Aug. Sept. Oct. Nov. Dec.

male

Dorsal (above)
bright metallic blue

long tails

Ventral (below)
iridescent blue patch

red spots

red underside of
abdomen

91

Larva

Comments: The dainty Eastern Pygmy-Blue is our smallest butterfly. It is found only along coastal portions of southeastern Georgia. Adults have a low, weak flight and flutter erratically just above the surface of their fleshy host plants. Nonetheless, their diminutive size often makes them a challenge to follow when on the wing. Easily identified, it is the only blue in the state with a row of four silvery black spots along the ventral hindwing margin. Although occasionally abundant in certain locations, individual colonies are often sporadic and highly localized.

Eastern Pygmy-Blue
Brephidium isophthalma

Family/Subfamily: Gossamer Wings (Lycaenidae)/
Blues (Polyommatinae)

Wingspan: 0.50–0.75" (1.3–1.9 cm)

Above: brown with some blue basal scaling and a row of
dark spots along the outer margin of the hindwing

Below: brown with numerous white streaks and bands;
hindwing margin has row of black spots with silver
highlights

Sexes: similar

Egg: greenish blue, laid singly on all parts of host

Larva: green with dark head

Larval Host Plants: Saltwort and glassworts

Habitat: salt marshes and adjacent coastal areas

Broods: multiple generations

Abundance: uncommon to locally abundant

Compare: Ceraunus Blue (pg. 77) is larger, gray beneath
with prominent white-rimmed black spots on base of
hindwing. Cassius Blue (pg. 75) is larger, strongly
banded beneath with two black hindwing eyespots.
Both lack row of black marginal spots on the hindwing
below.

Resident

Jan. Feb. Mar. Apr. May June July Aug. Sept. Oct. Nov. Dec.

Dorsal (above)
dull brown wings
brown fringe
faint blue basal
scaling
row of small black
spots

Ventral (below)
brown fringe
four prominent black
spots

93

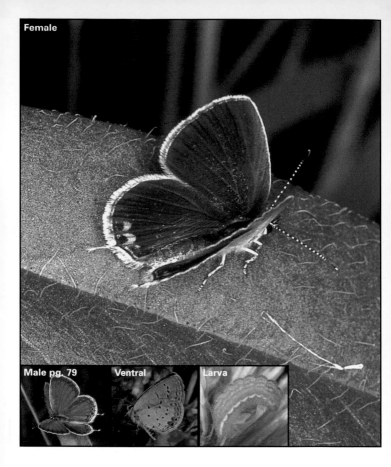

Female

Male pg. 79 | **Ventral** | **Larva**

Comments: The Eastern Tailed-Blue is widespread and common throughout most of the eastern United States. Named for its distinctive hindwing tail, it is the only blue in Georgia with this characteristic hairstreak-like feature. Do not rely solely on the presence of tails for identification, as they are fragile and may be lost with normal wing wear. Adults have a weak, dancing flight. They are fond of flowers and are easily attracted to gardens. Males often gather in small puddle clubs at damp sand or gravel. It typically rests and feeds with its wings closed, so its blue color is seen primarily in flight or when the butterfly is basking in the sun.

Eastern Tailed-Blue
Everes comyntas

Family/Subfamily: Gossamer Wings (Lycaenidae)/ Blues (Polyommatinae)

Wingspan: 0.75–1.00" (1.9–2.5 cm)

Above: male is blue with brown border; female is brownish gray; both sexes have one or two small orange and black hindwing spots above single tail

Below: silvery gray with numerous dark spots and bands; hindwing has two small orange-capped black spots above tail

Sexes: dissimilar; female is primarily brownish gray

Egg: pale green, laid singly on flowers or young leaves of host

Larva: variable, typically green with dark dorsal stripe and light lateral stripes

Larval Host Plants: various herbaceous Fabaceae including clovers, bush clovers and beggarweeds

Habitat: open, disturbed sites including roadsides, vacant lots and old fields

Broods: multiple generations

Abundance: occasional to common

Compare: Summer Azure (pg. 83) lacks hindwing tails. Gray Hairstreak (pg. 255) has distinct black-and-white (occasionally orange) ventral hindwing stripe.

Resident

Jan. Feb. Mar. Apr. May June July Aug. Sept. Oct. Nov. Dec.

male

Dorsal (above)
bright blue

one or two orange-capped black spots

tail

Ventral (below)
black spots and bars outlined in white

one or two orange-capped black spots

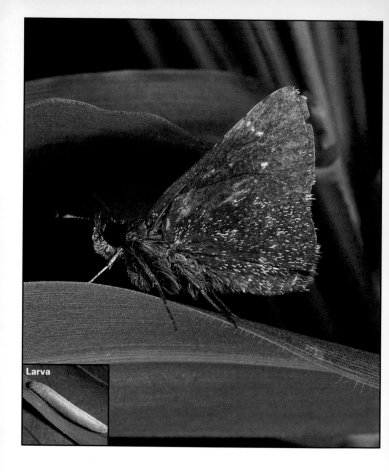

Larva

Comments: This small drab skipper is an inhabitant of open pine woodlands. Superficially similar to the more widespread and abundant Common Roadside-Skipper, it lacks the more extensive ventral gray overscaling and heavily checkered wing fringes. Rare throughout its limited range, much is yet to be learned about this reclusive, poorly understood butterfly.

Dusky Roadside-Skipper
Amblyscirtes alternata

Family/Subfamily: Skippers (Hesperiidae)/
Banded Skippers (Hesperiinae)

Wingspan: 0.85–1.00" (2.2–2.5 cm)

Above: primarily dark blackish brown, often with a few small white spots near the forewing apex

Below: dark grayish black with faint gray dusting and lightly checkered fringes

Sexes: similar

Egg: currently undocumented

Larva: blue green with faint dark dorsal stripe

Larval Host Plants: various grasses

Habitat: open pine woodlands

Broods: two generations

Abundance: rare to uncommon

Compare: Common Roadside-Skipper (pg. 137) has increased gray frosting below and more prominently checkered wing fringes. Forewing typically has a triangular white spot toward apex.

Resident

| Jan. | Feb. | Mar. | Apr. | May | June | July | Aug. | Sept. | Oct. | Nov. | Dec. |

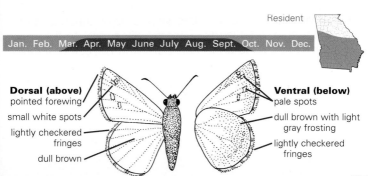

Dorsal (above)
pointed forewing
small white spots
lightly checkered fringes
dull brown

Ventral (below)
pale spots
dull brown with light gray frosting
lightly checkered fringes

97

Larva

Comments: This small but richly colored, tailless butterfly has only a single brief spring flight. Typically spotty
and highly localized in occurrence, it seldom wanders
far from stands of its larval hosts. Nonetheless, it
remains one of our most commonly encountered
elfins. The adults generally remain close to the ground,
often perching on low vegetation or resting on the
ground itself. If disturbed, they rapidly dart off but
travel only a short distance before alighting once more.
They nectar from a variety of early season flowers
including host blossoms.

Brown Elfin
Callophrys augustinus

Family/Subfamily: Gossamer Wings (Lycaenidae)/ Hairstreaks (Theclinae)

Wingspan: 0.8–1.1" (2.0–2.8 cm)

Above: dark brown; male has dark forewing stigma

Below: forewing brown; hindwing dark brown at base with outer portion lighter reddish brown to mahogany

Sexes: similar

Egg: whitish, laid singly host flower buds

Larva: yellow green with pale yellow oblique dorsal dashes and a yellow lateral stripe

Larval Host Plants: primarily plants in the heath family including Black Huckleberry, Leatherleaf, Highbush Blueberry, and Blue Ridge Blueberry

Habitat: open woodlands, forest margins and clearings, scrub and bogs

Broods: single generation

Abundance: occasional to common

Compare: Eastern Pine Elfin (pg. 109) has strongly patterned hindwings with numerous dark bands outlined in white. Frosted Elfin's (pg. 101) hindwing has extensive frosting and a short, stubby tail. Henry's Elfin (pg. 111) has some white on outer portion of dark basal hindwing patch, frosting along margin of hindwing and a short, stubby tail.

Resident

| Jan. | Feb. | Mar. | Apr. | May | June | July | Aug. | Sept. | Oct. | Nov. | Dec. |

Dorsal (above)
brown wings
lobed anal angle of hindwing

Ventral (below)
hindwing much darker at base
reddish brown toward outer margin

99

Larva

Comments: Living up to its name, the Frosted Elfin
looks as if it were dusted lightly with powdered sugar
on its ventral hindwings. Like most elfins, it tends to
be rather uncommon and highly localized, most often
encountered close to its leguminous larval hosts.
Despite its small size, generally slow, low flight and
close host association, the butterfly is considered an
effective colonizer and able to disperse some distance
to establish new populations in suitable habitat areas.
Larvae feed on host flowers and developing seed
pods.

Frosted Elfin
Callophrys irus

Family/Subfamily: Gossamer Wings (Lycaenidae)/ Hairstreaks (Theclinae)

Wingspan: 0.8–1.1" (2.0–2.8 cm)

Above: unmarked dark brown; male has dark forewing stigma

Below: forewing brown; hindwing dark brown at wing base, outer portion somewhat lighter with extensive gray frosting along outer margin; frosted area contains a distinct single black spot near the short, stubby tail

Sexes: similar, although female lacks forewing stigma

Egg: whitish, laid singly host flower buds

Larva: blue-green with pale white oblique dorsal dashes and a pale white lateral stripe

Larval Host Plants: Wild Lupine and Wild Indigo

Habitat: open woodlands, forest margins and clearings, open, brushy fields, roadsides and scrub

Broods: single generation

Abundance: rare to occasional

Compare: Eastern Pine Elfin (pg. 109) has strongly patterned hindwings with numerous dark bands outlined in white. Henry's Elfin (pg. 111) lacks black spot near short, stubby tail. Brown Elfin (pg. 99) lacks hindwing frosting and short, stubby tail.

Resident

| Jan. | Feb. | Mar. | Apr. | May | June | July | Aug. | Sept. | Oct. | Nov. | Dec. |

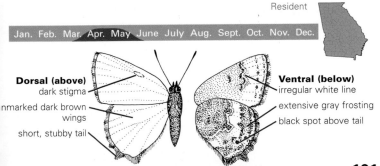

Dorsal (above)
dark stigma
nmarked dark brown wings
short, stubby tail

Ventral (below)
irregular white line
extensive gray frosting
black spot above tail

101

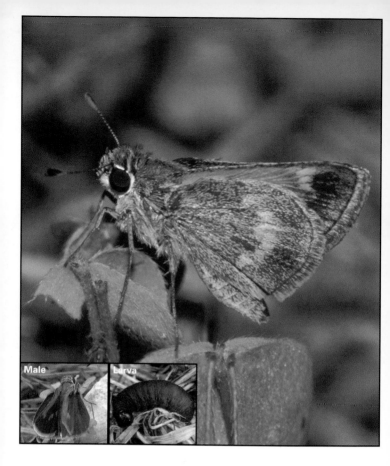

Male

Larva

Comments: Although the range of this small subtropical skipper is limited almost entirely to Florida, it just barely extends northward across the border into southern Georgia. The Baracoa Skipper is a butterfly of dry woodlands and scrub where it tends to be fairly local and uncommon. It is unlikely to be a frequent garden visitor. Adults maneuver close to the ground with a rapid flight. Males perch on low-growing vegetation, debris or bare earth to await passing females.

Baracoa Skipper
Polites baracoa

Family/Subfamily: Skippers (Hesperiidae)/
Banded Skippers (Hesperiinae)

Wingspan: 0.85–1.10" (2.2–2.8 cm)

Above: dark brown; male has golden orange scaling
along costal margin and a short black stigma toward
the base of the forewing

Below: forewing has golden orange scaling along costal
margin; hindwing is light brown with pale spot band

Sexes: similar, although female lacks black stigma and
has additional pale golden orange forewing spots

Egg: white, laid singly on host leaves

Larva: brown with dark brown longitudinal stripes and a
black head marked by two pale dashes on the top

Larval Host Plants: various grasses including Bermuda
Grass

Habitat: open, disturbed sites, suburban lawns and dry,
scrubby woodlands

Broods: multiple generations

Abundance: uncommon

Compare: Tawny-Edged Skipper (pg. 107) is larger and
typically lacks pale hindwing spot band. Crossline
Skipper (pg. 127) is larger and has a relatively straight
pale hindwing spot band.

Resident

Jan.	Feb.	Mar.	Apr.	May	June	July	Aug.	Sept.	Oct.	Nov.	Dec.

male

Dorsal (above)
tawny orange scaling
brown wing

Ventral (below)
orange scaling along
costal margin
pale hindwing band

103

Dorsal

Larva

Comments: This drab brown skipper is distinctly plain. The Swarthy Skipper is reliably identified in the field by its unmarked ventral wings with light colored veins. However, its small size and uneventful appearance make it an easy butterfly to quickly overlook. Frequently encountered in open grassy sites, colonies may be somewhat small and localized near patches of its larval host. Like most small skippers, it has a very quick, erratic flight but may be observed closely when nectaring at a variety of low-growing flowers. Larvae construct individual rolled leaf shelters on the host.

Swarthy Skipper
Nastra lherminier

Family/Subfamily: Skippers (Hesperiidae)/
Banded Skippers (Hesperiinae)

Wingspan: 0.9–1.1" (2.3–2.8 cm)

Above: dull dark brown, occasionally with small faint
forewing spots

Below: olive brown to yellow brown with light veins

Sexes: similar

Egg: white, laid singly on host leaves

Larva: elongate; pale green with a darker green dorsal
stripe, a pale lateral stripe and a reddish brown head
marked with vertical cream bands

Larval Host Plants: Little Bluestem and Kentucky
Bluegrass

Habitat: old fields, roadsides, meadows, open, grassy
areas, abandoned lots and gardens

Broods: two generations

Abundance: occasional to common

Compare: unique

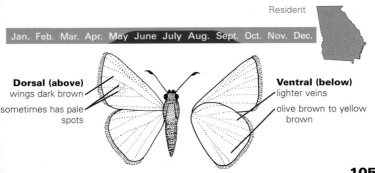

Resident

Jan. Feb. Mar. Apr. May June July Aug. Sept. Oct. Nov. Dec.

Dorsal (above)
wings dark brown

sometimes has pale
spots

Ventral (below)
lighter veins

olive brown to yellow
brown

105

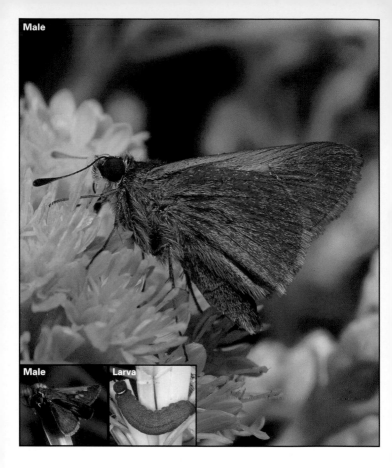

Male

Male Larva

Comments: The Tawny-edged Skipper's distinct orange band along the leading margin of the forewing is visible from both the dorsal and ventral surfaces. It is superficially quite similar to the Crossline Skipper. A common species, it may be frequently encountered in suburban locations including home gardens. Adults have a low, rapid flight and often alight on bare soil or low vegetation.

Tawny-edged Skipper
Polites themistocles

Family/Subfamily: Skippers (Hesperiidae)/
Banded Skippers (Hesperiinae)

Wingspan: 0.8–1.2" (2.0–3.0 cm)

Above: male is dark brown with prominent black stigma
and tawny orange scaling along forewing costa;
female is dark brown with small yellow spots across
forewing and reduced orange along costal margin

Below: light brown to olive brown with distinct contrasting orange scaling along costal margin of forewing

Sexes: dissimilar; female darker with reduced orange coloration

Egg: greenish white, laid singly on host leaves

Larva: reddish brown with dark dorsal stripe and black
head

Larval Host Plants: various grasses including panic
grass, Slender Crabgrass, mannagrass and bluegrass

Habitat: stream corridors, wet meadows, fields, pastures and suburban yards

Broods: two or more generations

Abundance: occasional to common

Compare: Crossline Skipper (pg. 127) is larger, and usually has a faint band of small, pale spots through the
center of the yellow-brown ventral hindwing. Tolerates
drier habitats.

Resident

Jan.	Feb.	Mar.	Apr.	May	June	July	Aug.	Sept.	Oct.	Nov.	Dec.

male

Dorsal (above)
orange along costal margin

sinuous black stigma

Ventral (below)
orange scaling along costal margin

unmarked olive to brassy brown hindwing, rarely with faint spot band

107

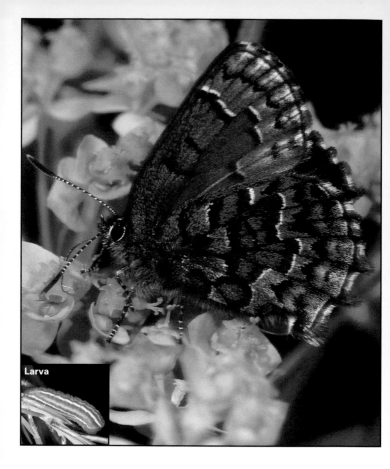

Larva

Comments: With its boldly patterned hindwings, this beautiful little spring species is our most distinctive elfin. Inhabiting a variety of open and semi-open landscapes that support stands of hard pines, the butterfly is commonly found in close association with younger trees. Adults spend much of their time perched on host branches, often high above the ground, but frequently venture down to nectar at nearby blossoms or sip moisture at damp soil.

Eastern Pine Elfin
Callophrys niphon

Family/Subfamily: Gossamer Wings (Lycaenidae)/ Hairstreaks (Theclinae)

Wingspan: 0.80–1.25" (2.0–3.2 cm)

Above: unmarked dark brown; male has a pale gray forewing stigma

Below: brown, strongly banded with black, reddish brown and gray; hindwing has gray marginal band

Sexes: similar, although female is tawnier above and lacks pale forewing stigma

Egg: pale green, laid singly at the base of host needles

Larva: bright green with cream longitudinal stripes

Larval Host Plants: various hard pines including Virginia Pine, Loblolly Pine, Pitch Pine and Shortleaf Pine; also Eastern White Pine

Habitat: open woodlands, forest margins and clearings, open, brushy fields, roadsides, scrub and utility easements

Broods: single generation

Abundance: occasional to common

Compare: All other elfins lack the strongly patterned ventral hindwing.

Resident

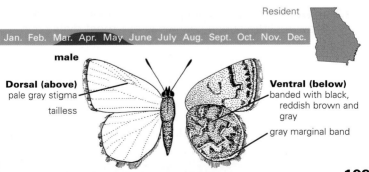

Jan. Feb. Mar. Apr. May June July Aug. Sept. Oct. Nov. Dec.

male

Dorsal (above)
pale gray stigma

tailless

Ventral (below)
banded with black, reddish brown and gray

gray marginal band

109

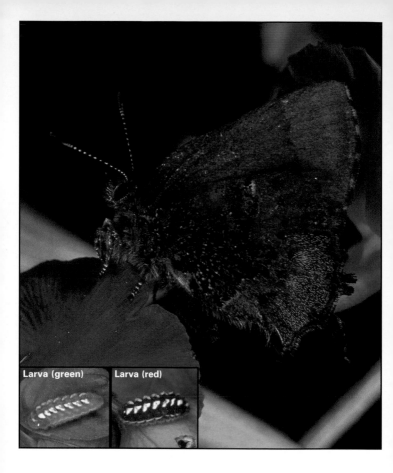

Larva (green) Larva (red)

Comments: Henry's Elfin is a small, primarily brown butterfly with delicate markings and a stubby tail. Although it is widespread in the Southeast, it is generally rare and encountered only in small, localized colonies. Found in variety of semi-open areas, this spring species rarely strays far from stands of its larval host. Adults have a fast, erratic flight but regularly perch on the tips of tree branches or on shrubby vegetation. Males may be encountered sipping moisture at damp earth.

Henry's Elfin
Callophrys henrici

Family/Subfamily: Gossamer Wings (Lycaenidae)/ Hairstreaks (Theclinae)

Wingspan: 0.9–1.2" (2.3–3.0 cm)

Above: brown with amber scaling along hindwing margin; hindwing has short, stubby tail

Below: brown; hindwing distinctly two-toned with dark brown basal half and light brown outer half; gray frosting along outer margin

Sexes: similar

Egg: whitish, laid singly on host twigs or flower buds

Larva: variable; green to reddish with oblique white dorsal markings

Larval Host Plants: Redbud, Dahoon Holly, American Holly and Yaupon Holly

Habitat: deciduous woodlands, forest edges and clearings, shrubby areas, old fields and roadsides

Broods: single spring generation

Abundance: occasional; localized

Compare: Eastern Pine Elfin (pg. 109) has strongly patterned ventral hindwing with numerous dark bands outlined in white. Frosted Elfin (pg. 101) has more frosting on hindwing and small dark spot near tail. Brown Elfin (pg. 99) lacks tail and gray frosting.

Resident

Jan. Feb. Mar. Apr. May June July Aug. Sept. Oct. Nov. Dec.

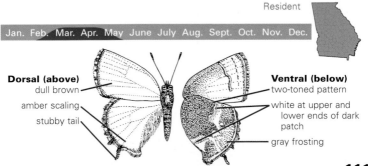

Dorsal (above)
dull brown
amber scaling
stubby tail

Ventral (below)
two-toned pattern
white at upper and lower ends of dark patch
gray frosting

111

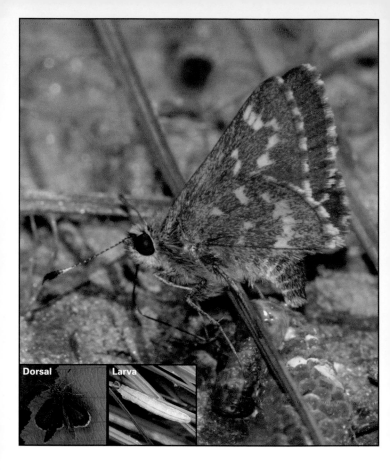

Dorsal

Larva

Comments: Well named, this distinctive skipper does indeed look as if it was sprinkled with ample amounts of salt and pepper. Widespread throughout the east, it is a butterfly of wet habitats preferring moist meadows, forest glades, and stream corridors. Seldom common, it is most often encountered in localized colonies. Males may frequently be seen puddling at moist ground. The adults are not strongly restricted to wet sites and often wander extensively into nearby habitats in search of nectar. Larvae overwinter.

Pepper and Salt Skipper
Amblyscirtes hegon

Family/Subfamily: Skippers (Hesperiidae)/
Banded Skippers (Hesperiinae)

Wingspan: 0.9–1.2" (2.3–3.0 cm)

Above: dark brown with checkered fringes and a band of
small white spots on the forewing

Below: variable; hindwing is greenish gray with cream
spot band; wing fringes are strongly checkered

Sexes: similar

Egg: light green, laid singly on host leaves

Larva: whitish green with a dark green dorsal line, a
paler green subdorsal line and a reddish brown head
with a pale brown crescent on each side

Larval Host Plants: various grasses including Fowl
Mannagrass, Indian Grass, Kentucky Bluegrass and
Indian Woodoats

Habitat: woodland margins, wet meadows, stream margins

Broods: single generation

Abundance: occasional

Compare: Bell's Roadside-Skipper (pg. 155) is generally
darker below with reduced white overscaling.

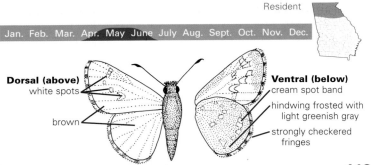

Resident

Jan. Feb. Mar. Apr. May June July Aug. Sept. Oct. Nov. Dec.

Dorsal (above)
white spots

brown

Ventral (below)
cream spot band

hindwing frosted with
light greenish gray

strongly checkered
fringes

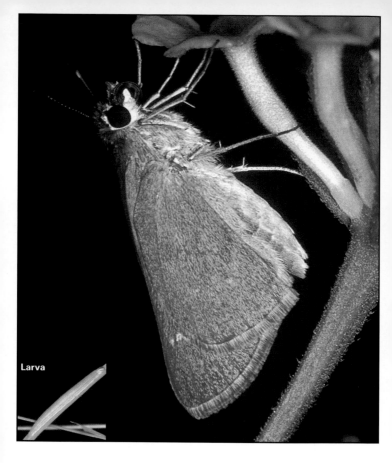

Larva

Comments: The underside of the Eufala Skipper's wings appear distinctly washed-out. A year-round resident of the warm Gulf Coast and Florida, it regularly establishes temporary breeding colonies throughout much of Georgia but is unable to survive prolonged exposure to freezing temperatures. Adults avidly visit available flowers and frequent home gardens. They have a rapid, erratic flight but pause regularly to perch on low vegetation where they are easy to observe.

Eufala Skipper
Lerodea eufala

Family/Subfamily: Skippers (Hesperiidae)/
Banded Skippers (Hesperiinae)

Wingspan: 0.90–1.25" (2.3–3.2 cm)

Above: grayish brown with several tiny semitransparent
spots on forewing; subapical spots form small, straight
band

Below: light brown to tan, often with faint, light hindwing
spots

Sexes: similar

Egg: cream, laid singly on or near host leaves

Larva: green with green and yellow stripes; head is
brownish orange below and cream above

Larval Host Plants: various grasses, including
Bermuda Grass, Barnyardgrass and Hooked
Bristlegrass

Habitat: open, grassy areas including old fields, roadsides, vacant lots, pineland edges and clearings, and
utility easements

Broods: two or more generations

Abundance: occasional to common

Compare: Swarthy Skipper (pg. 105) has a yellow brown
ventral hindwing with light veins.

Resident Visitor

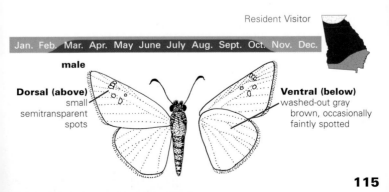

Jan. Feb. Mar. Apr. May June July Aug. Sept. Oct. Nov. Dec.

male

Dorsal (above)
small
semitransparent
spots

Ventral (below)
washed-out gray
brown, occasionally
faintly spotted

115

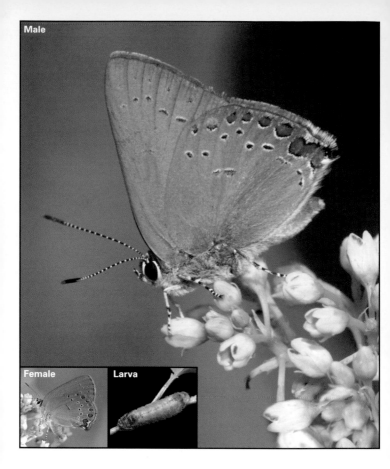

Male

Female

Larva

Comments: This distinctive tailless hairstreak can be confused with no other small Georgia butterfly. It frequents a variety of semi-open, brushy habitats in close association with its somewhat weedy, thicket-forming hosts. Although widespread, the Coral Hairstreak is often quite localized in occurrence and is seldom encountered in large numbers. Adults have a quick, erratic flight and readily perch on the top of small trees or shrubs. Both sexes frequently visit flowers and are exceedingly fond of milkweed blossoms.

Coral Hairstreak
Satyrium titus

Family/Subfamily: Gossamer Wings (Lycaenidae)/
Hairstreaks (Theclinae)

Wingspan: 0.90–1.25" (2.3–3.2 cm)

Above: unmarked brown; male has a small gray
forewing stigma and somewhat triangular wings

Below: light gray brown with a row of small, white-
rimmed black spots across both wings and a second
row of larger bright coral spots along the hindwing
margin; tailless

Sexes: similar, although female has more rounded wings
and lacks forewing stigma

Egg: cream, laid singly on host twigs, low on the trunks
of small host trees or occasionally on leaf litter below
the host

Larva: yellow green with pinkish red patches on each end

Larval Host Plants: Black Cherry, Wild Cherry,
American Plum and Chickasaw Plum

Habitat: overgrown fields near forest margins, brushy
woodland clearings, shrubby roadsides and trails, and
unmanaged pastures or fencerows

Broods: single generation

Abundance: uncommon to common

Compare: unique

Resident

| Jan. | Feb. | Mar. | Apr. | May | June | July | Aug. | Sept. | Oct. | Nov. | Dec. |

Dorsal (above)
tailless

Ventral (below)
white-rimmed black
spots

prominent row of
bright coral spots

117

Larvae

Comments: The Banded Hairstreak is Georgia's most abundant representative of the *Satyrium* genus, which is comprised primarily of dull brown species. A small, inconspicuous butterfly of mixed hardwood forests with hickories and oaks, it may be readily encountered at flowers in nearby clearings or along adjacent road-sides. The adults are particularly fond of white sweet clover. Males perch on shrubs or low, overhanging limbs and aggressively dart out at other hairstreaks or passing males.

Banded Hairstreak
Satyrium calanus

Family/Subfamily: Gossamer Wings (Lycaenidae)/ Hairstreaks (Theclinae)

Wingspan: 1.00–1.25" (2.5–3.2 cm)

Above: unmarked dark brown with two hindwing tails

Below: variable; brown to slate gray; hindwing has dark postmedian band outlined on outer side with white and a red-capped black spot and blue patch near tails

Sexes: similar

Egg: pinkish brown, laid singly on twigs of host

Larva: variable, green to grayish brown with a light lateral stripe

Larval Host Plants: various oaks, hickories and walnuts including White Oak, Northern Red Oak, Turkey Oak, Southern Red Oak, Pignut Hickory, Shagbark Hickory, Black Walnut and Bitternut

Habitat: mixed deciduous forests, oak woodlands, forest clearings, roads and adjacent open areas

Broods: single generation

Abundance: occasional to common

Compare: Striped Hairstreak (pg. 135) has wider, more extensive bands beneath and an orange-capped blue patch near tail. Hickory Hairstreak (pg. 123) has wider, more offset dark ventral bands edged in white on both sides.

Resident

| Jan. | Feb. | Mar. | Apr. | May | June | July | Aug. | Sept. | Oct. | Nov. | Dec. |

Dorsal (above)
unmarked brown

two tails

Ventral (below)
band of darkened dashes edged outwardly in white

red-capped black spot

blue patch not capped in red

119

Larva

Comments: Edward's Hairstreak is generally associated with areas dominated by short, scrubby oaks. Its relatively short flight period and resemblance to other, more abundant hairstreaks makes it an easy butterfly to overlook. The developing slug-like larvae are regularly tended (and thus guarded from many predators) by ants, which in turn feed on the larvae's sugary honeydew secretions. Depending on the degree of this association, the butterfly may rely heavily on the ant species for survival, which may contribute to its spotty, localized distribution.

Edwards' Hairstreak
Satyrium edwardsii

Family/Subfamily: Gossamer Wings (Lycaenidae)/ Hairstreaks (Theclinae)

Wingspan: 1.00–1.25" (2.5–3.2 cm)

Above: unmarked brown with a small orange spot near short tail; male has small dark forewing stigma

Below: light gray brown with a row of small, white-rimmed black spots; hindwing has a large blue patch and a series of orange spots near tails

Sexes: similar, although female has slightly more rounded wings and lacks dark forewing stigma above

Egg: cream pink, laid singly on host twigs near buds; eggs overwinter

Larva: dark brown with dark dorsal band and a series of pale oblique dashes along the sides

Larval Host Plants: various oaks including Bear Oak, Black Oak, Blackjack Oak and White Oak

Habitat: oak woodlands, thickets and scrub, forest margins, roadsides, utility easements and trail edges

Broods: single generation

Abundance: uncommon to locally common

Compare: Striped Hairstreak (pg. 135), King's Hairstreak (pg. 125), and Banded Hairstreak (pg. 119) all have bands of white-edged dashes, not spots on ventral wing surface.

Resident

Jan. Feb. Mar. Apr. May June July Aug. Sept. Oct. Nov. Dec.

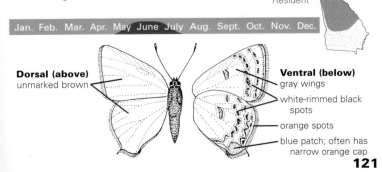

Dorsal (above)
unmarked brown

Ventral (below)
gray wings
white-rimmed black spots
orange spots
blue patch; often has narrow orange cap

121

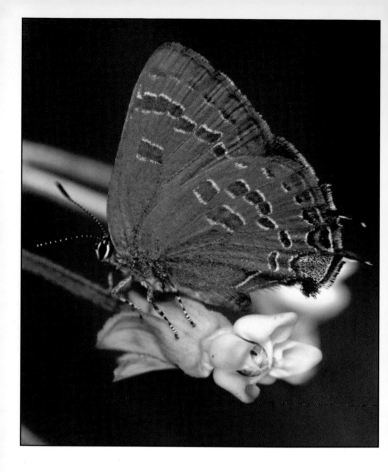

Comments: The range of this rare and reclusive hairstreak extends southward through the Appalachian Mountains and just barely enters the northern tip of Georgia. A butterfly of mixed deciduous forests and second growth woodlands, the Hickory Hairstreak is typically local and sporadic in occurrence. It may further be overlooked because of its close resemblance to the more widespread and common Banded Hairstreak. The adults often perch high on the branches of their hosts and occasionally dart out with a fast, erratic flight before alighting again.

Hickory Hairstreak
Satyrium caryaevorum

Family/Subfamily: Gossamer Wings (Lycaenidae)/ Hairstreaks (Theclinae)

Wingspan: 1.00–1.25" (2.5–3.2 cm)

Above: uniform dark brown with a short hindwing tail; male has a gray forewing stigma

Below: brown with a row of fairly wide and somewhat offset dark dashes edged in white across both wings, a large blue hindwing patch and orange-capped black spot near the tail

Sexes: similar, although female lacks forewing stigma

Egg: pinkish brown, laid singly on twigs; eggs overwinter

Larva: yellow green, often with dark green dorsal stripe, yellow lateral stripe and dark dashes edged in white

Larval Host Plants: various hickories, walnuts and oaks including Pignut Hickory, Shagbark Hickory, Bitternut Hickory, Northern Red Oak and Bitternut

Habitat: mixed deciduous forests, clearings, roads and margins, and adjacent open, often brushy, areas

Broods: single generation

Abundance: rare to uncommon

Compare: Banded Hairstreak (pg. 119) typically lacks white edging along inner margin of dark band. Difficult to reliably separate in the field.

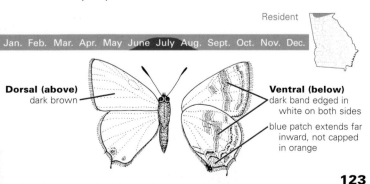

Resident

Jan. Feb. Mar. Apr. May June July Aug. Sept. Oct. Nov. Dec.

Dorsal (above)
dark brown

Ventral (below)
dark band edged in white on both sides

blue patch extends far inward, not capped in orange

123

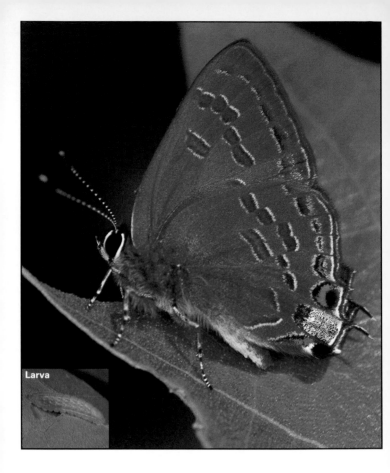

Larva

Comments: This lovely hairstreak is quite rare through-out its range and should be considered a "good find" when encountered. Restricted to the shady confines of hardwood forests and wooded swamps, it occurs in highly localized populations in close association with its sole larval host. Due to its reclusive nature, the King's Hairstreak remains one of our more poorly known and studied butterflies. Adults frequently perch on broad sunlit leaves but seldom venture into nearby open landscapes. Young larvae bore into host buds and feed on developing leaves.

King's Hairstreak
Satyrium kingi

Family/Subfamily: Gossamer Wings (Lycaenidae)/ Hairstreaks (Theclinae)

Wingspan: 1.00–1.25" (2.5–3.2 cm)

Above: uniform dark brown with two short hindwing tails

Below: gray brown with a row of prominent dark dashes edged in white across both wings, a large blue hindwing patch capped in orange, an orange-capped black spot near the tail, and iridescent wing fringes; freshly emerged individuals have a subtle violet blue cast

Sexes: similar

Egg: laid singly on host twigs; eggs overwinter

Larva: green with darker green oblique lines

Larval Host Plants: Common Sweetleaf

Habitat: hardwood forests, stream margins and wooded swamps

Broods: single generation

Abundance: rare, local

Compare: Striped Hairstreak (pg. 135) has more extensive, wider ventral bands. Banded Hairstreak (pg. 119) is more abundant, and lacks an orange cap on the ventral blue hindwing patch. Hickory Hairstreak (pg. 123) lacks an orange cap on the ventral blue hindwing patch.

Resident

Jan. Feb. Mar. Apr. May June July Aug. Sept. Oct. Nov. Dec.

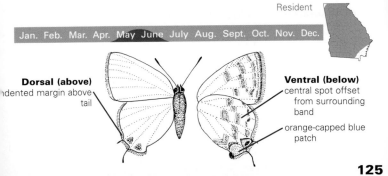

Dorsal (above)
indented margin above tail

Ventral (below)
central spot offset from surrounding band

orange-capped blue patch

125

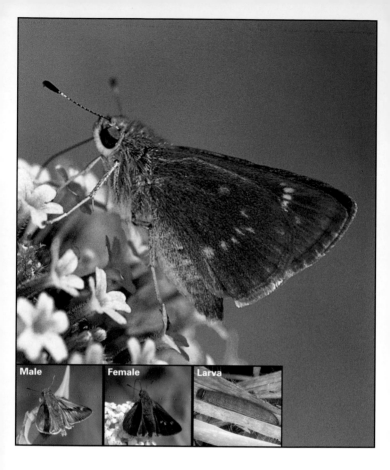

Male

Female

Larva

Comments: Although frequently confused with the similar Tawny-edged Skipper, the Crossline Skipper can often be readily distinguished from its relative on the basis of habitat, preferring drier, open areas. The species may be frequently encountered in more suburban locations including home gardens and lawns where the adults can be observed nectaring at a variety of flowers. Adults have a low, rapid flight and often alight on bare soil or low vegetation.

Crossline Skipper
Polites origenes

Family/Subfamily: Skippers (Hesperiidae)/
Banded Skippers (Hesperiinae)

Wingspan: 1.00–1.25" (2.5–3.2 cm)

Above: male is dark olive brown; forewing has tawny
orange scaling along costal margin and yellow orange
spots along the outer edge of black stigma

Below: hindwing is yellow brown with a faint, straight
band of small pale spots; forewing has dull tawny
orange scaling along costal margin, not strongly contrasting with color of hindwing

Sexes: dissimilar; female darker above with cream spots
on forewing and reduced orange along costal margin

Egg: greenish, laid singly on host leaves

Larva: dark brown with faint white mottling and a round
black head

Larval Host Plants: various grasses including Little
Bluestem, Purpletop Grass, mannagrass and bluegrass

Habitat: dry, grassy areas including old fields, woodland
meadows, pastures, forest clearings and easements

Broods: two generations

Abundance: occasional to common

Compare: Tawny-edged Skipper (pg. 107) prefers wetter
habitats, is smaller, and usually has unmarked, darker
hindwings.

Resident

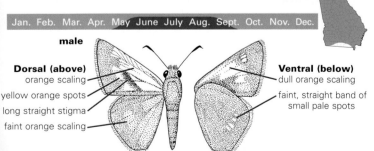

| Jan. | Feb. | Mar. | Apr. | May | June | July | Aug. | Sept. | Oct. | Nov. | Dec. |

male

Dorsal (above)
orange scaling
yellow orange spots
long straight stigma
faint orange scaling

Ventral (below)
dull orange scaling
faint, straight band of
small pale spots

127

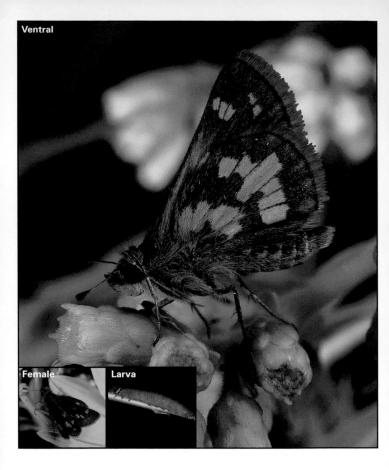

Ventral

Female

Larva

Comments: Common throughout most of its range,
Peck's Skipper just enters the northern tip of Georgia.
Primarily a butterfly of moist meadows and marshes, it
tolerates a wide range of more human-disturbed
grassy areas including roadsides and suburban lawns.
The small adults maneuver close to the ground with a
rapid, darting flight but regularly alight on low vegetation. Its distinctive light ventral hindwing patch is fairly
variable in appearance and may be solid or somewhat
broken into spot bands.

Peck's Skipper
Polites peckius

Family/Subfamily: Skippers (Hesperiidae)/
Banded Skippers (Hesperiinae)

Wingspan: 1.00–1.25" (2.5–3.2 cm)

Above: dark brown; forewing has orange scaling toward
base and a few tiny orange spots near apex; hindwing
has a band of elongated narrow orange spots

Below: variable; hindwing is dark brown with a distinctive irregular central golden yellow patch

Sexes: similar, although female has reduced orange scaling at forewing base

Egg: whitish green, laid singly on host leaves

Larva: dark maroon brown with short light hairs and a
black head and anal patch

Larval Host Plants: various grasses including Rice
Cutgrass and Kentucky Bluegrass

Habitat: open grassy areas including pastures, roadsides, old fields, wet meadows, marshes, utility
easements and lawns

Broods: two or three generations

Abundance: occasional to common

Compare: Sachem (pg. 151) is larger and has long, narrow wings; male has large rounded black stigma on
the forewing above.

Resident

| Jan. | Feb. | Mar. | Apr. | May | June | July | Aug. | Sept. | Oct. | Nov. | Dec. |

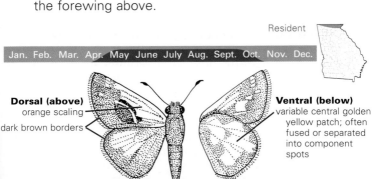

Dorsal (above)
orange scaling
dark brown borders

Ventral (below)
variable central golden
yellow patch; often
fused or separated
into component
spots

129

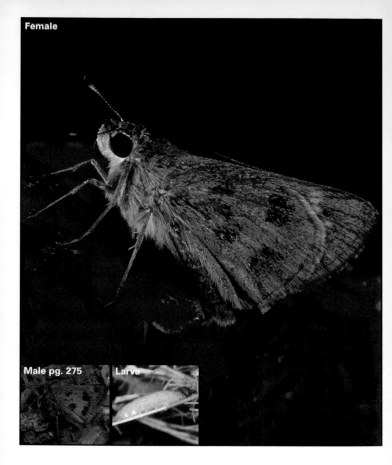

Female

Male pg. 275

Larva

Comments: The Whirlabout is a diminutive skipper with two distinct rows of squarish spots on the hindwings below. This species is sexually dimorphic. Males are tawny orange and considerably brighter than their drab brown female counterparts. It regularly expands its range each summer, establishing temporary breeding colonies throughout the southeast from Maryland to Texas. Living up to its name, adults have a low, erratic flight and scurry quickly around, periodically stopping to perch or nectar. Avidly fond of flowers, the butterfly is a frequent garden visitor.

Whirlabout
Polites vibex

Family/Subfamily: Skippers (Hesperiidae)/
Banded Skippers (Hesperiinae)

Wingspan: 1.00–1.25" (2.5–3.2 cm)

Above: elongated wings; golden orange with black borders and black stigma; female is dark brown with cream spots on forewing

Below: hindwing yellow in male or bronze brown in female with two loose bands of large dark brown spots

Sexes: dissimilar; female brown above with little orange scaling; olive brown below with similar pattern as male

Egg: white, laid singly on host leaves

Larva: brownish green with thin, dark dorsal stripe and black head

Larval Host Plants: various grasses including Bermuda Grass, St. Augustine Grass and crabgrass

Habitat: open, disturbed areas including old fields, roadsides, vacant lots, open woodlands, forest edges, parks, lawns and gardens

Broods: multiple generations

Abundance: occasional to abundant

Compare: Fiery Skipper (pg. 273) has more elongated forewings and scattered, tiny dark spots on ventral hindwing.

Resident Visitor

Jan. Feb. Mar. Apr. May June July Aug. Sept. Oct. Nov. Dec.

male

Dorsal (above)
golden orange
large black stigma
jagged black border
orange
smooth black
border

Ventral (below)
two bands of large
dark brown spots
golden orange

131

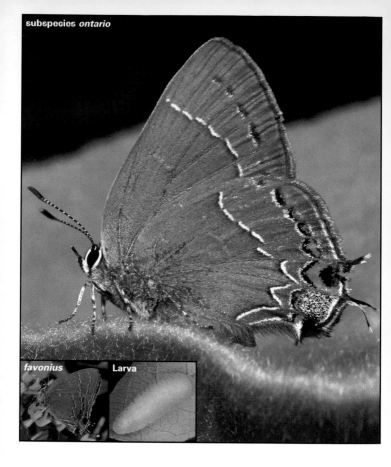

subspecies *ontario*

favonius

Larva

Comments: Populations of Southern Hairstreaks outside of the Florida peninsula and extreme southern Atlantic coast to southeastern South Carolina were previously treated as an entirely separate species (the Northern Hairstreak). They are now recognized as geographic races of the same butterfly. Adults have a quick, erratic flight and frequently perch high on the leaves of surrounding vegetation. They regularly venture down to nectar at a variety of small-flowered blossoms. Subspecies *favonius* replaces *ontario* in extreme southeastern Georgia.

Southern Hairstreak
Fixsenia favonius ontario and *F. favonius favonius*

Family/Subfamily: Gossamer Wings (Lycaenidae)/ Hairstreaks (Theclinae)

Wingspan: 1.0–1.3" (2.5–3.3 cm)

Above: dark brown with dark forewing stigma and a small orange spot near the tails

Below: subspecies *ontario* is gray brown with a white postmedian line that zigzags toward the tails, a large blue patch often capped lightly in orange, and a short row of small orange spots, the largest of which borders a black spot; subspecies *favonius* has a much larger, broad reddish orange patch on the hindwing, a small white spot along leading margin of the hindwing and longer hindwing tails

Sexes: similar

Egg: pinkish brown, laid singly on twigs; eggs overwinter

Larva: pale green; covered with tiny yellow dots

Larval Host Plants: various oaks

Habitat: woodland edges, oak scrub, adjacent open areas

Broods: single generation

Abundance: occasional to common

Compare: White M Hairstreak (pg. 89) has single red ventral hindwing spot. Gray Hairstreak (pg. 255) is light gray below with a less jagged white line.

Resident

Jan. Feb. Mar. Apr. May June July Aug. Sept. Oct. Nov. Dec.

male

Dorsal (above)
dull, gray brown wings

Ventral (below)
jagged black-and-white line

blue patch with orange cap

133

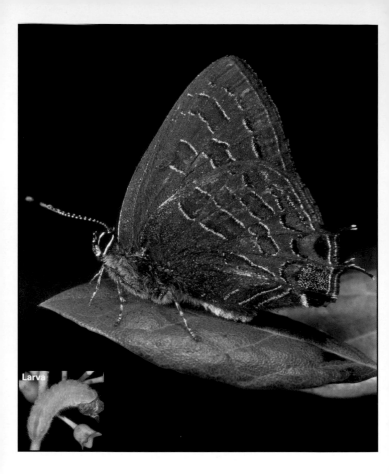

Larva

Comments: The Striped Hairstreak's name comes from the numerous dark dashes edged in white that give it an overall striped appearance. Although widespread throughout the state, it is generally uncommon, highly localized and seldom seen in any numbers. Adults are often encountered alongside a variety of other similar early season hairstreaks at available flowers. Females lay the small, flattened eggs singly on host twigs. The eggs overwinter and the young larvae hatch the following spring to feed on the buds and young leaves.

Striped Hairstreak
Satyrium liparops

Family/Subfamily: Gossamer Wings (Lycaenidae)/ Hairstreaks (Theclinae)

Wingspan: 1.0–1.3" (2.5–3.3 cm)

Above: unmarked dark brown with two hindwing tails

Below: brown to slate gray with numerous wide, dark bands outlined in white; hindwing has an orange-capped blue patch and several red spots near tails

Sexes: similar

Egg: pinkish brown, flattened, laid singly on twigs of host

Larva: bright green with yellow-green oblique stripes and dark dorsal line

Larval Host Plants: various trees and shrubs in the heath and rose families including Flame Azalea, Highbush Blueberry, Sparkleberry, Black Cherry, Wild Cherry, serviceberry and hawthorn

Habitat: mixed deciduous forests, thickets, forest clearings, woodland edges and adjacent open areas

Broods: single generation

Abundance: uncommon and often local

Compare: Banded Hairstreak (pg. 119), Hickory Hairstreak (pg. 123) and King's Hairstreak (pg. 125) have less extensive, narrower ventral bands. Banded and Hickory lack the extensive orange cap on the blue hindwing patch.

Resident

Jan. Feb. Mar. Apr. May June July Aug. Sept. Oct. Nov. Dec.

Dorsal (above)
unmarked brown

Ventral (below)
wide, dark bands outlined in white

blue patch with orange cap

135

Dorsal

Larva

Comments: Widespread throughout much of the East, the Common Roadside-Skipper is a denizen of grassy woodland clearings, forest margins and stream corridors where it is rather local in occurrence and seldom encountered in large numbers. The adults are often found on low sunlit perches or at nearby flowers, where they tend to be rather wary and difficult to closely approach. Males regularly visit moist earth to imbibe water and nutrients. Larvae construct individual leaf shelters on the host. Larvae overwinter.

Common Roadside-Skipper
Amblyscirtes vialis

Family/Subfamily: Skippers (Hesperiidae)/ Banded Skippers (Hesperiinae)

Wingspan: 1.0–1.3" (2.5–3.3 cm)

Above: primarily dark blackish brown with a few small white spots near the forewing apex

Below: dark grayish black with faint gray frosting; forewing has a few small white spots (sometimes fused into a tapering band) near the apex

Sexes: similar

Egg: pale green, laid singly on host leaves

Larva: pale green with a whitish head marked with reddish brown vertical lines

Larval Host Plants: various grasses including Indian Woodoats, Bermuda Grass and bentgrass

Habitat: open grassy areas in or near woodlands and along stream corridors

Broods: two generations

Abundance: uncommon to occasional

Compare: Bell's Roadside-Skipper (pg. 155) has extensive white spotting on the hindwing below. Dusky Roadside-Skipper (pg. 97) lacks prominent white spots below forewing apex.

Resident

Jan. Feb. Mar. Apr. May June July Aug. Sept. Oct. Nov. Dec.

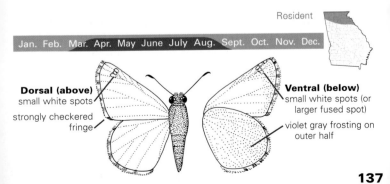

Dorsal (above)
small white spots
strongly checkered fringe

Ventral (below)
small white spots (or larger fused spot)
violet gray frosting on outer half

137

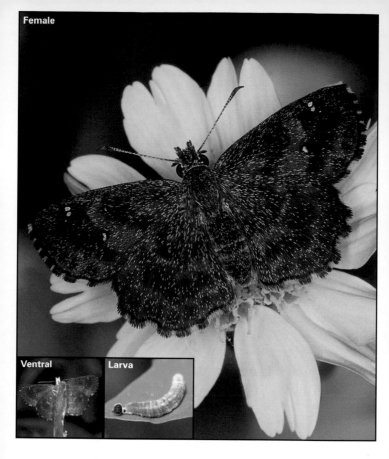

Female

Ventral

Larva

Comments: Hayhurst's Scallopwing is named for the distinctive scalloped hindwing margins that quickly distinguish it from all other small dark skippers in the Southeast. A butterfly of open, disturbed sites including suburban gardens, it is often found in close association with its introduced weedy larval host. The butterfly likely utilizes several native members of the Amaranth family as well. Adults have a quick, scurrying flight and regularly perch or nectar with their wings outstretched, providing a prominent view of their namesake wing shape.

Hayhurst's Scallopwing
Staphylus hayhurstii

Family/Subfamily: Skippers (Hesperiidae)/
Spread-wing Skippers (Pyrginae)

Wingspan: 1.0–1.4" (2.5–3.6 cm)

Above: dark blackish brown with black bands and subtle
gold flecking; forewing has a few small white spots;
hindwing has distinctly scalloped margin

Below: forewing is marked as above but paler

Sexes: similar, although female is lighter brown with an
overall more banded appearance

Egg: pink, laid singly on the underside of host leaves

Larva: green with a pinkish hue, a dark green dorsal
stripe, a thin yellow lateral stripe, and a black head

Larval Host Plants: Lamb's Quarters

Habitat: sunlit wooded stream margins, weedy disturbed sites, fallow agricultural land, forest edges and
gardens

Broods: two generations

Abundance: rare to uncommon

Compare: unique

Resident

Jan. Feb. Mar. Apr. May June July Aug. Sept. Oct. Nov. Dec.

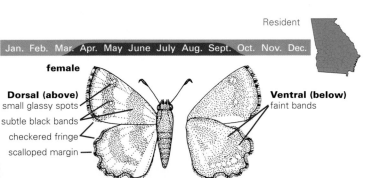

female

Dorsal (above)
small glassy spots
subtle black bands
checkered fringe
scalloped margin

Ventral (below)
faint bands

Larva

Comments: The Salt Marsh Skipper's light wing veins and distinct white dash on the hindwing quickly separate it from all other similar-looking skippers. As its name suggests, it is a locally common inhabitant of coastal salt marshes. Adults have a low, rapid flight and frequently visit available flowers along nearby roads or in adjacent fields. Many aspects of the butterfly's biology and life history remain poorly known.

Salt Marsh Skipper
Panoquina panoquin

Family/Subfamily: Skippers (Hesperiidae)/
Banded Skippers (Hesperiinae)

Wingspan: 1.1–1.3" (2.8–3.3 cm)

Above: brown with small light spots across forewing

Below: light brown with light veins and distinct cream
dash in center of hindwing

Sexes: similar

Egg: light green, laid singly on host leaves

Larva: yellow green

Larval Host Plants: grasses including Salt Grass

Habitat: salt marshes and adjacent open areas, roadsides

Broods: multiple generations

Abundance: occasional to locally common

Compare: Brazilian Skipper (pg. 225) and Ocola Skipper
(pg. 207) lack pale ventral wing venation and distinct
cream dash in center of hindwing.

Resident

Jan. Feb. Mar. Apr. May June July Aug. Sept. Oct. Nov. Dec.

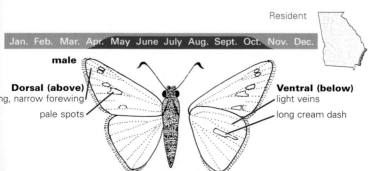

male

Dorsal (above)
ng, narrow forewing

pale spots

Ventral (below)
light veins

long cream dash

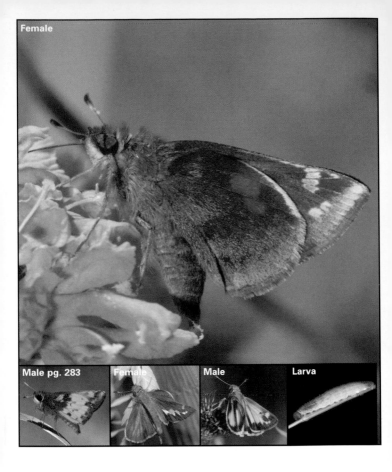

Female

Male pg. 283 | Female | Male | Larva

Comments: Sexually dimorphic, the Zabulon Skipper is a small butterfly with a bright orange male and a drab brown female. Primarily a butterfly of woodlands and adjacent open sites, it occasionally wanders into suburban gardens. Adults have a rapid flight and are strongly attracted to flowers. Males perch on sunlit branches along trails or clearings and engage passing objects or rival males. Females generally prefer to remain within the confines of nearby shady sites.

Zabulon Skipper
Poanes zabulon

Family/Subfamily: Skippers (Hesperiidae)/
Banded Skippers (Hesperiinae)

Wingspan: 1.0–1.4" (2.5–3.6 cm)

Above: male is golden orange with dark brown borders
and small brown spot near forewing apex; female is
dark brown with band of cream spots across forewing

Below: male hindwing yellow with a brown base enclosing a yellow spot; female is dark brown with small
light subapical spots, lavender scaling on wing margins, and white bar along leading margin of hindwing

Sexes: dissimilar, female brown with little orange color

Egg: pale green, laid singly on host leaves

Larva: tan with dark dorsal stripe, white lateral stripe and
short, light-colored hairs; reddish brown head

Larval Host Plants: various grasses including
Purpletop Grass, Whitegrass and lovegrass

Habitat: open woodlands, forest edges, roadsides, pastures, wetland edges, stream corridors and old fields

Broods: two generations

Abundance: occasional

Compare: Female "Pocahontas" form of Hobomok
Skipper (pg. 191) lacks white bar along the leading
margin of the ventral hindwing.

Resident

Jan. Feb. Mar. Apr. May June July Aug. Sept. Oct. Nov. Dec.

male

Dorsal (above)
dark spot
narrow black cell
end bar
golden orange
clear golden
orange

Ventral (below)
dark base encloses
yellow spot
yellow with darker
spots

143

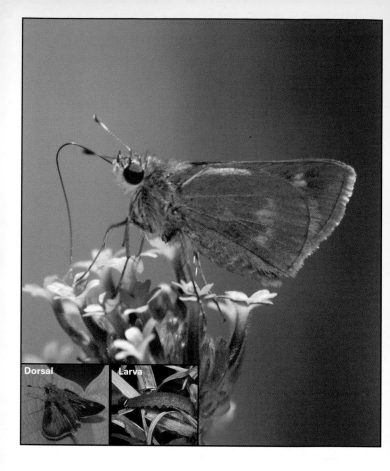

Dorsal

Larva

Comments: This widespread eastern skipper was once considered the same species as the Southern Broken-Dash. Like its close relative with which it often flies, the species' unique name comes from the dark forewing stigma that is separated or "broken" into two distinct dashes. Encountered in open habitats bordering woodlands, it readily ventures into nearby gardens in search of nectar. Adults are highly active butterflies but frequently stop to perch or feed where they can be easily and closely observed. Larvae overwinter.

Northern Broken-Dash
Wallengrenia egeremet

Family/Subfamily: Skippers (Hesperiidae)/
Banded Skippers (Hesperiinae)

Wingspan: 1.0–1.5" (2.5–3.8 cm)

Above: dark brown; forewing has yellow orange scaling
along the costal margin, a distinct separated stigma
and an elongated bright yellow orange spot extending
outward from the tip of the stigma

Below: hindwing is yellow brown with central band of
faint, light spots

Sexes: dissimilar; female is primarily dark brown above
with a few elongated cream yellow forewing spots
and reduced yellow orange markings

Egg: green, laid singly on host leaves

Larva: light green with darker green mottling, yellow lateral stripes; dark brown head with faint vertical stripes

Larval Host Plants: various grasses including
Switchgrass and Deertongue

Habitat: open, sunny areas near woodlands including
forest clearings and margins, roadsides, fallow agricultural land, pastures, old fields and gardens

Broods: two generations

Abundance: occasional to common

Compare: Southern Broken-Dash (pg. 147) is reddish
brown below.

Resident

| Jan. | Feb. | Mar. | Apr. | May | June | July | Aug. | Sept. | Oct. | Nov. | Dec. |

male

Dorsal (above)
yellow orange spot
at end of stigma

"broken" black
stigma

Ventral (below)
dull yellow brown,
often with violet
sheen

light spot band

145

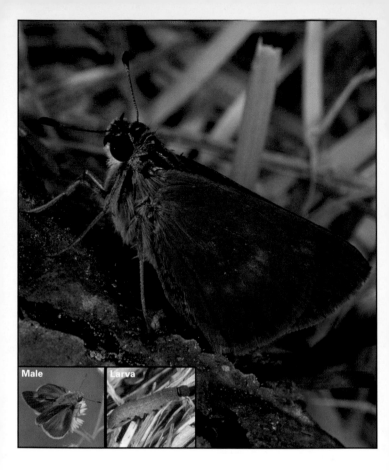

Male

Larva

Comments: The Southern Broken-Dash's unusual name comes from the noticeable separation of the forewing stigma that resembles two disconnected black lines. It can be quickly identified by its warm reddish brown ventral hindwings. It is a frequent garden visitor. Fond of flowers, the adults sit quietly on available blossoms and are easy to closely observe or photograph. Often found alongside the similar Northern Broken-Dash, it can be distinguished by the reddish orange ventral hindwings.

Southern Broken-Dash
Wallengrenia otho

Family/Subfamily: Skippers (Hesperiidae)/
Banded Skippers (Hesperiinae)

Wingspan: 1.0–1.5" (2.5–3.8 cm)

Above: male is dark brown with golden orange scaling
along costal margin and in center of hindwing;
forewing has broken black stigma near elongated
orange spot; female is dark brown with several small
cream-orange spots across forewing

Below: hindwing reddish brown with faint band of light
spots

Sexes: dissimilar; female darker with reduced orange
markings and pale forewing spots

Egg: pale green, laid singly on host leaves

Larva: light green with dark mottling and dark head

Larval Host Plants: various grasses including St.
Augustine Grass and crabgrass

Habitat: moist woodlands, forest edges, wetlands, roadsides, pastures, old fields and gardens

Broods: multiple generations

Abundance: occasional to common

Compare: Sachem (pg. 151) has more elongated wings
and broad pale ventral hindwing patch. Northern
Broken-Dash (pg. 145) is duller brown below.

Resident Visitor

Jan. Feb. Mar. Apr. May June July Aug. Sept. Oct. Nov. Dec.

male

Dorsal (above)
orange dash
separated black stigma

Ventral (below)
contrasting gray fringe
reddish brown
pale spot band

147

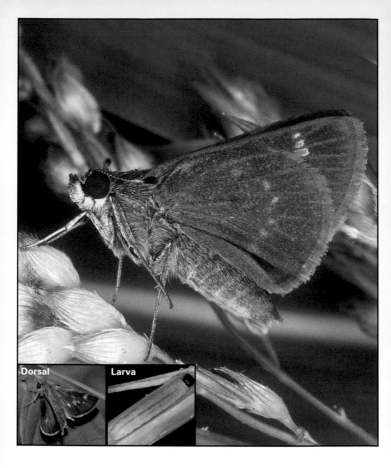

Dorsal

Larva

Comments: The Little Glassywing is named for the prominent translucent or "glassy" white spots on its forewing. It is a butterfly of shaded forest margins and adjacent, moist habitats or even open fields but is not usually encountered in home gardens. Adults have a low, quick flight and readily visit available wildflowers. Males perch on low growing vegetation in sunny areas for females.

Little Glassywing
Pompeius verna

Family/Subfamily: Skippers (Hesperiidae)/
Banded Skippers (Hesperiinae)

Wingspan: 1.0–1.5" (2.5–3.8 cm)

Above: male is dark brown with black stigma and several semitransparent spots across forewing; female is dark brown with several semitransparent spots across forewing

Below: dark brown; hindwing purplish brown with band of faint, light spots

Sexes: similar; female darker with more rounded wings and larger forewing spots

Egg: white, laid singly on host leaves

Larva: green to greenish brown with dark mottling and stripes; head is reddish brown

Larval Host Plants: grasses including Purpletop Grass

Habitat: moist, open woodlands, forest edges, wetlands, roadsides, pastures, old fields and gardens

Broods: two generations

Abundance: occasional to common

Compare: Dun Skipper (pg. 163) lacks semitransparent dorsal forewing spots and faint ventral hindwing band.

Resident

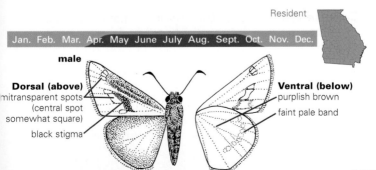

Jan. Feb. Mar. Apr. May June July Aug. Sept. Oct. Nov. Dec.

male

Dorsal (above)
semitransparent spots
(central spot
somewhat square)
black stigma

Ventral (below)
purplish brown
faint pale band

149

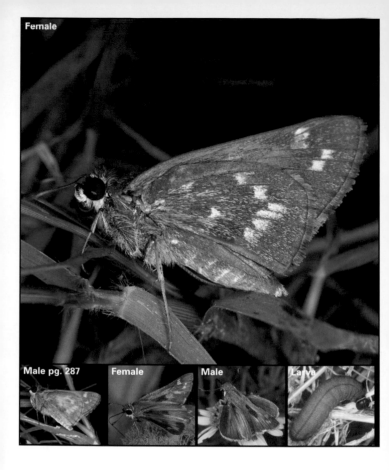

Female

Male pg. 287   Female   Male   Larva

Comments: The Sachem shares its affinity for open, disturbed sites with the Whirlabout and Fiery Skipper
with which it often flies. Adults have a quick, darting
flight that is usually low to the ground. All three
species are somewhat nervous butterflies, but readily
congregate at available flowers. Together, they often
form a circus of activity with several pausing briefly to
perch or nectar before one flies up and disturbs the
others, only to alight again moments later.

Sachem
Atalopedes campestris

Family/Subfamily: Skippers (Hesperiidae)/
Banded Skippers (Hesperiinae)

Wingspan: 1.0–1.5" (2.5–3.8 cm)

Above: elongated wings; male is golden orange with
brown borders and large, black stigma; female is dark
brown with golden markings in wing centers; forewing
has black median spot and several semitransparent
spots

Below: variable; hindwing golden brown in male, brown
in female with pale postmedian patch or band of spots

Sexes: dissimilar; female darker with semitransparent
forewing spots and reduced orange markings

Egg: white, laid singly on host leaves

Larva: greenish brown with thin, dark dorsal stripe and
black head

Larval Host Plants: various grasses including Bermuda
Grass and Crabgrass

Habitat: open, disturbed areas including old fields, pastures, roadsides, parks, lawns and gardens

Broods: multiple generations

Abundance: occasional to common

Compare: Fiery Skipper (pg. 273) and Whirlabout (pg.
131) have dark spots on the ventral hindwing.

Visitor Stray

| Jan. | Feb. | Mar. | Apr. | May | June | July | Aug. | Sept. | Oct. | Nov. | Dec. |

male

Dorsal (above)
elongated forewing
large squarish stigma
golden orange

Ventral (below)
large pale patch or
postmedian spot
band

151

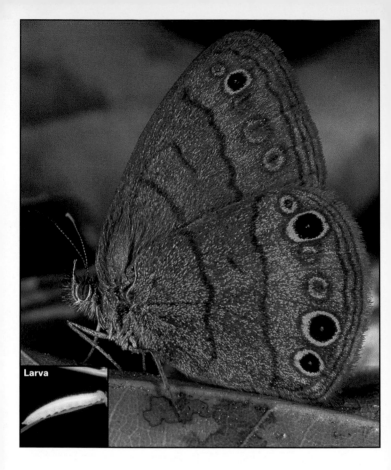

Larva

Comments: The small Carolina Satyr is one of the most abundant satyrs in the Southeast. Although it frequents shady woodlands, it regularly strays into nearby residential gardens. Adults have a low, erratic flight and bob slowly among understory vegetation and tall grass. Between periodic bursts of activity, adults perch on grasses or leaf litter with their wings tightly closed and can be easily approached for observation.

Carolina Satyr
Hermeuptychia sosybius

Family/Subfamily: Brush-foots (Nymphalidae)/ Satyrs and Wood Nymphs (Satyrinae)

Wingspan: 1.0–1.5" (2.5–3.8 cm)

Above: dark brown with no distinct markings or eyespots

Below: brown with two narrow, dark brown lines through center of wings; hindwing has row of yellow-rimmed dark eyespots

Sexes: similar

Egg: green, laid singly on host leaves

Larva: pale green with darker green longitudinal stripes and short yellow hairs

Larval Host Plants: various grasses including St. Augustine Grass, Broadleaf Carpetgrass and Bermuda Grass

Habitat: woodlands, forest clearings, trails and roadsides and adjacent disturbed, grassy areas

Broods: multiple generations

Abundance: occasional to abundant

Compare: Viola's Wood Satyr (pg. 223) and Little Wood Satyr (pg. 209) are larger and have two large, yellow-rimmed dorsal and ventral eyespots on both wings. Gemmed Satyr (pg. 183) lacks ventral eyespots.

Resident

| Jan. | Feb. | Mar. | Apr. | May | June | July | Aug. | Sept. | Oct. | Nov. | Dec. |

Dorsal (above)
brown without eyespots

Ventral (below)
dark lines
many small eyespots

153

Dorsal

Comments: Like other roadside-skippers, Bell's is an uncommon butterfly that is typically encountered singly or in small numbers. Males perch on low vegetation in sunlit sites and readily puddle at moist ground. The developing larvae construct individual shelters on the host by rolling individual leaves or tying several leaves together with silk. Fourth instar larvae from the last generation overwinter and complete development the following spring.

Bell's Roadside-Skipper
Amblyscirtes belli

Family/Subfamily: Skippers (Hesperiidae)/
Banded Skippers (Hesperiinae)

Wingspan: 1.1–1.4" (2.8–3.6 cm)

Above: dark blackish brown with small white forewing
spots

Below: dark grayish black with a dusting of white scales,
a white postmedian spot band on the hindwing, and a
checkered fringe

Sexes: similar

Egg: white, laid singly on host leaves

Larva: pale green with a darker green dorsal line and a
whitish head marked with orange brown vertical lines

Larval Host Plants: various grasses including St.
Augustine Grass and Indian Woodoats

Habitat: open grassy areas in or near woodlands and
along stream corridors

Broods: two generations

Abundance: rare to occasional

Compare: Common Roadside-Skipper (pg. 137) lacks
extensive white spotting on the hindwing below.

Resident

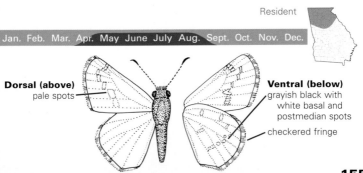

Jan. Feb. Mar. Apr. May June July Aug. Sept. Oct. Nov. Dec.

Dorsal (above)
pale spots

Ventral (below)
grayish black with
white basal and
postmedian spots

checkered fringe

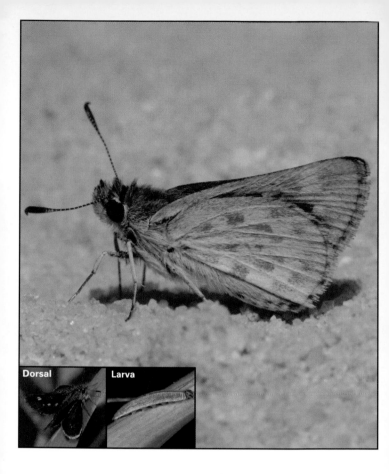

Dorsal

Larva

Comments: Named for the region from which it was first described, the Carolina Roadside-Skipper is a butterfly of dense wet woods, forested swamps and stream corridors that support stands of cane. Generally uncommon throughout its limited southeastern range, it is seldom encountered in large numbers. Colonies tend to be somewhat spotty and localized. Adults are often encountered in sunlit clearings or margins where they tend to alight on vegetation. This remains a poorly known butterfly.

Carolina Roadside-Skipper
Amblyscirtes carolina

Family/Subfamily: Skippers (Hesperiidae)/
Banded Skippers (Hesperiinae)

Wingspan: 1.1–1.4" (2.8–3.6 cm)

Above: dark brown with small cream yellow spots

Below: dirty yellow brown with pale forewing spots and
small reddish brown hindwing spots; abdomen has a
row of dark spots

Sexes: similar

Egg: currently undocumented

Larva: gray green with a dark dorsal stripe; reddish head
marked with vertical cream lines

Larval Host Plants: Switchcane

Habitat: moist woodlands, stream corridors and swamps

Broods: three generations

Abundance: rare to occasional

Compare: Reversed Roadside-Skipper (pg. 165) has a
reversed color pattern with a reddish brown ventral
hindwing with yellow spots.

Resident

Jan. Feb. Mar. Apr. May June July Aug. Sept. Oct. Nov. Dec.

Dorsal (above)
small cream yellow
spots

Ventral (below)
yellow brown
hindwing

reddish brown spots

157

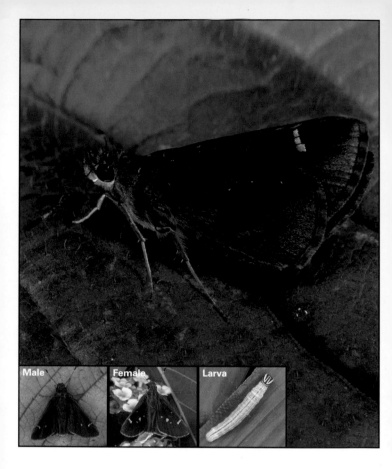

Male
Female
Larva

Comments: The Clouded Skipper is our only member of this primarily tropical genus. Although superficially appearing drab, closer inspection is needed to appreciate the delicate lavender scaling on the hindwings below. It regularly explores the surrounding landscape and may show up occasionally in suburban yards or gardens. Adults have a quick, nervous flight but readily alight on low vegetation or leaf litter. It is an easy butterfly to approach.

Clouded Skipper
Lerema accius

Family/Subfamily: Skippers (Hesperiidae)/
Banded Skippers (Hesperiinae)

Wingspan: 1.0–1.5" (2.5–3.8 cm)

Above: dark chocolate brown; forewing has several
small semitransparent spots

Below: dark brown; forewing has row of small semitransparent spots near apex; both wings have lavender
scaling in center and toward margin

Sexes: similar, female has larger forewing spots

Egg: laid singly on host leaves

Larva: green with a dark dorsal stripe and white lateral
stripes; head is white with a black margin and three
black stripes; body is covered with fine white spots

Larval Host Plants: various grasses including St.
Augustine Grass, Plumegrass and Rustyseed
Paspalum

Habitat: open woodlands, forest edges, roadsides, wetland edges, swamps, stream corridors and old fields

Broods: two or more generations

Abundance: occasional

Compare: Zabulon Skipper (pg. 143) female has larger
forewing spots and a white bar along leading edge of
ventral hindwing. Dusted Skipper (pg. 197) has small
white spot near base of ventral hindwing.

Resident Visitor

| Jan. | Feb. | Mar. | Apr. | May | June | July | Aug. | Sept. | Oct. | Nov. | Dec. |

male

Dorsal (above)
small semitransparent
spots

Ventral (below)
three small
semitransparent
spots

lavender frosting

dark central band

159

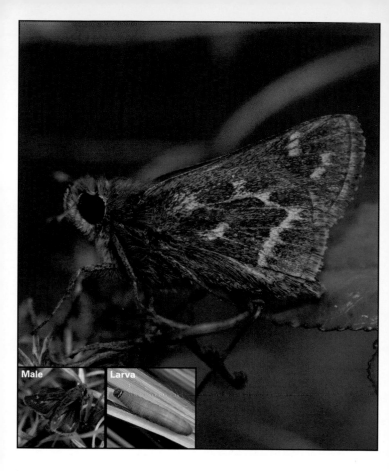

Male

Larva

Comments: The Cobweb Skipper is named for its distinctly jagged pattern on the ventral hindwing that resembles a spider's web. On the wing for a single spring flight, look for it in clearings, disturbed areas or other grassy sites in close association with stands of its larval hosts. Colonies are typically of low density, spotty and highly localized, although it can be fairly common when encountered. The adults have a rapid and extremely low flight. It is a wary butterfly but readily perches on or near the ground and visits a variety of low-growing spring flowers. Larvae construct individual leaf shelters on the host. Mature larvae overwinter.

Cobweb Skipper
Hesperia metea

Family/Subfamily: Skippers (Hesperiidae)/
Banded Skippers (Hesperiinae)

Wingspan: 1.1–1.4" (2.8–3.6 cm)

Above: olive brown; forewing has tawny orange spots
and a narrow black stigma; hindwing has angled band
of tawny orange spots

Below: hindwing is olive brown with irregular white
bands and veins giving an overall cobweb appearance

Sexes: dissimilar; female is primarily dark brown with a
few pale forewing spots near the apex

Egg: white, laid singly on or near host leaves

Larva: gray brown with a dark dorsal stripe and a round
black head

Larval Host Plants: various grasses including Little
Bluestem and Big Bluestem

Habitat: open areas within woodlands, pine barrens, utility easements and recently cleared or burned sites

Broods: single generation

Abundance: rare to occasional

Compare: unique

Resident

Jan. Feb. Mar. Apr. May June July Aug. Sept. Oct. Nov. Dec.

male

Dorsal (above)
narrow black stigma
orange scaling
ngled band of tawny
orange spots

Ventral (below)
"cobweb"
appearance—
irregular white
bands and veins

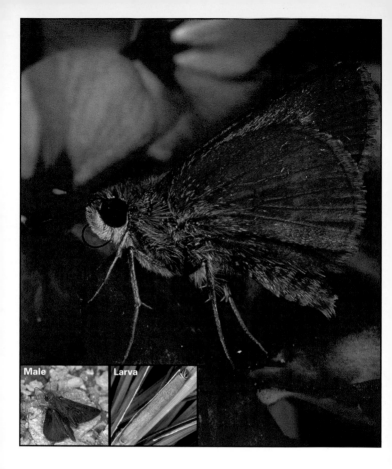

Male

Larva

Comments: The Dun Skipper is a plain chocolate brown butterfly with few markings. Although it prefers moist, grassy or sedge-dominated areas associated with deciduous woods, it frequently ventures into surrounding areas, and is periodically encountered in home gardens. Adults have a quick, low flight and dart around erratically over the vegetation. Males occasionally visit damp ground.

Dun Skipper
Euphyes vestris

Family/Subfamily: Skippers (Hesperiidae)/
Banded Skippers (Hesperiinae)

Wingspan: 1.0–1.5" (2.5–3.8 cm)

Above: male is dark chocolate brown with black stigma;
female is dark brown with several whitish spots on
forewing

Below: brown; typically unmarked hindwing, but occasionally has faint spot band

Sexes: similar; female has small, white forewing spots

Egg: green, laid singly on host leaves

Larva: green with thin white lines; head is brown with
light outer stripes and dark center

Larval Host Plants: various sedges including Upright
Sedge

Habitat: moist areas in or near deciduous woodlands,
wet meadows, marshes, forest edges, stream corridors, roadsides, pastures, utility easements and old
fields

Broods: two generations

Abundance: occasional to common

Compare: Little Glassywing (pg. 149) has distinct glassy
white spots on forewing and defined ventral hindwing
band.

Resident

Jan. Feb. Mar. Apr. May June July Aug. Sept. Oct. Nov. Dec.

male

Dorsal (above)
brown black wings
dark black stigma

Ventral (below)
unmarked or with faint
spot band

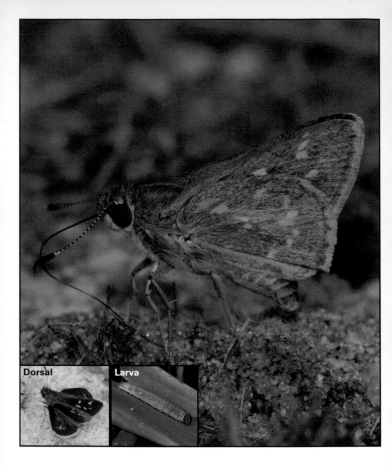

Dorsal

Larva

Comments: Most of this skipper's limited southeastern range occurs within the Carolinas and Georgia. With reddish brown hindwings and yellow spots, it has the reversed pattern of the Carolina Roadside-Skipper and was once considered to be a mere color form of that species. It, too, is a butterfly of wet woodlands, forested swamps and stream corridors that support abundant stands of cane. Little detailed information is known about this rare butterfly's biology and behavior. Although it has been reared, the details of its life history remain poorly known.

Reversed Roadside-Skipper
Amblyscirtes reversa

Family/Subfamily: Skippers (Hesperiidae)/
Banded Skippers (Hesperiinae)

Wingspan: 1.1–1.4" (2.8–3.6 cm)

Above: dark brown with small cream yellow spots

Below: reddish brown with pale yellow spots

Sexes: similar

Egg: currently undocumented

Larva: gray green with dark dorsal stripe; reddish head
marked with pale vertical stripes

Larval Host Plants: Switchcane

Habitat: moist woodlands, stream corridors and swamps

Broods: two generations

Abundance: rare to occasional

Compare: Carolina Roadside-Skipper (pg. 157) has a yellow ventral hindwing with small reddish brown spots.

Resident

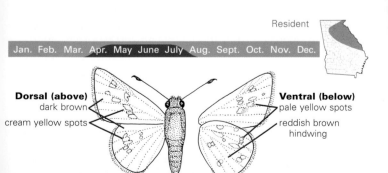

Jan. Feb. Mar. Apr. May June July Aug. Sept. Oct. Nov. Dec.

Dorsal (above)
dark brown
cream yellow spots

Ventral (below)
pale yellow spots
reddish brown
hindwing

165

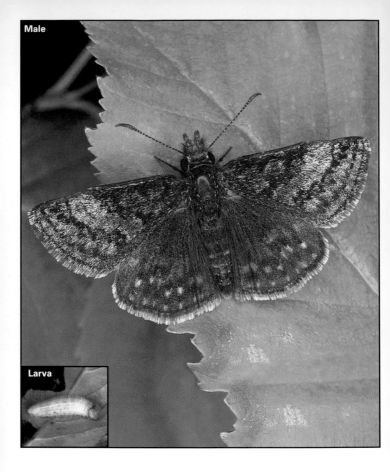

Male

Larva

Comments: The Dreamy Duskywing is a small, early
spring species that just barely makes its way into
northern portions of Georgia. The Dreamy and the similar but larger and more widespread Sleepy
Duskywing, lack glassy forewing spots that character-
ize all other members of this group. Adults scurry low
to the ground along forest trails or margins with a fast,
bouncing flight. Males are frequently encountered puddling at moist areas. Larvae construct individual leaf
shelters on host and overwinter in a similar structure.

Dreamy Duskywing
Erynnis icelus

Family/Subfamily: Skippers (Hesperiidae)/
Spread-wing Skippers (Pyrginae)

Wingspan: 1.0–1.6" (2.5–4.1 cm)

Above: dark brown; forewing has extensive gray scaling
toward outer margin, two black chain-like bands
enclosing a broad gray patch, a dark base, lacks glassy
spots; hindwing has two rows of pale spots; labial
palpi are noticeably long and project forward

Below: dark brown, hindwing has two rows of pale spots

Sexes: similar, although female is lighter with more heavily patterned forewings

Egg: green turning reddish, laid singly on stems or leaves

Larva: pale green with a dark dorsal stripe, a white lateral stripe, numerous tiny white tubercles, and a black
head marked with yellow and red spots

Larval Host Plants: various willows, poplars and
birches

Habitat: open woodlands, forest edges and clearings,
roadsides, moist woodland depressions

Broods: single generation

Abundance: uncommon to occasional

Compare: Sleepy Duskywing (pg. 193) flies earlier and is
larger with shorter, more rounded forewings.

Resident

| Jan. | Feb. | Mar. | Apr. | May | June | July | Aug. | Sept. | Oct. | Nov. | Dec. |

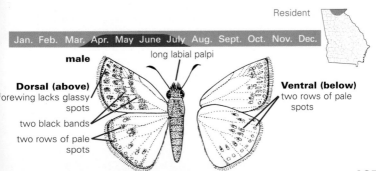

male

long labial palpi

Dorsal (above)
forewing lacks glassy
spots

two black bands

two rows of pale
spots

Ventral (below)
two rows of pale
spots

167

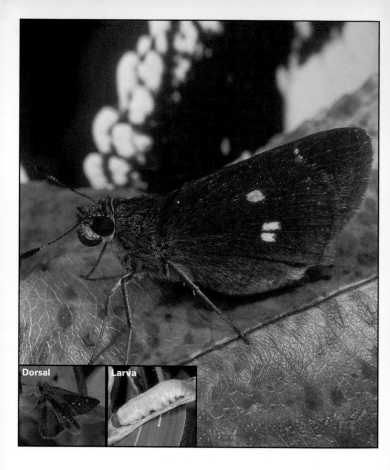

Dorsal

Larva

Comments: This is a large skipper of open pinelands and coastal marshes. Its unique hindwing spot pattern quickly distinguishes it from all other dark skippers in the state. Adults have a quick, darting flight but regularly alight on low vegetation or visit available wildflowers. Little detailed information is known about the biology and behavior of this distinctive southeastern butterfly.

Twin-Spot Skipper
Oligoria maculata

Family/Subfamily: Skippers (Hesperiidae)/
Banded Skippers (Hesperiinae)

Wingspan: 1.25–1.40" (3.2–3.6 cm)

Above: dark chocolate brown with small white spots
across forewing

Below: brown with three distinct white hindwing spots;
two close together and one isolated

Sexes: similar

Egg: brownish, laid singly on host leaves

Larva: pinkish green with brown head

Larval Host Plants: various grasses

Habitat: marshes, forest edges and pinelands

Broods: two or more generations

Abundance: occasional

Compare: Clouded Skipper (pg. 159) and Little
Glassywing (pg. 149) are smaller and lack the distinct
ventral hindwing white spots.

Resident

Jan. Feb. Mar. Apr. May June July Aug. Sept. Oct. Nov. Dec.

Dorsal (above)
white spots

Ventral (below)
brown with three
distinct white
spots: two next
to each other and
one separate

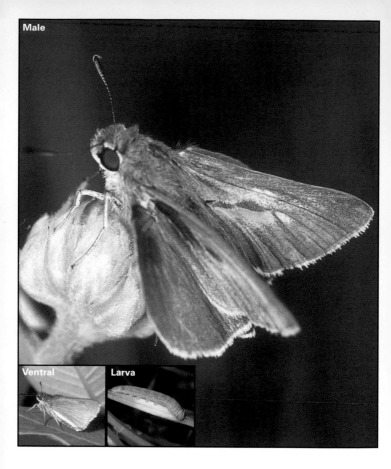

Male

Ventral

Larva

Comments: This primarily northeastern skipper is named for the two small white spots on the upper surface of the forewing in females. Restricted to open, sedge-dominated wetlands in close proximity to wooded areas, the Two-spotted Skipper is rare and highly local within Georgia. A fairly plain butterfly, it may be readily identified by the light veins and bright white anal margin on the hindwing below. Males perch low of sedges or grasses and readily fly out to engage other males. Larvae construct individual leaf shelters on the host. Larvae overwinter.

Two-spotted Skipper
Euphyes bimacula

Family/Subfamily: Skippers (Hesperiidae)/
Banded Skippers (Hesperiinae)

Wingspan: 1.25–1.40" (3.2–3.6 cm)

Above: dark brown with white fringes; forewing has
small tawny orange patch and black stigma

Below: brownish orange with pale veins and a whitish
anal hindwing margin

Sexes: dissimilar; female is primarily dark brown with
two cream spots in the center of the forewing above

Egg: green, laid singly on host leaves

Larva: pale green with a darker dorsal stripe and numerous tiny wavy white dashes; reddish brown head
marked with a black oval ringed in cream on the forehead, and a cream band around the outer margin

Larval Host Plants: various sedges including Upright
Sedge

Habitat: wet meadows, marshes and swamps near
woodlands

Broods: two generations

Abundance: locally rare to occasional

Compare: Berry's Skipper (pg. 307) has more orange
scaling above, a restricted range and lacks the white
wing fringes.

Resident

Jan. Feb. Mar. Apr. May June July Aug. Sept. Oct. Nov. Dec.

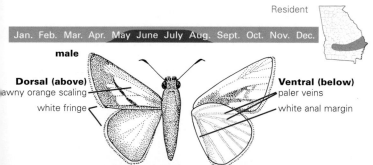

male

Dorsal (above)
tawny orange scaling
white fringe

Ventral (below)
paler veins
white anal margin

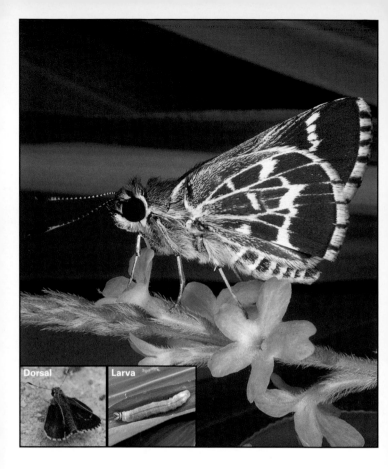

Dorsal

Larva

Comments: This skipper's white cobweb pattern on the gray brown ventral hindwing is distinctive and difficult to confuse with any other butterfly. It is an inhabitant of moist woodlands and associated margins or road-sides with cane. The species produces two generations and is on the wing in early summer and again toward early fall. As is the case with most road-side-skippers, little detailed information is know about the butterfly's biology and behavior.

Lace-winged Roadside-Skipper
Amblyscirtes aesculapius

Family/Subfamily: Skippers (Hesperiidae)/
Banded Skippers (Hesperiinae)

Wingspan: 1.2–1.5" (3.0–3.8 cm)

Above: dark brown with checkered fringes and a band of
small white spots on the forewing

Below: hindwing is gray brown with checkered fringes
and a network of white bands and veins, giving an
overall lacy appearance

Sexes: similar

Egg: currently undocumented

Larva: blue green with a dark dorsal stripe; reddish
brown head marked with pale crescents on each side

Larval Host Plants: Switchcane

Habitat: moist dense woodlands

Broods: two generations

Abundance: rare to locally common

Compare: Cobweb Skipper (pg. 161) lacks checkered
fringes, has less extensive pattern on ventral hindwing
and inhabits dry, open grassy areas.

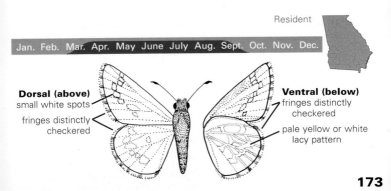

Resident

Jan. Feb. Mar. Apr. May June July Aug. Sept. Oct. Nov. Dec.

Dorsal (above)
small white spots

fringes distinctly
checkered

Ventral (below)
fringes distinctly
checkered

pale yellow or white
lacy pattern

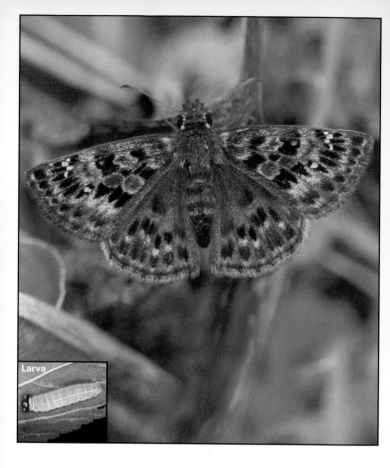

Larva

Comments: Finally an easy-to-identify duskywing! This small skipper can reliably be told apart from all other members of this complicated genus by its distinctively mottled wings. It is a rare to uncommon butterfly throughout its range and typically found in isolated, sporadic colony sites. In Georgia, the Mottled Duskywing can be encountered in open woodlands or in nearby brushy fields, often where the terrain is somewhat hilly and undulating. Males often puddle at damp ground with other duskywings but are rarely the most prevalent species present.

Mottled Duskywing
Erynnis martialis

Family/Subfamily: Skippers (Hesperiidae)/
Spread-wing Skippers (Pyrginae)

Wingspan: 1.2–1.6" (3.0–4.1 cm)

Above: brown and strongly patterned with numerous
dark blotches giving a distinctive mottled appearance;
forewing has several small glassy spots toward the
apex; fresh individuals have a subtle violet sheen

Below: brown with numerous light and dark spots

Sexes: similar, although female is lighter with increased
gray scaling and more heavily patterned wings

Egg: green soon turning pinkish, laid singly on host
leaves

Larva: pale green with numerous tiny white tubercles
and a black head marked with orange spots around the
margin

Larval Host Plants: New Jersey Tea

Habitat: open upland woodland, forest edges and clearings, barrens and old fields

Broods: two generations

Abundance: rare to uncommon

Compare: unique

Resident

Jan. Feb. Mar. Apr. May June July Aug. Sept. Oct. Nov. Dec.

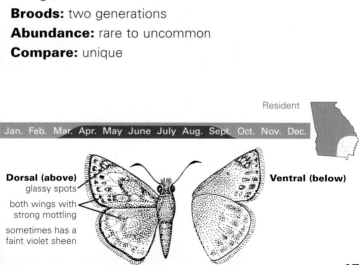

Dorsal (above)
glassy spots

both wings with
strong mottling

sometimes has a
faint violet sheen

Ventral (below)

175

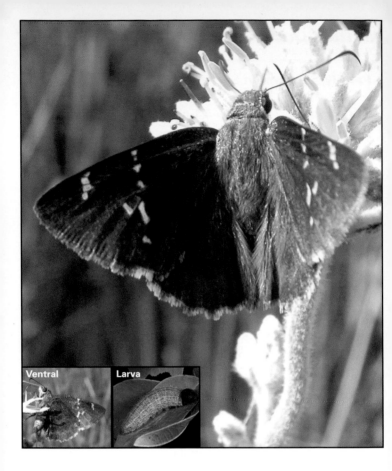

Ventral

Larva

Comments: Aptly named, the Confused Cloudywing is often very tricky to accurately distinguish from the more abundant Southern and Northern Cloudywings with which it often flies. Causing much of the problem is its band of glassy forewing spots that varies from highly reduced to prominent. An uncommon and often overlooked southern butterfly, it wanders northward each year to temporarily colonize many locations. Many aspects of the species' life history and behavior remain poorly known.

Confused Cloudywing
Thorybes confusis

Family/Subfamily: Skippers (Hesperiidae)/
Spread-wing Skippers (Pyrginae)

Wingspan: 1.2–1.6" (3.0–4.1 cm)

Above: brown with a variable band of several glassy
white spots across the forewing and a light, checkered
fringe; hindwing is tapered slightly toward bottom;
antennal clubs are all brown

Below: forewing is marked as above but paler and with
gray frosting along outer margin; hindwing has two
faint dark brown bands across center and faint light
frosting along outer margin; pale face

Sexes: similar

Egg: pale green, laid singly on host leaves

Larva: greenish brown with a dark dorsal stripe and pale
lateral stripes; blackish head

Larval Host Plants: various legumes such as beggarweeds and bush clover

Habitat: open sites in or near woodlands including clearings, trails, old fields, pastures and forest margins

Broods: two generations

Abundance: uncommon to occasional

Compare: Northern Cloudywing (pg. 181) has a dark
face. Southern Cloudywing (pg. 179) has a prominent,
straight forewing spot band and a white spot on the
antennal club.

Resident Visitor

Jan. Feb. Mar. Apr. May June July Aug. Sept. Oct. Nov. Dec.

male

brown antennal clubs

Dorsal (above)
bottom glassy spot
offset outwardly

hindwing slightly
tapered

Ventral (below)
two dark bands

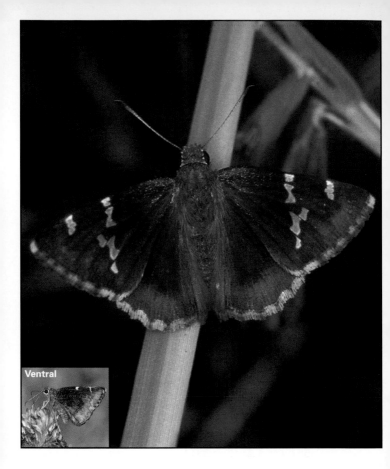

Ventral

Comments: The Southern Cloudywing frequents forest edges and open disturbed sites but is also a regular garden visitor. Adults have a strong, erratic flight but frequently stop to nectar. Males perch on low vegetation and aggressively dart out to investigate intruders before returning to the same general location moments later. Adults rest with their wings partially open but are often rather nervous and difficult to closely approach.

Southern Cloudywing
Thorybes bathyllus

Family/Subfamily: Skippers (Hesperiidae)/
Spread-wing Skippers (Pyrginae)

Wingspan: 1.2–1.6" (3.0–4.1 cm)

Above: brown with straight, glassy white spots across forewing and light, checkered wing fringe; hindwing tapered slightly toward bottom; antennal club has a white spot

Below: brown; hindwing darker at base with two dark brown bands; light face

Sexes: similar

Egg: green, laid singly on the leaves of host

Larva: greenish brown with black head, thin, dark dorsal stripe and narrow light lateral stripe; body covered with numerous short, light-colored hairs

Larval Host Plants: various legumes (Fabaceae) including beggarweeds, bush clovers, Butterfly Pea and Hog Peanut, Groundnut and milk vetch

Habitat: open, disturbed sites including roadsides, old fields, forest edges, meadows and gardens

Broods: two or more generations

Abundance: occasional to common

Compare: Northern Cloudywing (pg. 181) and Confused Cloudywing (pg. 177) have smaller white dorsal forewing spots.

Resident

Jan. Feb. Mar. Apr. May June July Aug. Sept. Oct. Nov. Dec.

male

Dorsal (above)
aligned band of prominent glassy spots

checkered fringe

Ventral (below)
antennal club has white spot

two dark bands

179

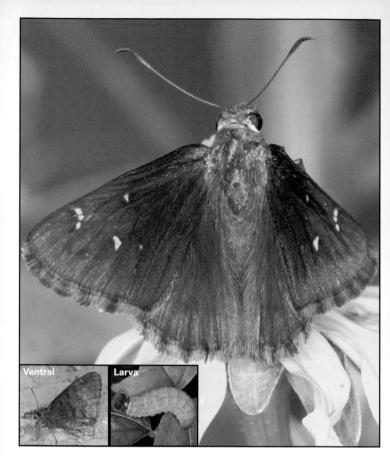

Ventral

Larva

Comments: The Northern Cloudywing is one of several similar-looking dark brown skippers found throughout the Southeast. The butterfly has a low, skipping flight and quickly darts along trails or clearings occasionally stopping to nectar. It readily visits nearby gardens. Males perch on the ground or low on vegetation and quickly speed out to engage rival males or passing females. At rest, they hold their wings in a relaxed, partially open position.

Northern Cloudywing
Thorybes pylades

Family/Subfamily: Skippers (Hesperiidae)/ Spread-wing Skippers (Pyrginae)

Wingspan: 1.2–1.7" (3.0–4.3 cm)

Above: brown with several small, elongated, misaligned glassy white spots on forewing and light, checkered wing fringe

Below: brown; hindwing darker at base with two dark brown bands; forewing has lavender gray scaling toward apex; dark face

Sexes: similar

Egg: pale greenish white, laid singly on the leaves of host

Larva: greenish brown with black head, thin, dark dorsal stripe and narrow pinkish brown lateral stripe; body covered with numerous short, light-colored hairs

Larval Host Plants: various legumes including beggar-weeds, bush clovers, milk vetch, alfalfa and clovers

Habitat: open woodlands, forest clearings, forest edges, roadsides, utility easements and old fields

Broods: two generations

Abundance: occasional to common

Compare: Southern Cloudywing (pg. 179) has larger dorsal forewing spots that form an aligned band.

Resident

| Jan. | Feb. | Mar. | Apr. | May | June | July | Aug. | Sept. | Oct. | Nov. | Dec. |

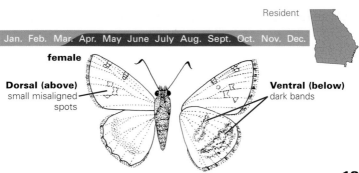

female

Dorsal (above)
small misaligned spots

Ventral (below)
dark bands

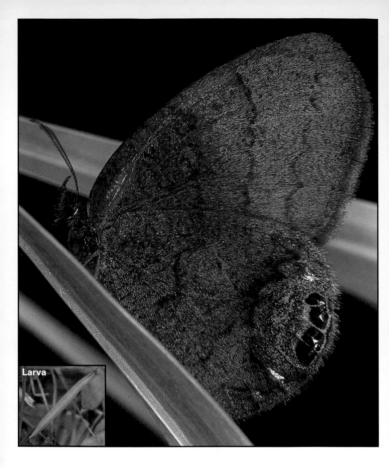

Larva

Comments: Often overlooked, the Gemmed Satyr is one of our most attractive satyrs and the only one without eyespots. It dances along the forest floor with a weak, low flight. Although they can be challenging to follow through the understory vegetation, adults regularly alight on grass blades or leaf litter. It is seldom very abundant, occurring in spotty, localized colonies, and may be overlooked due to its resemblance to the Carolina Satyr. The slender larvae have both a green and brown form.

Gemmed Satyr
Cyllopsis gemma

Family/Subfamily: Brush-foots (Nymphalidae)/
Satyrs and Wood Nymphs (Satyrinae)

Wingspan: 1.25–1.70" (3.2–4.3 cm)

Above: warm brown with very small dark spots along
hindwing margin

Below: light speckled brown with two narrow, dark wavy
lines through the center of the wings; hindwing has a
large purplish patch containing black spots with silver
highlights

Sexes: similar

Egg: green, laid singly on host leaves

Larva: green or brown with thin pale stripes, two small
tails and two brownish pink horns on the head

Larval Host Plants: Bermuda Grass and other grasses

Habitat: moist woodlands. stream corridors and associated shady grassy areas

Broods: three generations

Abundance: occasional to locally common

Compare: Carolina Satyr (pg. 153) has a row of yellow-
rimmed ventral eyespots on both the forewing and
hindwing.

Resident

Jan. Feb. Mar. Apr. May June July Aug. Sept. Oct. Nov. Dec.

Dorsal (above)
unmarked
brown wings

Ventral (below)
lacks eyespots on
both wings

large purplish patch
with shiny black
spots

183

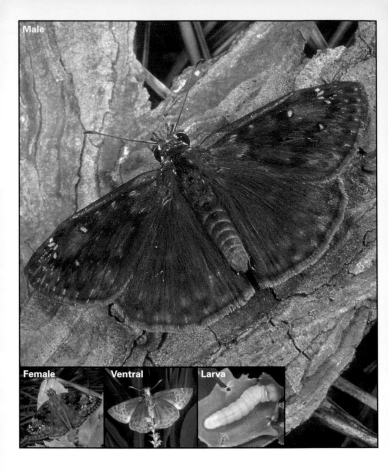

Comments: This abundant skipper commonly wanders into disturbed sites near its habitat in search of nectar. It is often a common garden visitor. It holds its wings outstretched when feeding or at rest. Adults flutter about with quick, somewhat erratic flight usually low to the ground. Males perch on low vegetation and occasionally puddle at damp sand or gravel. The larvae construct individual shelters on the host by folding over leaves with silk. Once fully mature, the larvae from the late season generation overwinter among the leaf litter until the following spring.

Horace's Duskywing
Erynnis horatius

Family/Subfamily: Skippers (Hesperiidae)/
Spread-wing Skippers (Pyrginae)

Wingspan: 1.25–1.75" (3.2–4.4 cm)

Above: dark brown overall with gray scaling usually lacking; forewing has cluster of small clear spots near apex and one at end of forewing cell; female is lighter with more contrasting pattern

Below: brown with faint rows of light spots along outer edge of hindwing

Sexes: similar, although female is lighter with more heavily patterned forewings and larger forewing spots

Egg: pale yellow green, laid singly on new growth of host

Larva: pale green with tiny white spots; reddish brown head marked with orange spots around the margin

Larval Host Plants: various oaks including Live Oak, Turkey Oak, Water Oak, Myrtle Oak, Scrub Oak and Post Oak

Habitat: oak woodlands, oak scrub, forest edges, woodland clearings, roadsides and utility easements

Broods: two to three generations

Abundance: occasional to common

Compare: Juvenal's Duskywing (pg. 211) has two light spots along leading margin of ventral hindwing and extensive gray scaling on dorsal forewing.

Resident

| Jan. | Feb. | Mar. | Apr. | May | June | July | Aug. | Sept. | Oct. | Nov. | Dec. |

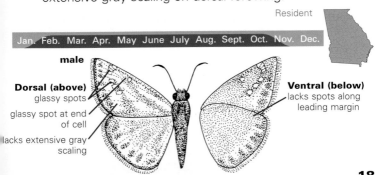

male

Dorsal (above)
glassy spots
glassy spot at end
of cell
lacks extensive gray
scaling

Ventral (below)
lacks spots along
leading margin

185

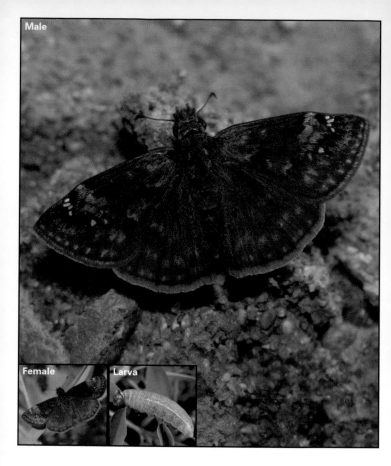

Male

Female

Larva

Comments: The Wild Indigo Duskywing is named for one of its preferred larval hosts. It has become more widespread because of its ability to colonize and use plantings of the introduced groundcover crown vetch. It is often extremely abundant in late summer and early fall. At such time, I have found it easy to locate several larvae and their leaf shelters on virtually every plant of Carolina Indigo examined. Larvae from the last generation overwinter and complete development in the spring. The butterfly has a fast, erratic flight but readily stops to nectar or perch on sunlit leaves or twigs. Males frequently puddle at damp ground.

Wild Indigo Duskywing
Erynnis baptisiae

Family/Subfamily: Skippers (Hesperiidae)/ Spread-wing Skippers (Pyrginae)

Wingspan: 1.3–1.7" (3.3–4.3 cm)

Above: dark brown with pale spots; forewing has darker base with several small glassy spots toward the apex and a distinctive reddish brown patch at the end of the cell; hindwing typically has faint cell-end bar

Below: dark brown, hindwing has two rows of prominent light spots

Sexes: similar, although female is lighter with more heavily pattered wings and larger glassy spots

Egg: green, laid singly on host leaves

Larva: pale green with numerous tiny white tubercles, dark dorsal stripe, white lateral stripe; dark brown head marked with pale orange or yellow around the margin

Larval Host Plants: wide variety including Carolina Indigo, Wild Indigo, Blue Wild Indigo, White Wild Indigo, Canadian Milkvetch, Wild Lupine and Crown Vetch

Habitat: open woodlands, forest edges and clearings, roadsides, utility easements, old fields and roadsides

Broods: two or three generations

Abundance: occasional to common

Compare: Horace's Duskywing (pg. 185) has glassy spot at end of forewing cell.

Resident

Jan. Feb. Mar. Apr. May June July Aug. Sept. Oct. Nov. Dec.

male

Dorsal (above)
red-brown spot at end of cell

typically lacks glassy spot at end of cell

basal half of wing darker

faint cell-end bar

Ventral (below)
two rows of white spots

187

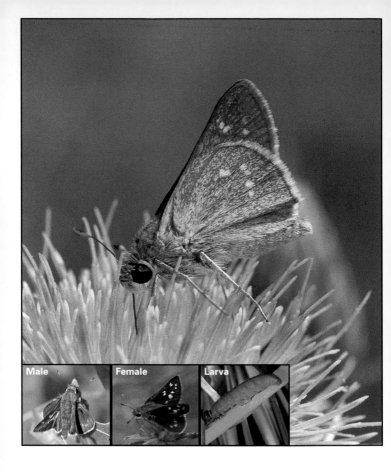

Male | Female | Larva

Comments: A butterfly of pine and oak barrens and
adjacent meadows, the Dotted Skipper is typically rare
and highly localized throughout its fragmented eastern
range. Within Georgia, it is restricted solely to the
extreme southeastern tip of the state. When encountered, this dull olive brown skipper is fairly easy to
identify by its distinctive small white dots on the ventral hindwing. Additional studies are needed to unravel
the details of this reclusive species' life history, ecology and behavior.

Dotted Skipper
Hesperia attalus

Family/Subfamily: Skippers (Hesperiidae)/
Banded Skippers (Hesperiinae)

Wingspan: 1.4–1.6" (3.6–4.1 cm)

Above: dark brown; forewing is elongated and pointed with several tawny orange spots; hindwing has post-median band of small tawny orange spots

Below: hindwing is olive brown with a band of small white dots

Sexes: similar, female is primarily dark brown with several pale forewing spots on both wings

Egg: laid singly on or near host leaves

Larva: green brown with a dark dorsal stripe; black head

Larval Host Plants: various grasses including Arrowfeather Threeawn and Carolina Crabgrass

Habitat: sandy pine barrens, woodland meadows

Broods: two generations

Abundance: rare to occasional

Compare: Leonard's Skipper (pg. 205) is larger, reddish brown beneath with prominent, large white hindwing spots. Forewings above have tawny orange scaling at base.

Resident

Jan. Feb. Mar. Apr. May June July Aug. Sept. Oct. Nov. Dec.

Dorsal (above)
pointed forewing

Ventral (below)
band of tiny white dots

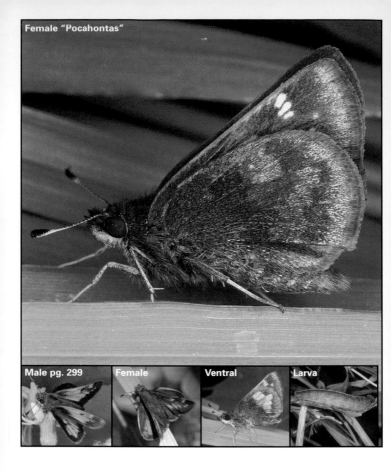

Female "Pocahontas"

Male pg. 299　Female　Ventral　Larva

Comments: This small woodland skipper has a single early summer flight. Males perch on sunlit leaves along forest margins and aggressively dart out at other passing butterflies. Although common throughout the northeast, its range just enters the extreme northern mountains of Georgia. The female produces two distinct forms. The lighter form closely resembles the male and the darker form "Pocahontas" is superficially similar to Zabulon Skipper females. Larvae construct individual leaf shelters on the host. Larvae overwinter and complete development the following spring.

Hobomok Skipper
Poanes hobomok

Family/Subfamily: Skippers (Hesperiidae)/
Banded Skippers (Hesperiinae)

Wingspan: 1.4–1.6" (3.6–4.1 cm)

Above: golden orange with irregular dark brown borders
and a narrow black cell-end bar on the forewing

Below: purplish brown with a broad yellow orange patch
through the hindwing

Sexes: dissimilar; female has two forms. Normal form
resembles male but has reduced orange scaling above.
"Pocahontas" form is dark brown above with pale
forewing spots; hindwing is purplish brown below with
faint band and violet gray frosting along outer margin.

Egg: white, laid singly on host leaves

Larva: brown green with numerous short, light-colored
hairs; round, brown head

Larval Host Plants: various grasses including Little
Bluestem, panic grasses, Poverty Oatgrass, bluegrass
and Rice Cutgrass

Habitat: open woodlands, forest edges, clearings and
trails, roadsides and along forested stream margins

Broods: single generation

Abundance: occasional to common

Compare: Female Zabulon Skipper (pg. 143) has a white
bar along leading edge of ventral hindwing.

Resident

Jan. Feb. Mar. Apr. May June July Aug. Sept. Oct. Nov. Dec.

male

Dorsal (above)
narrow cell-end bar
no stigma
irregular dark brown
borders

Ventral (below)
purplish brown
broad yellow orange
patch

191

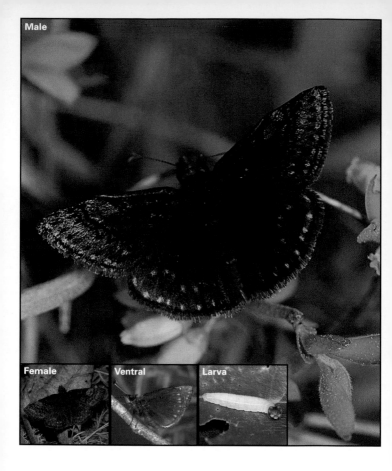

Male

Female · Ventral · Larva

Comments: An early season species, the Sleepy Duskywing has a single spring flight and is typically out before the smaller and similar-looking Dreamy Duskywing. Together, they are the only two dusky-wings that lack small glassy forewing spots. It is a widespread and generally common butterfly through-out the eastern U.S. but occasionally goes through marked fluctuations in abundance. Adults perch and rest with their mottled gray brown wings held in an open posture, a common characteristic of all dusky-wings. Larvae construct individual leaf shelters and overwinter inside, pupating the following spring.

Sleepy Duskywing
Erynnis brizo

Family/Subfamily: Skippers (Hesperiidae)/
Spread-wing Skippers (Pyrginae)

Wingspan: 1.30–1.75" (3.3–4.4 cm)

Above: dark brown; forewing has extensive gray scaling
toward outer margin and two black chain-like bands;
hindwing has two rows of faint pale spots

Below: dark brown, hindwing has two often faint rows
of pale spots

Sexes: similar, female is lighter with more heavily patterned forewing and more prominent hindwing spots

Egg: green, laid singly on host leaves

Larva: pale green with a yellow white lateral stripe and
numerous tiny white tubercles; brown head marked
with six orange spots around the margin

Larval Host Plants: various oaks including Scrub Oak
and Black Oak, also American Chestnut

Habitat: open oak woodlands and scrub, forest edges
and clearings, roadsides and adjacent open sites

Broods: single generation

Abundance: uncommon to common

Compare: Dreamy Duskywing (pg. 167) is smaller,
forewing has darker base and more distinct gray patch
between black bands; flies later.

Resident

Jan. Feb. Mar. Apr. May June July Aug. Sept. Oct. Nov. Dec.

Dorsal (above)
lacks glassy forewing
spots

distinct black, chainlike
bands

Ventral (below)
faint spots

193

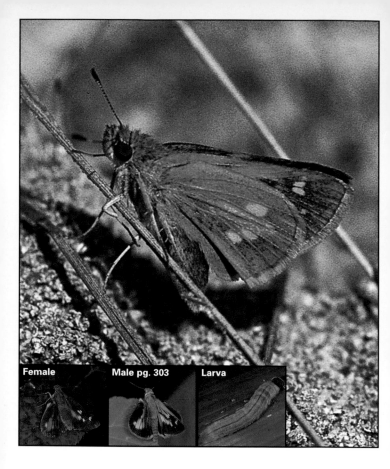

Female | Male pg. 303 | Larva

Comments: The Yehl Skipper is rare to uncommon large butterfly of southeastern forested swamps or moist woodlands. It is most frequently encountered in sunlit clearings, margins or roadsides. The adults are very wary and often difficult to closely approach. They visit a variety of moisture-loving flowers. Little detailed information is known about the biology and behavior of this reclusive species.

Yehl Skipper
Poanes yehl

Family/Subfamily: Skippers (Hesperiidae)/
Banded Skippers (Hesperiinae)

Wingspan: 1.30–1.75" (3.3–4.3 cm)

Above: golden orange with broad dark brown borders;
forewing has long, narrow black stigma; female is
overall brownish

Below: hindwing is yellow orange with a pale band of
spots (usually three prominent spots)

Sexes: dissimilar; female has pale forewing spots and
reduced golden orange scaling on the wing bases
above; ventral hindwing is brown with pale spot band

Egg: currently undocumented

Larva: green brown with a dark dorsal stripe; dark brown
head

Larval Host Plants: currently undocumented

Habitat: forested swamps and associated clearings and
margins

Broods: two generations

Abundance: rare to occasional

Compare: Broad-winged Skipper (pg. 317) has broad
pale ray through the spot band on the hindwing below.

Resident

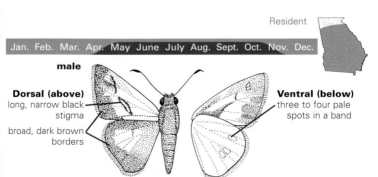

Jan. Feb. Mar. Apr. May June July Aug. Sept. Oct. Nov. Dec.

male

Dorsal (above)
long, narrow black
stigma

broad, dark brown
borders

Ventral (below)
three to four pale
spots in a band

195

Dorsal

loammi

loammi ventral

Larva

Comments: A butterfly of open, dry habitats, the Dusted Skipper is uncommon and typically quite localized in occurrence. On the wing in late spring or early summer, it has but one generation each year. The elongated slender larvae construct individual shelters on the host by tying several grass blades together with silk. The fully grown larvae overwinter in a similar shelter at the base of the host grass clump and pupate the following spring. Subspecies *loammi*, considered a separate species by some, occurs locally in coastal portions of Georgia.

Dusted Skipper
Atrytonopsis hianna and A. hianna loammi

Family/Subfamily: Skippers (Hesperiidae)/
Banded Skippers (Hesperiinae)

Wingspan: 1.4–1.7" (3.6–4.3 cm)

Above: dark chocolate brown with small glassy forewing
spots

Below: dark brown with gray frosting toward outer margin; forewing has small white forewing spots near
apex; hindwing has tiny white spot near base; face is
white with black mask; subspecies *loammi* has angled
bands of white spots

Sexes: similar

Egg: yellow, laid singly on host leaves

Larva: gray, pinkish dorsally, with numerous cream hairs,
a brown anal segment; reddish purple head

Larval Host Plants: various grasses including Little
Bluestem and Big Bluestem

Habitat: dry habitats including open woodlands, barrens,
utility easements and old fields

Broods: one to two generations

Abundance: rare to occasional

Compare: Clouded Skipper (pg. 159) lacks small white
spot at base of ventral hindwing. Female Zabulon
Skipper (pg. 143) has white bar along the leading edge
of the ventral hindwing.

Resident

| Jan. | Feb. | Mar. | Apr. | May | June | July | Aug. | Sept. | Oct. | Nov. | Dec. |

Dorsal (above)
glassy white spots

Ventral (below)
white spots
dusted gray
single white spot

197

Dorsal

Larva

Comments: The Hoary Edge is named for the large
frosty white (or hoary) patch on the ventral hindwing. It
readily ventures into disturbed sites near its habitat
and shows up occasionally in home gardens. The
Hoary Edge is common, but rarely found in any large
numbers. Adults have a low, strong flight and can be a
challenge to follow. Males perch on low, protruding
vegetation and aggressively investigate and chase
passing insects.

Hoary Edge
Achalarus lyciades

Family/Subfamily: Skippers (Hesperiidae)/
Spread-wing Skippers (Pyrginae)

Wingspan: 1.40–1.75" (3.6–4.4 cm)

Above: brown with broad band of gold spots across
forewing and checkered fringe

Below: brown; forewing as above but muted; hindwing
mottled dark brown at base with distinct broad white
marginal patch

Sexes: similar

Egg: cream, laid singly on host leaves

Larva: dark green with a dark dorsal stripe, numerous
tiny pale yellow dots and a thin, brownish orange lateral stripe; black head

Larval Host Plants: primarily beggarweeds, but also
occasionally uses bush clover and Horseflyweed

Habitat: open, sandy woodlands, forest edges and adjacent disturbed, brushy areas

Broods: two generations

Abundance: occasional

Compare: Silver-spotted Skipper (pg. 229) is larger, has a
clear white median ventral hindwing patch and round,
stubby tail. Golden-banded Skipper (pg. 217) lacks marginal white patch on ventral hindwing.

Resident

Jan. Feb. Mar. Apr. May June July Aug. Sept. Oct. Nov. Dec.

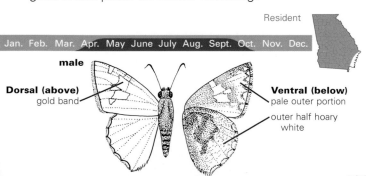

male

Dorsal (above)
gold band

Ventral (below)
pale outer portion

outer half hoary
white

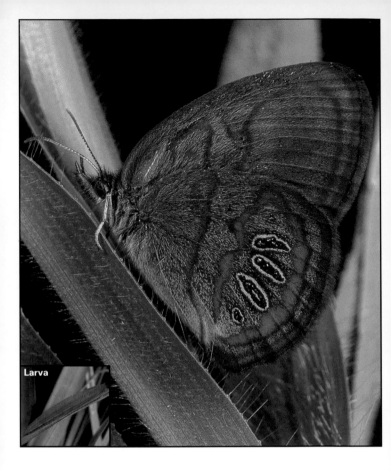

Larva

Comments: This delicately marked satyr bears the state's name. Unfortunately, it tends to occur in spotty, highly localized colonies that may be easily overlooked. The distinctive adults have a low, weak flight and bob slowly among the tall grasses and sedges, often flying only when disturbed. When seen on the wing, they typically fly only a short distance before alighting low within the surrounding wetland vegetation. Little detailed information is available about the biology and behavior of the species, including the exact larval hosts utilized in the wild.

Georgia Satyr
Neonympha areolata

Family/Subfamily: Brush-foots (Nymphalidae)/
Satyrs and Wood Nymphs (Satyrinae)

Wingspan: 1.40–1.75" (3.6–4.4 cm)

Above: uniform, unmarked brown

Below: brown with wavy reddish orange lines through
both wings; hindwing has a row of very elongated yellow-rimmed eyespots encircled in a thin reddish
orange oval

Sexes: similar

Egg: pale green to yellow, laid singly on host leaves

Larva: green with narrow light stripes, two short tails
and two reddish horns on the head

Larval Host Plants: currently undocumented; various
sedges likely, will accept grasses in captivity

Habitat: open, moist, grassy areas, wet meadows, pine
savannas, roadsides

Broods: two generations

Abundance: uncommon to occasional; locally common

Compare: Carolina Satyr (pg. 153), Little Wood Satyr
(pg. 209) and Gemmed Satyr (pg. 183) lack the distinct
red orange ventral markings and elongated hindwing
eyespots.

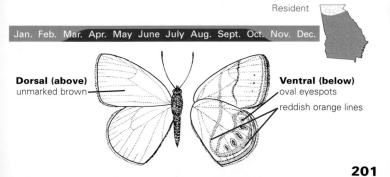

Resident

Jan. Feb. Mar. Apr. May June July Aug. Sept. Oct. Nov. Dec.

Dorsal (above)
unmarked brown

Ventral (below)
oval eyespots

reddish orange lines

201

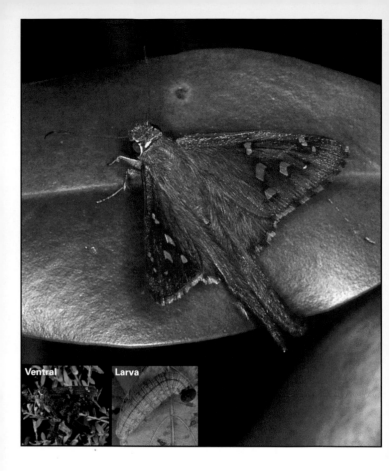

Ventral

Larva

Comments: Although only recently established in south Florida, the species is now a common butterfly of forest edges and adjacent open, disturbed sites there. It frequently wanders northward to colonize portions of north Florida, occasionally wandering across the border into Georgia. Nonetheless, it is an uncommon and only temporary colonist. Adults have a quick, darting flight and are frequently drawn to available flowers. Like the similar Long-tailed Skipper, its drab larvae construct individual shelters on the host by weaving together one or more leaves with silk.

Dorantes Skipper
Urbanus dorantes

Family/Subfamily: Skippers (Hesperiidae)/
Spread-wing Skippers (Pyrginae)

Wingspan: 1.4–1.8" (3.6–4.6 cm)

Above: brown with several semitransparent spots on
forewing and long hindwing tail

Below: brown; hindwing has two diffuse dark brown
bands, giving an overall mottled pattern

Sexes: similar

Egg: green, laid singly on the leaves of host

Larva: yellow-green with pinkish hue and a black head;
body has a thin dark dorsal stripe and lateral band of
dark-rimmed pale yellow spots

Larval Host Plants: various legumes including beggarweeds

Habitat: open woodlands, roadsides, old fields, fallow
agricultural land, utility easements, forest edges and
gardens

Broods: multiple generations

Abundance: rare to uncommon

Compare: Long-tailed Skipper (pg. 219) has a dorsal
green iridescence on body and wing bases.

Stray

Jan. Feb. Mar. Apr. May June July Aug. Sept. Oct. Nov. Dec.

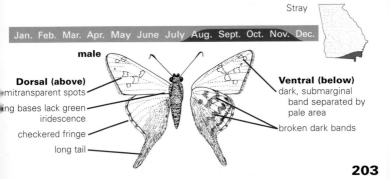

male

Dorsal (above)
semitransparent spots

wing bases lack green
iridescence

checkered fringe

long tail

Ventral (below)
dark, submarginal
band separated by
pale area

broken dark bands

203

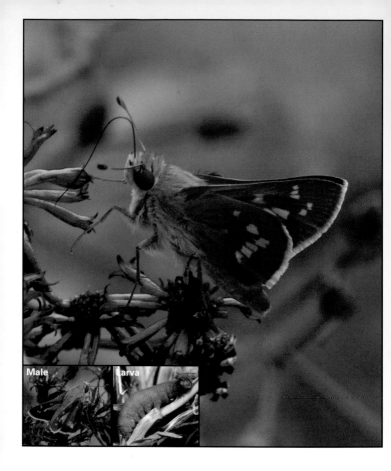

Male

Larva

Comments: Leonard's Skipper is a large, dark brown skipper with a distinctive white spot band on the hind-wing below. A late season species, it produces a single generation each year that emerges in mid to late August and continues flying well into September. Generally common throughout much of its primarily northern range, it extends southward through the Appalachians into the extreme northeastern tip of Georgia. Adults have a powerful and fast flight and tend to be quite wary and difficult to closely approach, even when nectaring at many late summer blossoms.

Leonard's Skipper
Hesperia leonardus

Family/Subfamily: Skippers (Hesperiidae)/
Banded Skippers (Hesperiinae)

Wingspan: 1.50–1.75" (3.8–4.4 cm)

Above: tawny orange with broad dark brown borders
and several small orange spots; forewings elongated
and pointed

Below: hindwing is reddish brown with a distinct row of
cream white spots

Sexes: similar, although female is primarily brown with
pale forewing spots

Egg: whitish green, laid singly on or near host leaves

Larva: olive green with a black head marked with cream

Larval Host Plants: a variety of grasses including bentgrass, panic grasses, and Poverty Oatgrass

Habitat: open, grassy areas including old fields, roadsides, wet meadows, woodland clearings and margins

Broods: single generation

Abundance: rare to uncommon

Compare: Indian Skipper (pg. 291) has a yellow orange
ventral hindwing with a pale spot band.

Resident

Jan. Feb. Mar. Apr. May June July Aug. Sept. Oct. Nov. Dec.

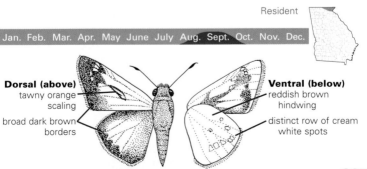

Dorsal (above)
tawny orange scaling
broad dark brown borders

Ventral (below)
reddish brown hindwing
distinct row of cream white spots

205

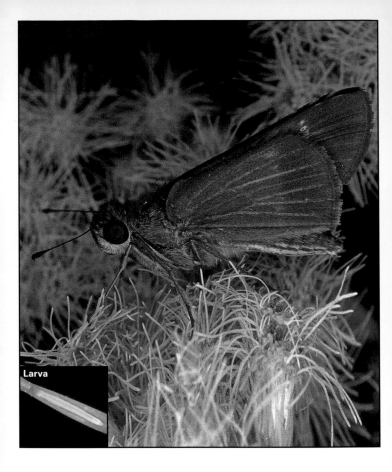

Larva

Comments: Freshly emerged Ocola Skippers often have a noticeable purplish sheen to the hindwings below. The butterfly can be encountered in a wide range of habitats including suburban gardens. Adults have a fast, darting flight typically within a few feet of the ground. A year-round resident of the southeast, it regularly expands its range northward each year and is particularly abundant in the fall.

Ocola Skipper
Panoquina ocola

Family/Subfamily: Skippers (Hesperiidae)/ Banded Skippers (Hesperiinae)

Wingspan: 1.50–1.75" (3.8–4.4 cm)

Above: forewings are long and slender with pale median spots

Below: brown with light veins and a subtle purple sheen; typically darker toward margin; often has faint post-median spot band

Sexes: similar

Egg: green, laid singly on host leaves

Larva: light green with yellow stripes and green head

Larval Host Plants: various grasses including Southern Cutgrass

Habitat: marshes, pond margins, forest edges, road-sides, old fields, utility easements and gardens

Broods: multiple generations

Abundance: uncommon to common

Compare: Salt Marsh Skipper (pg. 141) is lighter brown beneath with distinct cream dash in center of ventral hindwing. Brazilian Skipper (pg. 225) is larger and has a row of semitransparent spots on ventral hindwing.

Resident Visitor

Jan. Feb. Mar. Apr. May June July Aug. Sept. Oct. Nov. Dec.

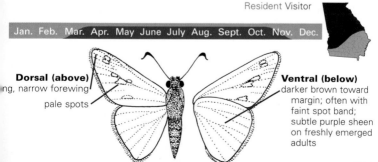

Dorsal (above)
ng, narrow forewing
pale spots

Ventral (below)
darker brown toward margin; often with faint spot band; subtle purple sheen on freshly emerged adults

207

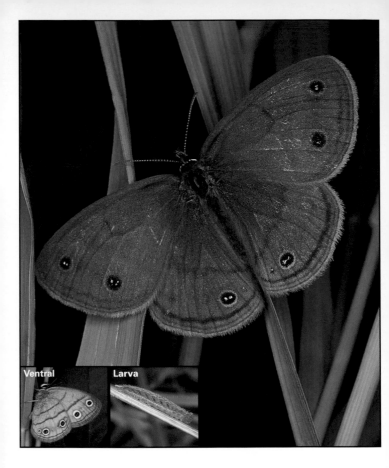

Ventral

Larva

Comments: The Little Wood Satyr is one of our most abundant and commonly encountered satyrs. It dances along the forest floor with a relatively slow, bobbing flight, but can move rapidly if disturbed. Adults periodically perch on leaf litter or low vegetation with their wings partially open. Adults feed at sap flows, animal dung, rotting fungi and fermenting fruit and do not visit flowers. Unlike the similar Viola's Wood Satyr, it has several successive generations each year.

Little Wood Satyr
Megisto cymela

Family/Subfamily: Brush-foots (Nymphalidae)/ Satyrs and Wood Nymphs (Satyrinae)

Wingspan: 1.5–1.9" (3.3–4.8 cm)

Above: brown; forewing has two prominent yellow-rimmed eyespots; hindwing has one to three (usually one is quite small) prominent yellow-rimmed eyespots

Below: light brown with two dark brown lines across both wings; each wing has some pearly silver markings between two large, yellow-rimmed eyespots

Sexes: similar, although female has larger eyespots

Egg: green, laid singly on host leaves

Larva: brown with a dark dorsal stripe, brown lateral dashes, two short stubby tails on the rear and two small horns on the head

Larval Host Plants: various grasses including St. Augustine Grass, bluegrass and Orchardgrass

Habitat: woodlands, forest clearings and margins

Broods: two to three generations

Abundance: common

Compare: Viola's Wood Satyr (pg. 223) is larger overall, has larger yellow-rimmed black eyespots, more pronounced pearly markings, and is primarily restricted to the southeastern portion of the state.

Resident

Jan. Feb. Mar. Apr. May June July Aug. Sept. Oct. Nov. Dec.

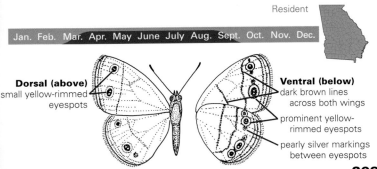

Dorsal (above)
small yellow-rimmed eyespots

Ventral (below)
dark brown lines across both wings

prominent yellow-rimmed eyespots

pearly silver markings between eyespots

209

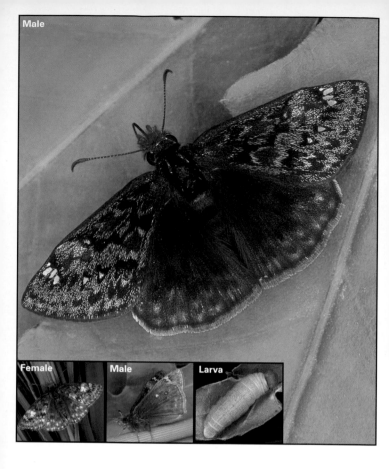

Male

Female   Male   Larva

Comments: A common spring species, Juvenal's Duskywing darts up and down sunlit trails and explores adjacent open sites with a quick, low flight. It frequently visits flowers or basks on bare ground with wings spread. Males perch on low vegetation and actively pursue passing objects. They occasionally puddle at damp sand or gravel. The larvae construct individual shelters on the host by folding over leaves with silk.

Juvenal's Duskywing
Erynnis juvenalis

Family/Subfamily: Skippers (Hesperiidae)/ Spread-wing Skippers (Pyrginae)

Wingspan: 1.5–1.9" (3.8–4.8 cm)

Above: dark brown; forewing has small cluster of tiny clear spots near wingtip and one at end of cell, and is heavily patterned with brown, gray, black and tan; female has increased gray scaling and heavier pattern

Below: brown, lightening toward wing margin; hindwing has two small, light spots along leading margin

Sexes: similar, although female is lighter and more heavily patterned with larger forewing spots

Egg: pale green, laid singly on host leaves

Larva: pale green with thin, light lateral stripe and reddish brown head; head capsule has a row of light orange spots around the margin

Larval Host Plants: various oaks including Live Oak, Turkey Oak, Water Oak, Myrtle Oak and White Oak

Habitat: oak woodlands, forest edges, woodland clearings, roadsides and utility easements

Broods: single generation

Abundance: occasional to abundant

Compare: Horace's Duskywing (pg. 185) lacks two light spots on ventral hindwing and extensive gray scaling on dorsal forewing.

Resident

Jan. Feb. Mar. Apr. May June July Aug. Sept. Oct. Nov. Dec.

male

Dorsal (above)
small glassy spots
glassy spot at end of cell
heavy gray scaling

Ventral (below)
two round light spots along leading margin

211

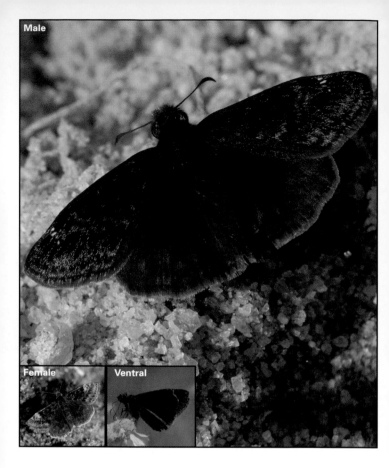

Male

Female Ventral

Comments: This is a common dark duskywing of the Deep South becoming increasingly rare northward. Extremely similar in appearance to the Wild Indigo Duskywing, close and careful observation is needed to ensure proper field identification but the exact determination of many (particularly worn) individuals may not be possible. Like most duskywings, the adults have a rapid, erratic flight usually within a few feet of the ground. They hold their wings open when perching or feeding. Larvae from last generation overwinter in individual leaf shelters.

Zarucco Duskywing
Erynnis zarucco

Family/Subfamily: Skippers (Hesperiidae)/ Spread-wing Skippers (Pyrginae)

Wingspan: 1.6–1.9" (4.1–4.8 cm)

Above: dark brown; forewing has several small glassy spots toward the apex and a distinctive pale brown patch at the end of the cell; small cell spot typically lacking

Below: dark brown with numerous light and dark spots

Sexes: similar, although female is lighter with more heavily patterned wings and larger glassy spots

Egg: yellow green, laid singly on host leaves

Larva: pale green with numerous tiny white tubercles, dark dorsal stripe, yellowish white lateral stripe; dark brown head with orange spots around the margin

Larval Host Plants: a variety of plants in the bean family including Carolina Indigo, Hairy Indigo, Black Locust, American Wisteria, vetch and milk peas

Habitat: open upland woodland, forest edges and clearings, roadsides, utility easements and old fields

Broods: three generations

Abundance: occasional to common

Compare: Wild Indigo Duskywing (pg. 187) has a faint (usually) cell-end bar on the hindwing above.

Resident

| Jan. | Feb. | Mar. | Apr. | May | June | July | Aug. | Sept. | Oct. | Nov. | Dec. |

Dorsal (above)
very dark forewing
pale patch at end of cell

Ventral (below)

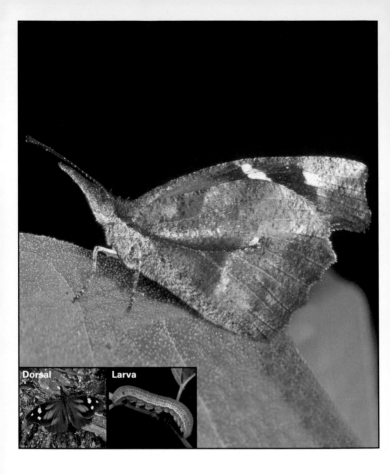

Dorsal

Larva

Comments: The American Snout gets its name from the
unusually long labial palpi that resemble an elongated
nose. This unique feature, combined with the cryptic
coloration of the wings beneath enhances the butterfly's overall "dead leaf" appearance when at rest.
Adults have a rapid, somewhat erratic flight and are
commonly drawn to flowers. Males readily puddle at
damp ground. This butterfly typically rests and feeds
with its wings closed, so its dorsal color is seen primarily in flight or when the butterfly is basking in the sun.

American Snout
Libytheana carinenta

Family/Subfamily: Brush-foots (Nymphalidae)/ Snouts (Libytheinae)

Wingspan: 1.6–1.9" (4.1–4.8 cm)

Above: brown with orange patches and white forewing spots; forewing apex is extended and squared off

Below: brown with orange basal forewing scaling and white spots; hindwing variable; plain gray brown or pinkish brown with heavy mottling

Sexes: similar

Egg: tiny white eggs laid in axils of host leaves

Larva: light green with numerous small yellow dots and yellow lateral stripe; rear portion has two small black lateral spots

Larval Host Plants: Common Hackberry and Sugarberry

Habitat: rich, deciduous woodlands, stream corridors, forest edges, woodland clearings and adjacent open brushy areas

Broods: multiple generations

Abundance: occasional to common

Compare: unique

Resident Visitor

Jan. Feb. Mar. Apr. May June July Aug. Sept. Oct. Nov. Dec.

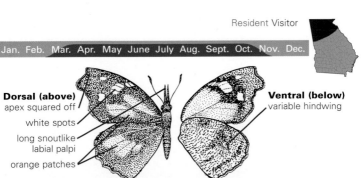

Dorsal (above)
apex squared off

white spots

long snoutlike labial palpi

orange patches

Ventral (below)
variable hindwing

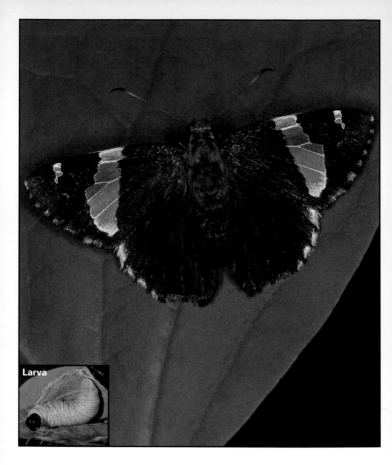

Larva

Comments: Aptly named, this robust skipper had a distinct glassy golden yellow band across each forewing. Generally rare and extremely local throughout most of its range, the Golden-banded Skipper is most often encountered singly or in very low numbers. Adults have a somewhat slow but highly erratic, darting flight close to the ground and can be a challenge to follow. Males perch on low vegetation with their wings outstretched.

Golden-banded Skipper
Autochton cellus

Family/Subfamily: Skippers (Hesperiidae)/
Spread-wing Skippers (Pyrginae)

Wingspan: 1.5–2.0" (3.8–5.1 cm)

Above: brown; forewing has a golden yellow band across the center and a white spot below the apex; checkered fringe

Below: forewing is marked as above, but paler and mottled with faint dark brown spots; hindwing has two irregular dark brown bands and a light gray frosted patch along the margin

Sexes: similar

Egg: yellow, laid in short strings on host leaves

Larva: yellow green with a broad yellow lateral stripe, numerous small yellow dots; reddish brown head has two round yellow spots on the lower half

Larval Host Plants: primarily beggarweeds, occasionally uses bush clover and Horseflyweed

Habitat: moist woodlands, stream corridors, wetland margins

Broods: two generations

Abundance: locally rare to occasional

Compare: Hoary Edge (pg. 199) has a broad, dirty white patch along the margin of the ventral hindwing.

Resident

Jan. Feb. Mar. Apr. May June July Aug. Sept. Oct. Nov. Dec.

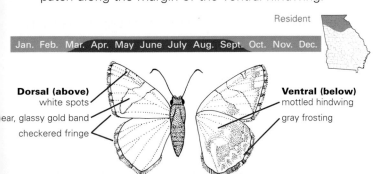

Dorsal (above)
white spots
ear, glassy gold band
checkered fringe

Ventral (below)
mottled hindwing
gray frosting

217

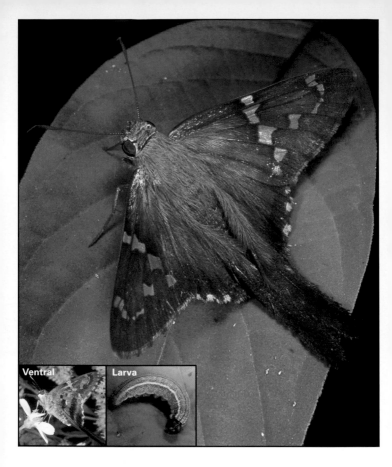

Ventral

Larva

Comments: Resembling a small swallowtail, the Long-tailed Skipper is one of the most common and distinctive skippers in the Southeast. At home in most open, disturbed sites, it regularly wanders into nearby yards and can be an abundant garden visitor. Adults have a quick, low flight but often stop to perch on low vegetation or nectar at blossoms. The colorful larvae construct individual shelters on the host by folding over small sections of a leaf with silk. Older larvae may use the entire leaf or connect several leaves. The butterfly is migratory and moves south each fall into the Florida peninsula to escape cold winter temperatures.

Long-tailed Skipper
Urbanus proteus

Family/Subfamily: Skippers (Hesperiidae)/
Spread-wing Skippers (Pyrginae)

Wingspan: 1.5–2.0" (3.8–5.1 cm)

Above: brown with iridescent blue-green scaling on wing
bases and body; long hindwing tail; forewing has several semitransparent spots

Below: brown; hindwing has two crisp dark brown
bands; forewing has a continuous brown submarginal
band

Sexes: similar

Egg: pale yellow, laid singly on the underside of host
leaves

Larva: yellow-green with a dark dorsal stripe, yellow lateral stripe and crimson head; body is covered with tiny
black spots

Larval Host Plants: a wide variety of legumes including beggarweeds, wisteria, beans and Kudzu

Habitat: open, disturbed sites including roadsides, old
fields, fallow agricultural land, utility easements, forest
edges and gardens

Broods: multiple generations

Abundance: common to abundant

Compare: Dorantes Skipper (pg. 203) lacks iridescent
blue-green dorsal coloration.

Resident Visitor Stray

Jan. Feb. Mar. Apr. May June July Aug. Sept. Oct. Nov. Dec.

Dorsal (above)
semitransparent spots

iridescent blue-green

blue-green body

Ventral (below)
continuous brown submarginal band

distinct dark bands and spots

long tail

219

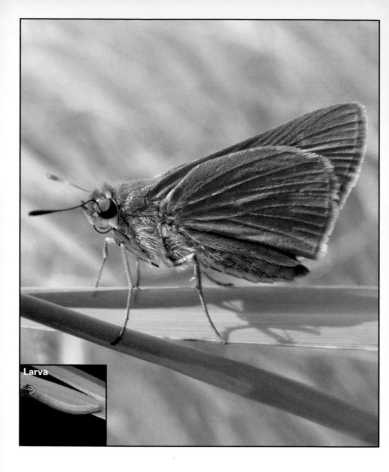

Larva

Comments: This is a large southern skipper restricted primarily to Florida. It just barely enters our area in the extreme southeastern portion of the state. As its name implies, the Palmetto Skipper inhabits scrubby woodland areas that support palmettos. It tends to be local and uncommon. Adults have a strong, rapid flight but are often encountered feeding at available blossoms. They are particularly fond of thistles.

Palmetto Skipper
Euphyes arpa

Family/Subfamily: Skippers (Hesperiidae)/
Banded Skippers (Hesperiinae)

Wingspan: 1.6–1.9" (4.1–4.8 cm)

Above: male is bright golden-orange with dark brown
borders, forewing bears a narrow black stigma; female
is primarily dark brown with pale yellow-orange
forewing spots; head and thorax yellow orange

Below: hindwing is unmarked golden orange

Sexes: dissimilar; female is primarily dark brown above
with pale forewing spots

Egg: light green, laid singly on host leaves

Larva: green with a black and white collar; white head
marked by tan stripes and a black spot on the forehead

Larval Host Plants: Saw Palmetto

Habitat: pinelands and scrub with palmetto

Broods: two generations

Abundance: uncommon; local

Compare: Unlikely to be confused with any other skipper based on habitat.

Resident

| Jan. | Feb. | Mar. | Apr. | May | June | July | Aug. | Sept. | Oct. | Nov. | Dec. |

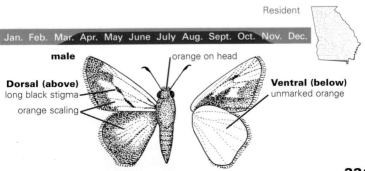

male — orange on head

Dorsal (above)
long black stigma
orange scaling

Ventral (below)
unmarked orange

221

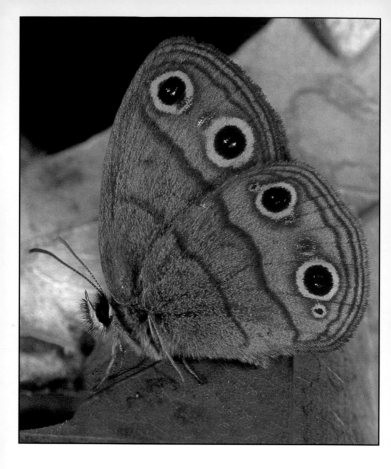

Comments: There remains considerable debate about the taxonomic status of this attractive woodland butterfly. Some treat it as a separate species, while others feel it is best considered a form of the widespread Little Wood Satyr. It scurries along the forest floor with a quick, bobbing flight and periodically lands on leaf litter or low vegetation. Like most satyrs, it does not visit flowers but instead is drawn to sap flows, dung, rotting fungi and fermenting fruit. The large yellow-rimmed eyespots presumably help deflect attack away from its vulnerable body.

Viola's Wood Satyr
Megisto viola

Family/Subfamily: Brush-foots (Nymphalidae)/
Satyrs and Wood Nymphs (Satyrinae)

Wingspan: 1.6–2.0" (4.1–5.1 cm)

Above: brown with large yellow-rimmed eyespots on
both wings; male has two conspicuous eyespots on
the forewing and one to two on the hindwing; female
has two on the hindwing

Below: light brown with two dark brown lines and large,
yellow-rimmed eyespots; silver markings between
eyespots

Sexes: similar, although female has larger eyespots

Egg: green, laid singly on host leaves

Larva: brown with dark dorsal stripe and two stubby tails

Larval Host Plants: various grasses including St.
Augustine Grass

Habitat: shady woodlands, forest edges and adjacent
open areas

Broods: single spring generation

Abundance: occasional to common

Compare: Little Wood Satyr (pg. 209) is smaller and has
smaller yellow-rimmed eyespots.

Resident

Jan. Feb. Mar. Apr. May June July Aug. Sept. Oct. Nov. Dec.

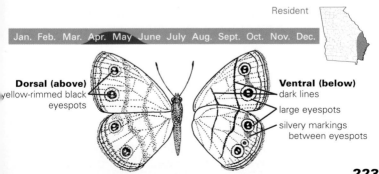

Dorsal (above)
yellow-rimmed black
eyespots

Ventral (below)
dark lines

large eyespots

silvery markings
between eyespots

223

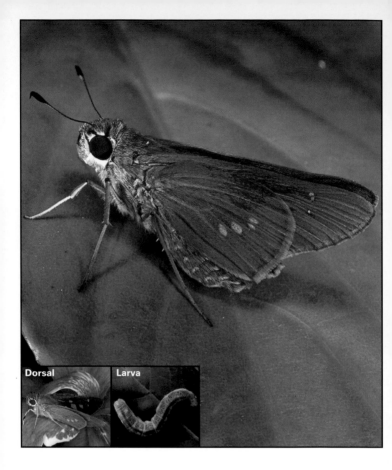

Dorsal

Larva

Comments: The Brazilian Skipper is also referred to as the Canna Skipper and can be a common nuisance or aesthetic pest on ornamental cannas. The transparent, alien-looking larvae construct individual shelters by rolling over sections of the host leaf with silk. Inside they hide safely out of the sight of would-be predators and come out to feed mainly at night. The adults have a strong, rapid flight, usually low to the ground, and visit a wide range of flowers. Primarily a tropical butterfly, it regularly colonizes southern portions of Georgia but is unable to survive freezing temperatures in any life stage.

Brazilian Skipper
Calpodes ethlius

Family/Subfamily: Skippers (Hesperiidae)/
Banded Skippers (Hesperiinae)

Wingspan: 1.75–2.25" (4.4–5.7 cm)

Above: brown; elongated forewing is lighter at base with
several semitransparent spots across the center; hindwing has postmedian band of three small
semitransparent spots and tapers toward bottom

Below: as above but lighter brown

Sexes: similar

Egg: gray-green, laid singly on host leaves

Larva: green, semitransparent with orange-brown head;
head has a central black dot

Larval Host Plants: Alligator Flag, Indian Shot, ornamental cannas

Habitat: marshes, pond edges, parks, gardens and various urban areas

Broods: multiple generations

Abundance: occasional to common

Compare: Ocola Skipper (pg. 207) is smaller and lacks
ventral hindwing band of semitransparent spots.

Visitor Stray

| Jan. | Feb. | Mar. | Apr. | May | June | July | Aug. | Sept. | Oct. | Nov. | Dec. |

male

Dorsal (above)
ng, narrow forewing

large translucent
spots

apers to stubby lobe

Ventral (below)
band of
semitransparent
spots

225

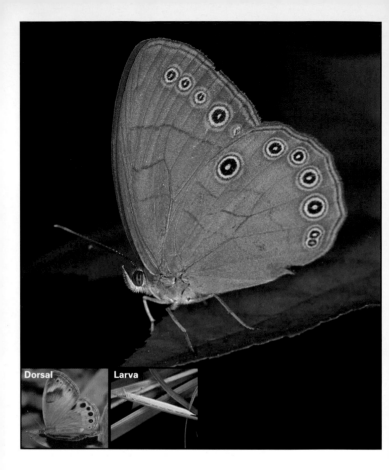

Dorsal

Larva

Comments: The Appalachian Brown is a medium-sized brown butterfly. Often spotty and localized, it prefers moist, shaded habitats. Adults have an erratic, bouncing flight and travel low through wetland vegetation, stopping frequently to perch. Even when disturbed, they typically fly only a short distance before alighting again. As a result of their reclusive behavior, active colonies may be easily overlooked. Like most satyrs, the adults feed at sap flows, fermenting fruit, animal dung or rotting fungi and do not visit flowers.

Appalachian Brown
Satyrodes appalachia

Family/Subfamily: Brush-foots (Nymphalidae)/ Satyrs and Wood Nymphs (Satyrinae)

Wingspan: 1.90–2.25" (4.8–5.7 cm)

Above: light brown with small, solid black eyespots

Below: soft brown; forewing has a row of four double-rimmed black eyespots, the middle two generally smaller than one above or below; hindwing has a row of five to six double-rimmed black eyespots with pale centers bordered inwardly by a dark sinuous post-median line

Sexes: similar, although female is generally paler brown with larger eyespots

Egg: greenish white, laid singly on or near host leaves

Larva: light green with narrow longitudinal yellow stripes, two short tails on the rear and two reddish horns on the head

Larval Host Plants: various grasses and sedges including Upright Sedge and Fowl Mannagrass

Habitat: wooded swamps, moist, grassy glades, stream corridors and forest margins

Broods: two generations

Abundance: occasional; localized

Compare: unique

Resident

Jan. Feb. Mar. Apr. May June July Aug. Sept. Oct. Nov. Dec.

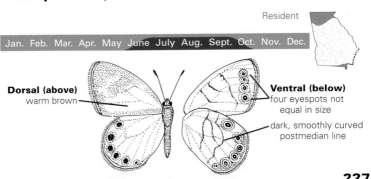

Dorsal (above)
warm brown

Ventral (below)
four eyespots not equal in size

dark, smoothly curved postmedian line

227

Dorsal

Larva

Comments: The Silver-spotted Skipper is a large, robust
butterfly named after the distinctive pure silver-white
patch on the hindwing below. Found along forest
edges and in adjacent open areas, adults have a powerful darting flight. Adults are fond of colorful flowers
and may be frequent garden visitors. They have a long
proboscis and can easily gain access to nectar from a
variety of flowers. Males perch on shrubs or overhanging branches and aggressively investigate passing
organisms. The colorful larvae construct individual
shelters on the host by tying one or more leaves
together with silk.

Silver-spotted Skipper
Epargyreus clarus

Family/Subfamily: Skippers (Hesperiidae)/ Spread-wing Skippers (Pyrginae)

Wingspan: 1.75–2.40" (4.4–6.1 cm)

Above: brown with median row of gold spots on forewing and checkered wing fringe; hindwing is tapered into small, rounded, lobe-like tail

Below: brown; forewing as above; hindwing has distinct, elongated clear silver-white patch in center

Sexes: similar

Egg: green, laid singly on host leaves

Larva: yellow-green with dark bands and reddish brown head

Larval Host Plants: wide variety of legumes including Black Locust, wisteria, bush clover, False Indigo, Kudzu, Groundnut, Butterfly Pea and beggarweeds

Habitat: forest edges, open woodlands, roadsides, utility easements, old fields and gardens

Broods: two or more generations

Abundance: occasional to common

Compare: Hoary Edge (pg. 199) is smaller and has marginal white ventral hindwing patch. Golden-banded Skipper (pg. 217) lacks prominent silver-white median patch on ventral hindwing.

Resident

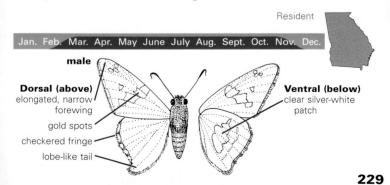

Jan. Feb. Mar. Apr. May June July Aug. Sept. Oct. Nov. Dec.

male

Dorsal (above)
elongated, narrow forewing

gold spots

checkered fringe

lobe-like tail

Ventral (below)
clear silver-white patch

229

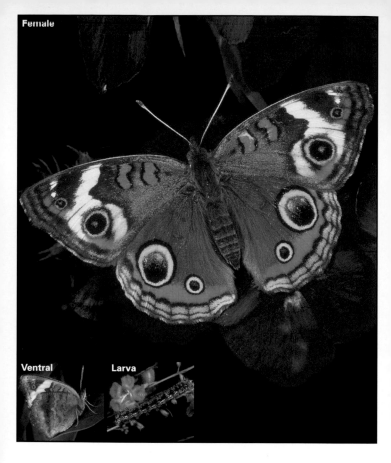

Female

Ventral

Larva

Comments: The Common Buckeye is one of our most distinctive butterflies. The large eyespots help deflect attack away from the insect's vulnerable body or serve to startle would-be predators. It is fond of most open, sunny locations with low-growing vegetation and may be an occasional garden visitor. Adults frequently alight on bare soil or gravel but are extremely wary and difficult to approach. Males establish territories and actively investigate most any passing insect. Flight is rapid and low to the ground. Unable to survive harsh freezing conditions, it annually undertakes a southward fall migration and overwinters in warmer Gulf Coast locations.

Common Buckeye
Junonia coenia

Family/Subfamily: Brush-foots (Nymphalidae)/
True Brush-foots (Nymphalinae)

Wingspan: 1.5–2.7" (3.8–6.9 cm)

Above: brown with prominent eyespots; forewing bears
a distinct white patch and two small orange bars

Below: forewing has prominent white band; hindwings
seasonally variable in color; summer forms are light
brown with numerous pattern elements; cool-season
forms are reddish brown with reduced markings

Sexes: similar, although female has broader wings and
larger hindwing eyespots

Egg: dark green, laid singly on host leaves

Larva: black with lateral white stripes, orange patches
and branched spines

Larval Host Plants: plants in many families including
toadflax, false foxglove, Frogfruit, plantain, twinflower
and wild petunia

Habitat: fields, pastures, roadsides, fallow agricultural
land, gardens, open pineland, disturbed sites

Broods: multiple generations, overwinters as adult

Abundance: occasional to common; locally abundant

Compare: unique

Resident Visitor

Jan. Feb. Mar. Apr. May June July Aug. Sept. Oct. Nov. Dec.

Dorsal (above)
white band that
surrounds
eyespot

orange bars

eyespots

orange band

Ventral (below)
seasonally variable:
reddish brown to
tan

231

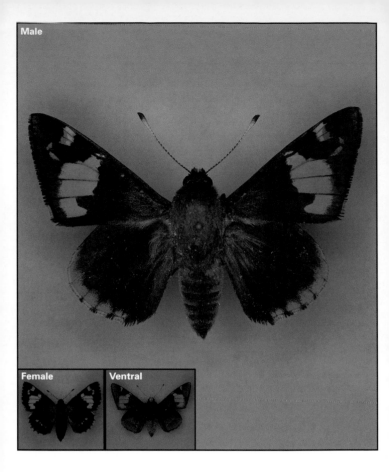

Comments: Although the Cofaqui Giant-Skipper is somewhat dwarfed by its larger relative, the Yucca Giant-Skipper, it is still an impressive butterfly. It is an inhabitant of open pine woodlands that support its larval host. Larvae burrow into the host stem and feed on the root. Larvae overwinter. Adults have a rapid, powerful flight that produces a noticeable buzz when close. Males perch on vegetation along trails or clearings and actively defend their territory. It is rare and seldom-seen throughout its limited range. Witnessing even one individual will make your day!

Cofaqui Giant-Skipper
Megathymus cofaqui

Family/Subfamily: Skippers (Hesperiidae)/
Giant-Skippers (Megathyminae)

Wingspan: 1.9–2.4" (4.8–6.1 cm)

Above: dark brown; male has a broad yellow forewing
band and pale hindwing border

Below: dull gray brown with variable small white spots
and light gray scaling toward outer margin

Sexes: similar, although female is larger with broader
wings and a postmedian row of small yellow spots on
the hindwing

Egg: cream, laid singly on host leaves

Larva: cream with a brownish black head

Larval Host Plants: yuccas including Spanish Dagger
and Stiff-leaved Bear Grass

Habitat: dry woodlands, pinelands and scrub

Broods: one generation

Abundance: rare to uncommon

Compare: Yucca Giant-Skipper (pg. 245) is larger with
more pointed and elongated forewings, a narrower
straight yellow forewing band above and darker ventral
wings with extensive frosting.

Resident

Jan. Feb. Mar. Apr. May June July Aug. Sept. Oct. Nov. Dec.

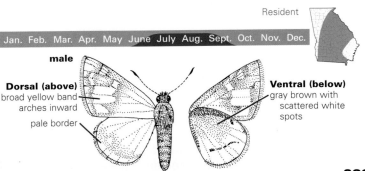

male

Dorsal (above)
broad yellow band
arches inward

pale border

Ventral (below)
gray brown with
scattered white
spots

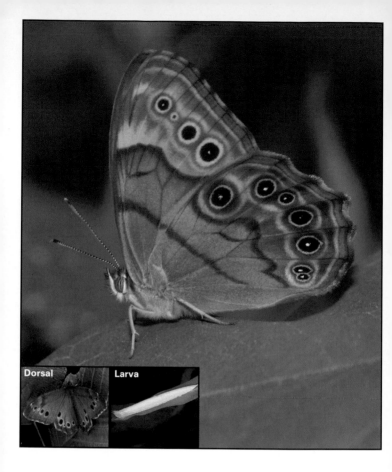

Dorsal

Larva

Comments: Although called the Northern Pearly Eye, this
butterfly's range extends into the Deep South, brushing
the northern tip of Georgia. It occurs in localized, spotty
colonies in close association with its larval hosts, but
may be common when encountered. Adults have a
quick, bobbing flight and maneuver close to the ground,
often through the dense forest undergrowth. They frequently alight on low vegetation, tree trunks or leaf
litter. They do not visit flowers but instead feed at sap
flows, rotting fruit, decaying vegetation, fungi and dung.
Unlike most butterflies, the adults are active even on
overcast days and often fly late into the evening.

Northern Pearly Eye
Enodia anthedon

Family/Subfamily: Brush-foots (Nymphalidae)/ Satyrs and Wood Nymphs (Satyrinae)

Wingspan: 1.75–2.60" (4.3–6.6 cm)

Above: light brown with black eyespots in a pale field; hindwing has a slightly scalloped margin; antennal clubs are black at base

Below: brown with a violet cast; forewing has a straight row of four yellow-rimmed dark eyespots; hindwing has a cream band enclosing a row of yellow-rimmed dark eyespots with light highlights

Sexes: similar, although female generally has broader, more rounded wings and larger eyespots

Egg: greenish white, laid singly on host leaves

Larva: yellow green with narrow longitudinal yellow stripes, a dark green dorsal stripe, two short red-tipped tails on the rear and two reddish horns on the head

Larval Host Plants: various grasses including Whitegrass, Indian Woodoats, Silver Plumegrass, Bearded Shorthusk and Reed Canarygrass

Habitat: moist, shady woods, stream corridors, marsh edges and semi-open grassy areas along forest edges

Broods: two generations

Abundance: uncommon to occasional; localized

Compare: Southern Pearly Eye (pg. 243) has orange-tipped antennae.

Resident

Jan. Feb. Mar. Apr. May June July Aug. Sept. Oct. Nov. Dec.

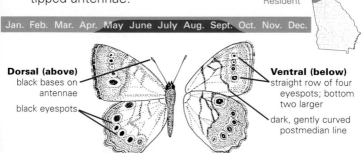

Dorsal (above)
black bases on antennae

black eyespots

Ventral (below)
straight row of four eyespots; bottom two larger

dark, gently curved postmedian line

235

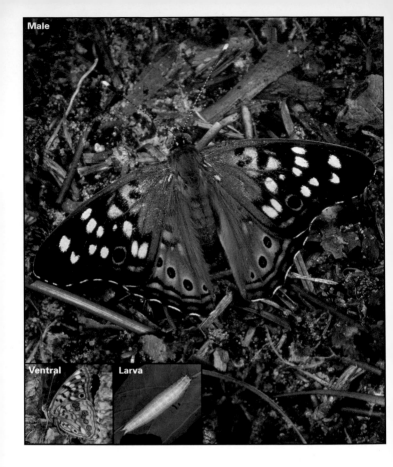

Male

Ventral

Larva

Comments: The Hackberry Butterfly is named for its
common larval host. Though it prefers shady woodlands, it may show up in suburban yards or parks. It
has a strong, rapid flight and perches on sunlit leaves,
overhanging branches or tree trunks along forest trails
and woodland edges. Adults are exceedingly inquisi-
tive and dart out to investigate passing objects,
sometimes even landing on humans. They are drawn
to sap flows or rotting fruit and do not visit flowers.
Although often spotty and localized, the species can
be quite abundant when encountered.

Hackberry Butterfly
Asterocampa celtis

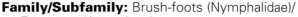

Family/Subfamily: Brush-foots (Nymphalidae)/ Emperors (Apaturinae)

Wingspan: 2.0–2.6" (5.1–6.6 cm)

Above: amber-brown with dark markings and borders; forewing bears several small white spots near the apex and a single submarginal black eyespot; hindwing has a postmedian row of dark spots

Below: as above with muted coloration; hindwing has postmedian row of yellow-rimmed black spots with blue green centers

Sexes: similar, although female has broader wings

Egg: cream-white, laid singly or in small clusters on leaves

Larva: light green with two narrow dorsal yellow stripe; mottled with small yellow spots; dark head bears two stubby, branched horns; rear end has a pair of short tails

Larval Host Plants: Common Hackberry, Sugarberry and Dwarf Hackberry

Habitat: moist, rich woodlands, forest margins and clearings, stream corridors, parks and yards

Broods: multiple generations

Abundance: occasional to common; localized

Compare: Tawny Emperor (pg. 241) is more orange-brown above and lacks white forewing spots and single forewing eyespot.

Resident

Jan. Feb. Mar. Apr. May June July Aug. Sept. Oct. Nov. Dec.

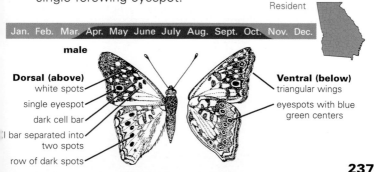

male

Dorsal (above)
white spots
single eyespot
dark cell bar
l bar separated into two spots
row of dark spots

Ventral (below)
triangular wings
eyespots with blue green centers

237

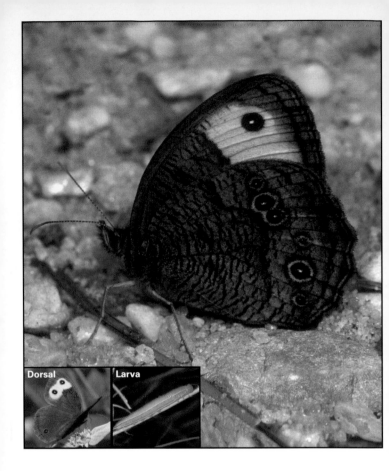

Dorsal

Larva

Comments: The Common Wood Nymph is a medium-sized butterfly primarily encountered in open, grassy meadows and fields, though it may also be found in forest clearings and margins. Adults have a low, relaxed flight and bob erratically through the vegetation. Well camouflaged when resting, it can be a challenge to locate or follow. Unlike most satyrs, it is an opportunistic feeder and frequently visits flowers along with sap flows and fermenting fruit.

Common Wood Nymph
Cercyonis pegala

Family/Subfamily: Brush-foots (Nymphalidae)/
Satyrs and Wood Nymphs (Satyrinae)

Wingspan: 1.8–2.8" (4.6–7.1 cm)

Above: brown; forewing has large postmedian yellow
patch containing two dark eyespots

Below: brown with dark striations; forewing has large
postmedian yellow patch containing two dark eyespots; hindwing has postmedian row of small,
yellow-rimmed dark eyespots

Sexes: similar, although female is paler and has larger
eyespots

Egg: cream, laid singly on host leaves

Larva: green with dark green dorsal stripe and light side
stripes

Larval Host Plants: various grasses including bluegrass, Poverty Oatgrass and Purpletop Grass

Habitat: open woodlands, forest edges, marshes, grassy
fields and roadsides

Broods: single generation

Abundance: occasional to common

Compare: unique

Resident

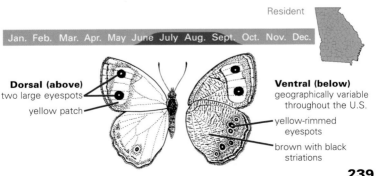

Jan. Feb. Mar. Apr. May June July Aug. Sept. Oct. Nov. Dec.

Dorsal (above)
two large eyespots
yellow patch

Ventral (below)
geographically variable
throughout the U.S.
yellow-rimmed
eyespots
brown with black
striations

239

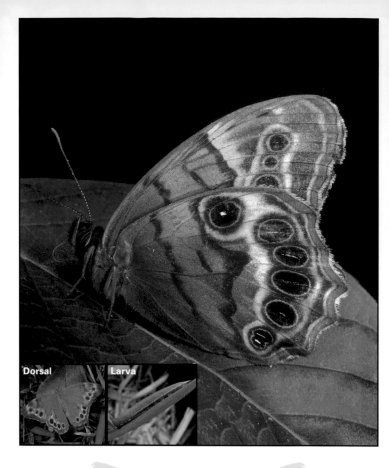

Dorsal

Larva

Comments: The Southern Pearly Eye is one of our largest satyrs. It prefers moist shady areas and is typically found in close association with its larval host. The butterfly has a spotty, localized distribution but may be common when found. Adults have a quick, bobbing flight and frequently alight on low vegetation or tree trunks. They do not visit flowers, but instead prefer to feed at sap flows, rotting fruit, decaying vegetation and dung. Unlike most butterflies, adults are often active on overcast days and fly until dusk.

Southern Pearly Eye
Enodia portlandia

Family/Subfamily: Brush-foots (Nymphalidae)/ Satyrs and Wood Nymphs (Satyrinae)

Wingspan: 2.00–2.75" (5.1–7.0 cm)

Above: light brown; forewing has dark eyespots in light postmedian patch

Below: purplish brown; hindwing has submarginal cream band and row of yellow-rimmed dark eyespots

Sexes: similar, although female is generally somewhat lighter in color

Egg: pale green, laid singly on host leaves

Larva: green with narrow light stripes, two short tails and two reddish horns on the head

Larval Host Plants: Giant Cane and Switchcane

Habitat: moist, shaded woodlands, stream corridors and swamp margins

Broods: three generations

Abundance: occasional to locally abundant

Compare: Creole Pearly Eye (pg. 247) has five yellow-rimmed black eyespots and a dark postmedian line through the ventral forewing that bulges outward near costal margin.

Resident

Jan. Feb. Mar. Apr. May June July Aug. Sept. Oct. Nov. Dec.

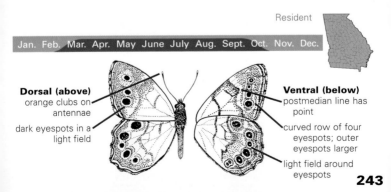

Dorsal (above)
orange clubs on antennae

dark eyespots in a light field

Ventral (below)
postmedian line has point

curved row of four eyespots; outer eyespots larger

light field around eyespots

243

Ventral

Comments: The Yucca Giant-Skipper is a beautifully marked butterfly with elongated wings. Adults have a rapid, powerful flight that produces a noticeable buzz. Males perch on vegetation along trails or clearings and actively defend their territory. The butterfly is particularly active in late afternoon or early evening. The larvae feed on host leaves when young but soon burrow into stem and large taproot, forming a long tunnel.

Yucca Giant-Skipper
Megathymus yuccae

Family/Subfamily: Skippers (Hesperiidae)/ Giant-Skippers (Megathyminae)

Wingspan: 2.0–2.8" (5.1–7.1 cm)

Above: blackish brown with yellow hindwing border and straight band of yellow spots on forewing; small white spots near the forewing apex; female has small post-median band of tiny orange spots on hindwing

Below: chocolate brown with marginal frosting and distinct white patch along upper margin of hindwing

Sexes: similar, although female is significantly larger with broader wings and an additional row of yellow spots on hindwing

Egg: pinkish brown, laid singly on host leaves

Larva: light tan with reddish brown head

Larval Host Plants: yuccas including Spanish Dagger and Stiff-leaved Bear Grass

Habitat: dry woodlands, pinelands and scrub

Broods: single generation

Abundance: uncommon to occasional

Compare: Cofaqui Giant-Skipper (pg. 233) has a broad, curved yellow forewing band and is duller gray-brown below with less prominent scattered small white hindwing spots.

Resident

Jan. Feb. Mar. Apr. May June July Aug. Sept. Oct. Nov. Dec.

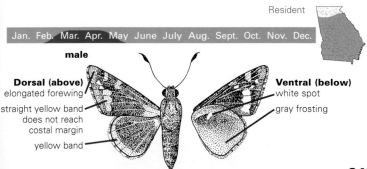

male

Dorsal (above)
elongated forewing

straight yellow band does not reach costal margin

yellow band

Ventral (below)
white spot

gray frosting

245

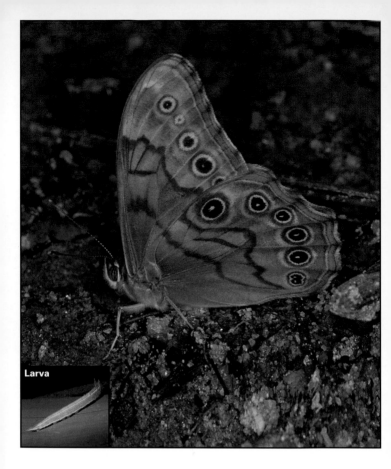

Larva

Comments: The Creole Pearly Eye is rarer and more localized in occurrence than its two other close relatives. It seldom wanders far from stands of its larval host. It is often encountered alongside the similar Southern Pearly Eye and as a result may go undetected. Adults have a quick, bobbing flight and maneuver close to the ground through the forest understory, making them a challenge to follow. They frequently perch on tree trunks or other vegetation. They do not visit flowers but instead prefer to feed at sap flows, rotting fruit, decaying vegetation, fungi and dung.

Creole Pearly Eye
Enodia creola

Family/Subfamily: Brush-foots (Nymphalidae)/ Satyrs and Wood Nymphs (Satyrinae)

Wingspan: 2.30–2.75" (5.8–7.0 cm)

Above: light brown; forewing has black eyespots in pale field; male has dark, raised scent-scale patches; hindwing has a row of large, solid black eyespots and slightly scalloped margin

Below: brown with a violet cast; forewing has a straight row of five yellow-rimmed dark eyespots and a dark postmedian line bulging outward near the costal margin

Sexes: similar, female lacks the scent-scale patches, and has broader, more rounded wings and larger eyespots

Egg: greenish white, laid singly on host leaves

Larva: yellow green with narrow longitudinal yellow stripes, two short red-tipped tails on the rear and two reddish horns on the head

Larval Host Plants: Switchcane

Habitat: canebrakes in moist, shaded woodlands, dense upland forests, stream corridors and swamp margins

Broods: two generations

Abundance: rare to occasional; localized

Compare: Southern (pg. 243) and Northern Pearly Eye (pg. 235) have four ventral forewing eyespots.

Resident

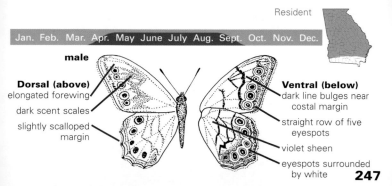

Jan. Feb. Mar. Apr. May June July Aug. Sept. Oct. Nov. Dec.

male

Dorsal (above)
elongated forewing
dark scent scales
slightly scalloped margin

Ventral (below)
dark line bulges near costal margin
straight row of five eyespots
violet sheen
eyespots surrounded by white

247

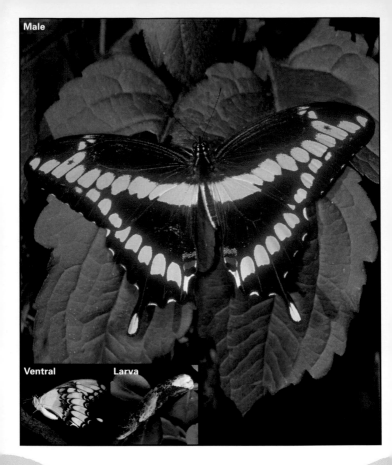

Male

Ventral   Larva

Comments: With a wingspan often approaching six inches, the Giant Swallowtail is one of the largest butterflies in North America. An inhabitant of semi-open areas, it is regularly encountered along woodland roads and stream margins in close association with its larval host. Although it is an occasional garden visitor, the species is seldom overly abundant in any location and not highly tolerant of urban development. When nectaring, adults continuously flutter their wings. This behavior coupled with a long proboscis enables them to visit a wide range of flowers, including many that otherwise might not easily support their weight.

Giant Swallowtail
Papilio cresphontes

Family/Subfamily: Swallowtails (Papilionidae)/ Swallowtails (Papilioninae)

Wingspan: 4.5–5.5" (11.4–14.0 cm)

Above: chocolate brown with broad crossing bands of yellow spots; characteristic diagonal band extends from tip of forewing to base of abdomen; hindwing tail has yellow center

Below: cream yellow with brown markings and blue median hindwing band

Sexes: similar, although female is generally larger

Egg: amber-brown, laid singly on upperside of host leaves

Larva: brown with yellow and cream patches; resembles bird dropping

Larval Host Plants: Hercules Club, Wafer Ash, Prickly Ash and cultivated citrus

Habitat: woodlands, pastures, forest edges, stream corridors, open pinelands and suburban gardens

Broods: multiple generations

Abundance: occasional

Compare: Palamedes Swallowtail (pg. 71) has cream markings and lacks crossing forewing bands.

Resident

Jan. Feb. Mar. Apr. May June July Aug. Sept. Oct. Nov. Dec.

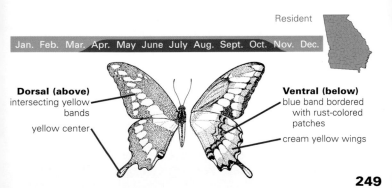

Dorsal (above)
intersecting yellow bands

yellow center

Ventral (below)
blue band bordered with rust-colored patches

cream yellow wings

249

Larva

Comments: The Red-Banded Hairstreak has a rapid,
erratic flight. Males typically perch on the sunlit leaves
of small trees and shrubs (often on their hosts) and
readily fly out to interact with other individuals often
spiraling high into the air before returning to a nearby
perch. Unlike most other butterflies, female Red-
Banded Hairstreaks do not lay their eggs directly on
the larval host. Instead, they land on the ground below
appropriate hosts and deposit the small eggs singly on
the undersides of dead, fallen leaves or other debris.
The resulting larvae feed primarily on this decaying
plant material.

Red-banded Hairstreak
Calycopis cecrops

Family/Subfamily: Gossamer Wings (Lycaenidae)/ Hairstreaks (Theclinae)

Wingspan: 0.75–1.00" (1.9–2.5 cm)

Above: male is slate gray above with no markings; female is slate gray with iridescent blue scaling on hindwing; hindwing bears two short tails

Below: light gray with broad, red band edged outwardly by a thin, wavy white line; blue scaling and a black eyespot near tails

Sexes: similar, although female has blue scaling above

Egg: cream brown, laid on dead leaves below host

Larva: pinkish brown with numerous short hairs

Larval Host Plants: Wax Myrtle, Winged Sumac, Mango, Staghorn Sumac and Fragrant Sumac; feed primarily on dead plant material below host

Habitat: woodland edges and adjacent disturbed, brushy areas, suburban gardens

Broods: multiple generations

Abundance: common

Compare: Southern Hairstreak (pg. 133) lacks complete red hindwing band.

Resident

Jan. Feb. Mar. Apr. May June July Aug. Sept. Oct. Nov. Dec.

Dorsal (above)
gray with varying amount of blue scaling

Ventral (below)
broad red band edged outwardly with black and white

251

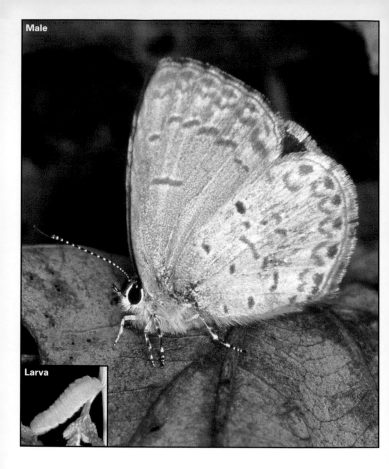

Male

Larva

Comments: This early-season blue is easily distinguished from the superficially similar Spring Azure with which it often flies by its dark, charcoal gray-infused wings. Although now considered a distinct species, individuals were previously through to be rare dark-colored forms of the Spring Azure. It typically occurs in small, isolated colonies that are often best discovered by first locating patches of its larval host. Adults have a quick, directed flight usually close to the ground. Males often join other azures at mud puddles or stream banks to sip moisture. It typically rests and feeds with its wings closed; dorsal color shows in flight or while basking.

Dusky Azure
Celastrina nigra

Family/Subfamily: Gossamer Wings (Lycaenidae)/ Blues (Polyommatinae)

Wingspan: 0.75–1.25" (1.9–3.2 cm)

Above: male is uniform dark charcoal gray; female is pale gray blue with extensive, broad dark wing borders

Below: light gray with small black spots; hindwing has pale but prominent dark zigzag band along margin enclosing a row of small dark spots

Sexes: dissimilar; female is pale gray blue with extensive, broad dark wing borders, some white scaling, and distinct narrow dark cell-end bars

Egg: blue gray eggs laid singly young shoots, new leaves or flower buds of host

Larva: yellow green with pale lateral stripes

Larval Host Plants: Goatsbeard or Bride's Feathers

Habitat: rich, shaded, deciduous woodlands, forest trails, woodland roads, shaded ravines, wooded ridges and stream corridors

Broods: single generation

Abundance: uncommon and local

Compare: Spring Azure (pg. 81) is blue above and has more extensive dark gray scaling below.

Resident

| Jan. | Feb. | Mar. | Apr. | May | June | July | Aug. | Sept. | Oct. | Nov. | Dec. |

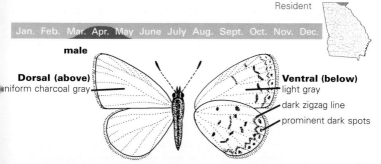

male

Dorsal (above)
uniform charcoal gray

Ventral (below)
light gray
dark zigzag line
prominent dark spots

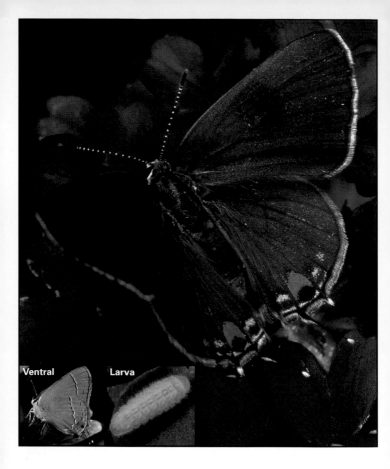

Ventral

Larva

Comments: Widespread and abundant, the Gray Hairstreak is one of our most commonly encountered hairstreaks. It is extremely fond of flowers and a frequent garden visitor. The small hairlike tails on the hindwing resemble antennae and presumably help deflect the attack of would-be predators away from the insect's vulnerable body. This charade, employed by many members of the family, is enhanced by the bright orange eyespots and converging lines on the wings below that draw attention to this unique "false head" feature.

Gray Hairstreak
Strymon melinus

Family/Subfamily: Gossamer Wings (Lycaenidae)/ Hairstreaks (Theclinae)

Wingspan: 1.0–1.5" (2.5–3.8 cm)

Above: slate gray with distinct reddish orange-capped black hindwing spot above tail

Below: light gray with black-and-white line across both wings (often with some orange); hindwing has reddish orange-capped black spot and blue scaling above tail

Sexes: similar; female larger with broader wings

Egg: light green, laid singly on flower buds or flowers of host

Larva: highly variable; bright green with lateral cream stripes to pinkish red

Larval Host Plants: wide variety of plants including Partridge Pea, beggarweeds, milk peas, milkvetch, lupine, bush clover, clover, vetch, mallow and Sida

Habitat: open, disturbed sites including roadsides, fallow agricultural land, old fields and gardens

Broods: multiple generations

Abundance: common

Compare: White M Hairstreak (pg. 89) has red ventral hindwing spot without a black pupil, distinct zigzag white line and a small white spot along the costal margin of hindwing.

Resident

Jan. Feb. Mar. Apr. May June July Aug. Sept. Oct. Nov. Dec.

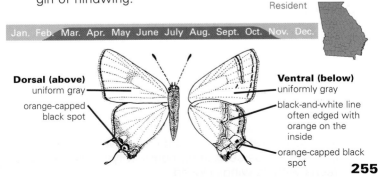

Dorsal (above)
uniform gray
orange-capped black spot

Ventral (below)
uniformly gray
black-and-white line often edged with orange on the inside
orange-capped black spot

255

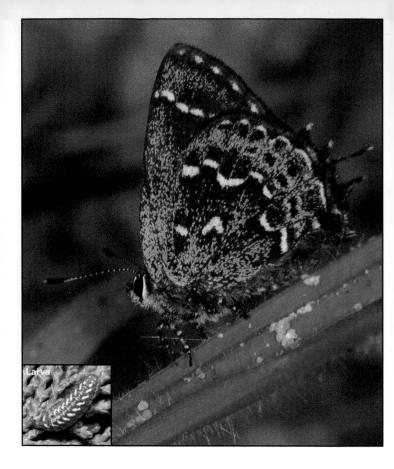

Larva

Comments: This rare hairstreak is a denizen of Atlantic White Cedar swamps and adjacent woodlands. Once widespread and more common along the southern Coastal Plain, much of this butterfly's freshwater wetland habitat has already disappeared due to extensive logging, fire suppression, hydrologic alteration and unabated urban development. As a result, Hessel's Hairstreak now occurs in isolated, highly localized colonies in often widely spaced pockets of remote remnant habitat.

Hessel's Hairstreak
Callophrys hesseli

Family/Subfamily: Gossamer Wings (Lycaenidae)/ Hairstreaks (Theclinae)

Wingspan: 0.8–1.1" (2.0–2.8 cm)

Above: variable; unmarked dark brown often with some amber scaling (spring brood individuals are generally lighter); forewing has pale gray stigma; hindwing has two short tails

Below: blue-green to emerald; forewing has reddish brown scaling along the trailing margin, a band of somewhat offset white spots and a single faint white cell spot; hindwing has two small white bars toward the base and an irregular white band across the middle, both heavily edged with dark brown

Sexes: similar, although female lacks pale forewing stigma and has increased amber scaling above

Egg: light green, laid singly on host

Larva: green with white dashes

Larval Host Plants: Atlantic White Cedar

Habitat: Atlantic White Cedar swamps and adjacent woodlands

Broods: two generations

Abundance: locally rare to uncommon

Compare: Juniper Hairstreak (pg. 261) is brighter green below; lacks white forewing cell spot.

Resident

Jan. Feb. Mar. Apr. May June July Aug. Sept. Oct. Nov. Dec.

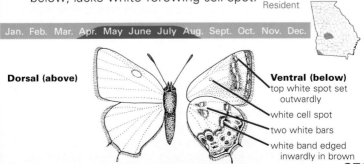

Dorsal (above)

Ventral (below)
top white spot set outwardly

white cell spot

two white bars

white band edged inwardly in brown

259

Larva

Comments: This diminutive, reclusive butterfly, although widespread, typically occurs in spotty, localized colonies but can be quite abundant when encountered. It is always found in extremely close association with stands of Eastern Redcedar. This relationship is so intimate that the butterfly spends the majority of its adult life directly on host trees, leaving only occasionally to nectar at nearby blossoms or disperse to pioneer new colonies. The adults regularly perch high in the branches and may go unnoticed. They are best discovered by gently tapping the trunk or branches.

Juniper Hairstreak
Callophrys gryneus

Family/Subfamily: Gossamer Wings (Lycaenidae)/ Hairstreaks (Theclinae)

Wingspan: 0.8–1.1" (2.0–2.8 cm)

Above: variable; unmarked brown to brown with extensive amber scaling; hindwing has two short tails; male has pale gray stigma on forewing

Below: bright olive green; forewing has a straight submarginal white band and reddish orange scaling along trailing edge; hindwing has two small white bars toward the base and an irregular white band across the middle that is edged on the inside with reddish brown

Sexes: similar, although female lacks pale forewing stigma

Egg: light green, laid singly on host

Larva: bright green with bold white dashes

Larval Host Plants: Eastern Redcedar

Habitat: old fields, forest edges, rocky outcrops, coastal areas, dry hillsides, bluffs, rural roadsides, windbreaks, old historical properties and even cemeteries

Broods: two or more generations

Abundance: locally uncommon to common

Compare: Hessel's Hairstreak (pg. 259) is emerald green with a ventral white forewing cell spot.

Resident

Jan.	Feb.	Mar.	Apr.	May	June	July	Aug.	Sept.	Oct.	Nov.	Dec.

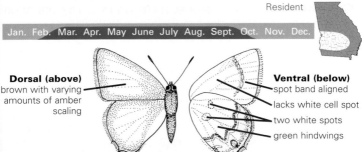

Dorsal (above)
brown with varying amounts of amber scaling

Ventral (below)
spot band aligned
lacks white cell spot
two white spots
green hindwings

261

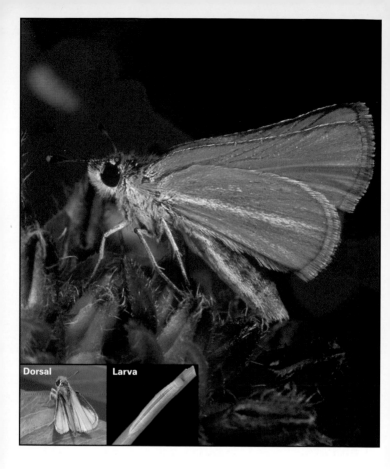

Dorsal

Larva

Comments: Easily overlooked, the Southern Skipperling is the smallest skipper in the Southeast. The species frequents open, sunny grass-dominated habitats and may be easily identified by its elongated wings and the distinctive light hindwing streak. Adults have a weak, darting flight and skim quickly over low vegetation stopping now and then to perch on available leaves or grass blades. Although a year-round resident of the Gulf Coast, it regularly expands its range northward each summer throughout the Deep South.

Southern Skipperling
Copaeodes minima

Family/Subfamily: Skippers (Hesperiidae)/
Banded Skippers (Hesperiinae)

Wingspan: 0.50–0.75" (1.3–1.9 cm)

Above: elongated wings; male is bright tawny orange;
female is brownish orange with darker scaling toward
wing bases and along margins

Below: yellow orange with narrow, distinctive cream
streak through hindwing

Sexes: similar, although female somewhat darker

Egg: laid singly on host leaves

Larva: green

Larval Host Plants: grasses including Bermuda Grass

Habitat: open, grassy areas including roadsides, utility
easements, old fields, meadows and forest edges

Broods: multiple generations

Abundance: occasional to common

Compare: Least Skipper (pg. 267) is larger, has more
rounded wings with dark dorsal borders and lacks
cream ventral hindwing streak.

Resident Visitor

Jan. Feb. Mar. Apr. May June July Aug. Sept. Oct. Nov. Dec.

Dorsal (above)
elongated wings

Ventral (below)
all yellow orange

cream streak

Ventral

Larva

Comments: This dazzling little butterfly is the only metalmark in the Southeast. It typically occurs in highly localized, spotty colonies in close association with its sole larval host, but may be abundant when encountered. While not currently in need of conservation, the species appears to be declining throughout much of its range. Adults scurry low to the ground among grassy vegetation and are easily overlooked. Both sexes stop to perch on vegetation with their colorful wings outstretched. During periods of inclement weather or if disturbed, they often fly quickly and land out of sight on the underside of large, broad leaves.

Little Metalmark
Calephelis virginiensis

Family/Subfamily: Gossamer Wings (Lycaenidae)/ Metalmarks (Riodininae)

Wingspan: 0.5–1.0" (1.3–2.5 cm)

Above: brownish orange with numerous delicate dark markings and two narrow, metallic gray bands along the outer edge of the wings

Below: similar to upper surface, but paler; brownish orange with dark spots and metallic gray bands

Sexes: similar, although female has broader, more rounded wings

Egg: laid singly on host leaves

Larva: pale green with long white hairs

Larval Host Plants: Yellow Thistle

Habitat: open grassy areas, pine savannas, moist meadows and forest edges

Broods: multiple generations

Abundance: occasional, locally common

Compare: unique

Resident

Jan. Feb. Mar. Apr. May June July Aug. Sept. Oct. Nov. Dec.

Dorsal (above)
brownish orange wings

dark reticulations

metallic bands

Ventral (below)
metallic bands

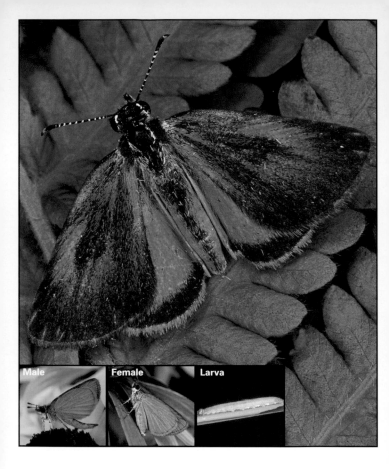

Male | Female | Larva

Comments: The tiny Least Skipper has a low, weak flight and flutters slowly through the vegetation, occasionally pausing to nectar or perch. They regularly visit flowers but prefer low plants with small blossoms. It is not a regular garden visitor. Adults have noticeably rounded wings. Although the sexes are similar, the male has a very long slender abdomen that protrudes well past the wings.

Least Skipper
Ancyloxypha numitor

Family/Subfamily: Skippers (Hesperiidae)/
Banded Skippers (Hesperiinae)

Wingspan: 0.7–1.0" (1.8–2.5 cm)

Above: forewing orange-brown with dark border; hind-wing orange with dark border; rounded wings; male has a long, pointed abdomen

Below: forewing dark brown with orange border; hind-wing orange-gold

Sexes: similar, although female has a shorter abdomen

Egg: yellow, laid singly on or near host leaves

Larva: long and slender, light yellow-green with thin dark dorsal stripe and reddish brown head; head has numerous cream stripes

Larval Host Plants: various grasses including Rice Cutgrass, Giant Cutgrass, panic grass and cordgrass

Habitat: moist, grassy areas including roadside ditches, utility easements, wet meadows, pond edges and old fields

Broods: multiple generations

Abundance: occasional to common

Compare: The Southern Skipperling (pg. 263) is smaller, has elongated wings and a distinct pale ray through the hindwing below.

Resident

| Jan. | Feb. | Mar. | Apr. | May | June | July | Aug. | Sept. | Oct. | Nov. | Dec. |

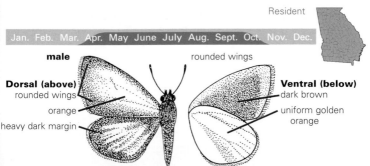

male

rounded wings

Dorsal (above)
rounded wings

orange

heavy dark margin

Ventral (below)
dark brown

uniform golden orange

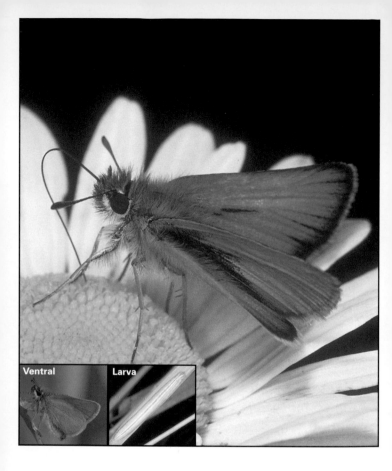

Ventral

Larva

Comments: This common skipper of the northeast just barely enters our area in the northern mountains of Georgia. As its name implies, the species was accidentally introduced into Ontario, Canada from Europe in 1910 and continues to expand its range. Superficially similar to the Least Skipper, the butterfly is more likely to be found in dryer areas of open grassy habitat. Univoltine (only one brood per year) over its entire range, the tiny white eggs overwinter and hatch the following spring.

European Skipper
Thymelicus lineola

Family/Subfamily: Skippers (Hesperiidae)/
Banded Skippers (Hesperiinae)

Wingspan: 0.9–1.1" (2.3–2.8 cm)

Above: bronzy orange wings with dark brown borders;
veins are darkened toward the outer wing margins

Below: unmarked orange

Sexes: similar, although female is somewhat darker with
veins darkened to base

Egg: white, laid on host stems

Larva: pale green with a darker green dorsal stripe,
white lateral stripes and a greenish tan head marked
with two vertical cream stripes on the face

Larval Host Plants: various grasses including Timothy
Grass, Orchardgrass, Common Velvetgrass and bentgrass

Habitat: open, grassy areas including roadsides, utility
easements, old fields, meadows and pastures

Broods: single generation

Abundance: occasional

Compare: Least Skipper (pg. 267) is more widespread,
has rounder wings, solid dark dorsal borders, and multiple generations.

Visitor

Jan. Feb. Mar. Apr. May June July Aug. Sept. Oct. Nov. Dec.

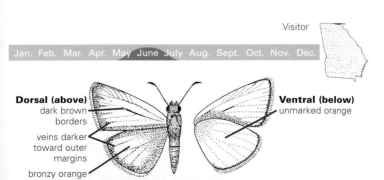

Dorsal (above)
dark brown borders
veins darker toward outer margins
bronzy orange

Ventral (below)
unmarked orange

269

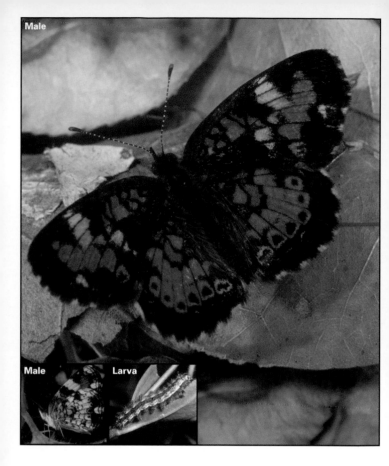

Male

Male   Larva

Comments: The Phaon Crescent is a small, colorful tropical butterfly. A year-round resident along extreme southern portions of the Gulf Coast and southeastern Georgia, it annually expands its range northward to temporarily colonize much of the Deep South. The species' exact occurrence is spotty and variable from year to year but it may be extremely abundant at times. It is an inhabitant of open, primarily moist sites where it remains in close proximity to patches of its low-growing larval host. Adults have a low, quick flight but frequently stop to nectar or perch on low vegetation. Males may occasionally gather at moist ground.

Phaon Crescent
Phyciodes phaon

Family/Subfamily: Brush-foots (Nymphalidae)/
True Brush-foots (Nymphalinae)

Wingspan: 0.90–1.25" (2.3–3.2 cm)

Above: orange with dark spots, bands and wing borders;
forewing has a distinctive pale yellow to cream postmedian band

Below: seasonally variable; cream with brown bands,
spots and patches; winter-form has increased brown
coloration on ventral hindwings

Sexes: similar

Egg: light green, laid in clusters on the underside of host
leaves

Larva: amber brown with dark brown lines and short,
branched spines

Larval Host Plants: Frogfruit

Habitat: open, disturbed sites including roadsides, old
fields, moist ditches, utility easements, fallow agricultural land and pond edges

Broods: multiple generations

Abundance: occasional to common; locally abundant

Compare: Pearl Crescent (pg. 295) is tawny orange
below and lacks dorsal pale yellow median forewing
band.

Resident Visitor

Jan. Feb. Mar. Apr. May June July Aug. Sept. Oct. Nov. Dec.

Dorsal (above)
pale median band

extensive black
markings and
borders

Ventral (below)
seasonally variable

tan with fine brown
lines

pale crescent in dark
marginal patch

271

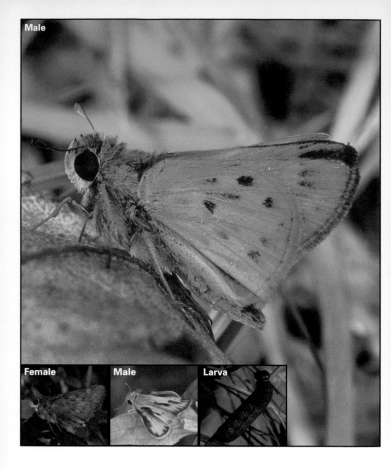

Male

Female   Male   Larva

Comments: The Fiery Skipper has a rapid, darting flight
but frequently stops to perch on low vegetation.
Adults are exceedingly fond of flowers and readily congregate at available blossoms. They have a strong
preference for colorful composites. The larvae utilize a
variety of grasses including many commonly planted
for lawns. As a result, the butterfly is often mentioned
as a minor turf pest. It is often found alongside the
similar-looking and equally abundant Sachem and
Whirlabout.

Fiery Skipper
Hylephila phyleus

Family/Subfamily: Skippers (Hesperiidae)/
Banded Skippers (Hesperiinae)

Wingspan: 1.00–1.25" (2.5–3.2 cm)

Above: elongated wings; male is golden orange with
jagged black border and black stigma; female is tawny
orange with dark brown bands

Below: hindwing golden orange in male or orange brown
in female with tiny dark brown spots

Sexes: dissimilar; female darker with reduced orange
markings and larger hindwing spots

Egg: whitish green, laid singly on host leaves

Larva: greenish brown with thin, dark brown dorsal
stripe and black head

Larval Host Plants: a variety of grasses including
Bermuda Grass, crabgrass, bentgrass and St.
Augustine Grass

Habitat: open, grassy areas including old fields, roadsides, vacant lots, open woodlands, forest edges,
parks, lawns and gardens

Broods: multiple generations

Abundance: occasional to abundant

Compare: Whirlabout (pg. 275) has two rows of
large dark spots on the ventral hindwing. Sachem
(pg. 287) lacks dark spots on
ventral hindwing.

Resident Visitor

Jan. Feb. Mar. Apr. May June July Aug. Sept. Oct. Nov. Dec.

male

Dorsal (above)
orange
jagged black
margins

Ventral (below)
small scattered dark
spots

273

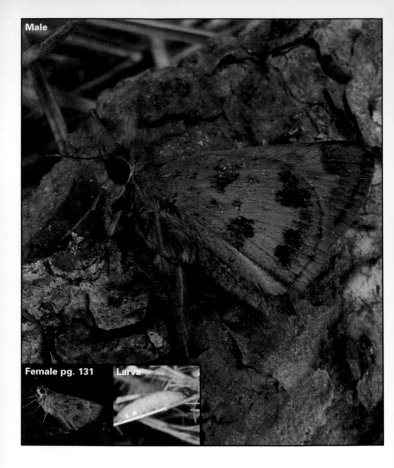

Male

Female pg. 131

Larva

Comments: The Whirlabout is a diminutive skipper with two distinct rows of squarish spots on the hindwings below. This species is sexually dimorphic. Males are tawny orange and considerably brighter than their drab brown female counterparts. It regularly expands its range each summer, establishing temporary breeding colonies throughout the southeast from Maryland to Texas. Living up to its name, adults have a low, erratic flight and scurry quickly around, periodically stopping to perch or nectar. Avidly fond of flowers, the butterfly is a frequent garden visitor.

Whirlabout
Polites vibex

Family/Subfamily: Skippers (Hesperiidae)/
Banded Skippers (Hesperiinae)

Wingspan: 1.00–1.25" (2.5–3.2 cm)

Above: elongated wings; golden orange with black borders and black stigma; female is dark brown with cream spots on forewing

Below: hindwing yellow in male or bronze brown in female with two loose bands of large dark brown spots

Sexes: dissimilar; female brown above with little orange scaling; olive brown below with similar pattern as male

Egg: white, laid singly on host leaves

Larva: brownish green with thin, dark dorsal stripe and black head

Larval Host Plants: various grasses including Bermuda Grass, St. Augustine Grass and Crabgrass

Habitat: open, disturbed areas including old fields, roadsides, vacant lots, open woodlands, forest edges, parks, lawns and gardens

Broods: multiple generations

Abundance: occasional to abundant

Compare: Fiery Skipper (pg. 273) has more elongated forewings and scattered, tiny dark spots on ventral hindwing.

Resident Visitor

Jan. Feb. Mar. Apr. May June July Aug. Sept. Oct. Nov. Dec.

male

Dorsal (above)
golden orange
large black stigma
jagged black border
orange
smooth black border

Ventral (below)
two bands of large dark brown spots
golden orange

275

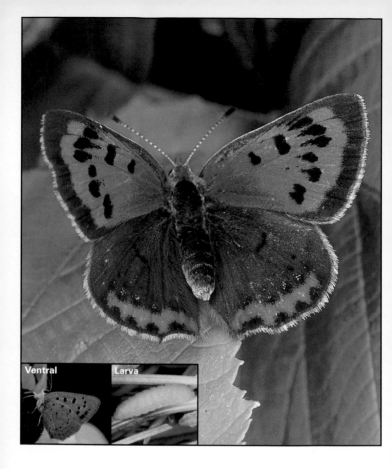

Comments: Although called the American Copper, some suggest that the eastern populations of the butterfly may actually be the result of historical introductions from Europe. This argument is fueled by the species' unique preference for open, disturbed habitats and primary use of a weedy, non-native larval host. It tends to occur in widespread and highly localized colonies, but is often fairly common when encountered. The adults frequently perch on bare soil or on low vegetation with the wings held in a characteristic, partially open posture. When first seen in bright sunlight, there remains little doubt as to why the butterfly is called a copper!

American Copper
Lycaena phlaeas

Family/Subfamily: Gossamer Wings (Lycaenidae)/
Coppers (Lycaeninae)

Wingspan: 0.9–1.4" (2.3–3.6 cm)

Above: bright red orange forewings with black spots and
dark borders; hindwing is gray with wide scalloped
submarginal orange band subtended by black spots
along outer margin

Below: forewing is pale orange with prominent white-
rimmed black spots and light gray apex and outer
margin; hindwing is silvery gray with small white-
rimmed black spots and narrow, irregular reddish
orange line along outer margin

Sexes: similar, although female is larger and has more
rounded wings

Egg: pale greenish white, laid singly host stems or leaves

Larva: variable; yellow green to rose, often with a narrow lateral stripe

Larval Host Plants: Sheep Sorrel and Curly Dock

Habitat: open, disturbed sites, old fields, utility easements, roadsides, pastures and meadows

Broods: two or more generations

Abundance: occasional to locally common

Compare: unique

Resident

Jan. Feb. Mar. Apr. May June July Aug. Sept. Oct. Nov. Dec.

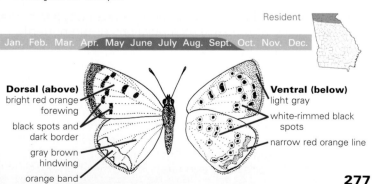

Dorsal (above)
bright red orange
forewing

black spots and
dark border

gray brown
hindwing

orange band

Ventral (below)
light gray

white-rimmed black
spots

narrow red orange line

277

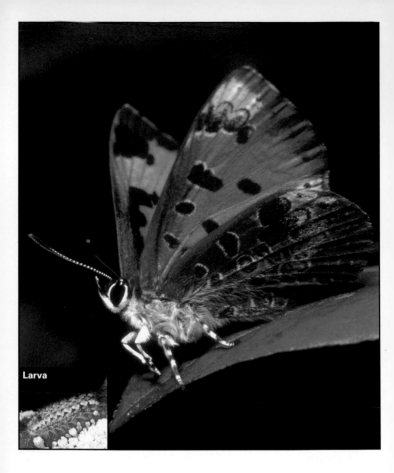

Larva

Comments: Unique in appearance and behavior, the Harvester is the only North American butterfly with carnivorous larvae. A denizen of woodland habitats, it tends to be found in small, localized colonies in close association with its host aphids. Males are regularly encountered perching on sunlit leaves or imbibing moisture at damp ground along forest trails, unpaved roads or stream margins. The butterfly has a fast, erratic flight reminiscent of most hairstreaks and can be a challenge to follow. Adults feed primarily on sugary aphid honeydew and rarely if ever visit flowers.

Harvester
Feniseca tarquinius

Family/Subfamily: Gossamer Wings (Lycaenidae)/
Harvesters (Miletinae)

Wingspan: 1.1–1.3" (2.8–3.3 cm)

Above: orange with brown to black spots, patches and
borders

Below: brown; forewing has orange central scaling and
several dark patches outlined in white; hindwing has
numerous dark spots outlined in white and silver scaling toward base

Sexes: similar

Egg: greenish white, laid singly among aphid colonies

Larva: gray with whitish yellow bumps bordered with
brown along top, reddish brown lateral stripes and
long gray hairs

Larval Host Plants: does not feed on plant material;
carnivorous on woolly aphids

Habitat: forest edges, stream corridors, swamp margins,
moist woodlands and associated clearings, trails and
roads

Broods: multiple generations

Abundance: occasional; often highly localized

Compare: unique

Resident

Jan. Feb. Mar. Apr. May June July Aug. Sept. Oct. Nov. Dec.

female

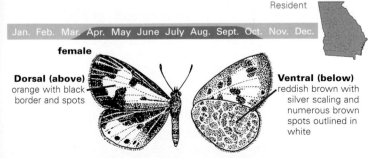

Dorsal (above)
orange with black
border and spots

Ventral (below)
reddish brown with
silver scaling and
numerous brown
spots outlined in
white

279

Female

Ventral

Larva

Comments: The Delaware Skipper is an orange butterfly with elongated, somewhat pointed forewings. The ventral wing surface is immaculate golden yellow. Found primarily in a variety of moist, grassy habitats from damp meadows to coastal marshes, the butterfly frequently finds its way into suburban yards. Adults have a quick, darting flight and are fond of flowers. Males perch on low leaves and grasses and make frequent exploratory flights.

Delaware Skipper
Anatrytone logan

Family/Subfamily: Skippers (Hesperiidae)/
Banded Skippers (Hesperiinae)

Wingspan: 1.0–1.4" (2.5–3.6 cm)

Above: orange with dark borders and veins; forewings
are elongated and somewhat pointed; male has a
small black cell-end bar on forewing; female has
brown scaling in forewing cell, wider borders, and
forewing cell-end bar is larger

Below: unmarked golden orange

Sexes: similar, although female darker with reduced
orange coloration

Egg: white, laid singly on host leaves

Larva: bluish white with dark tubercles and a black-and-
white head

Larval Host Plants: various grasses including
bluestems, Silver Plumegrass and Switch Grass

Habitat: open woodlands, forest edges, roadsides, pastures, wetland edges and old fields

Broods: two generations

Abundance: occasional to common

Compare: Byssus Skipper (pg. 309) has more pointed
forewings and pale yellow spots on the ventral hindwing. European Skipper (pg. 269) lacks black forewing
cell-end bar.

Resident

Jan. Feb. Mar. Apr. May June July Aug. Sept. Oct. Nov. Dec.

male

Dorsal (above)
dark border
hin black cell-end bar
dark veins

Ventral (below)
orange fringes
unmarked golden
orange

281

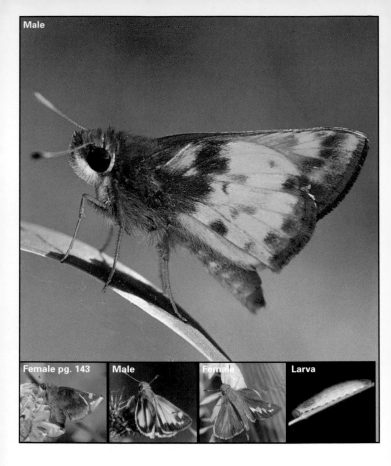

Male

Female pg. 143   Male   Female   Larva

Comments: Sexually dimorphic, the Zabulon Skipper is a small butterfly with a bright orange male and a drab brown female. Primarily a butterfly of woodlands and adjacent open sites, it occasionally wanders into suburban gardens. Adults have a rapid flight and are strongly attracted to flowers. Males perch on sunlit branches along trails or clearings and engage passing objects or rival males. Females generally prefer to remain within the confines of nearby shady sites.

Zabulon Skipper
Poanes zabulon

Family/Subfamily: Skippers (Hesperiidae)/ Banded Skippers (Hesperiinae)

Wingspan: 1.0–1.4" (2.5–3.6 cm)

Above: male is golden orange with dark brown borders and small brown spot near forewing apex; female is dark brown with band of cream spots across forewing

Below: male hindwing yellow with a brown base enclosing a yellow spot; female is dark brown with small light subapical spots, lavender scaling on wing margins, and white bar along leading margin of hindwing

Sexes: dissimilar, female brown with little orange color

Egg: pale green, laid singly on host leaves

Larva: tan with dark dorsal stripe, white lateral stripe and short, light-colored hairs; reddish brown head

Larval Host Plants: various grasses including Purpletop Grass, Whitegrass and lovegrass

Habitat: open woodlands, forest edges, roadsides, pastures, wetland edges, stream corridors and old fields

Broods: two generations

Abundance: occasional to common

Compare: Sachem (pg. 287) is similar to male Zabulon Skipper, but dark hindwing base does not enclose yellow patch.

Resident

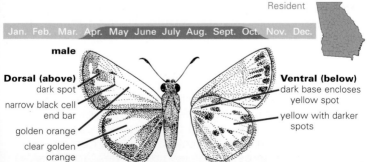

Jan. Feb. Mar. Apr. May June July Aug. Sept. Oct. Nov. Dec.

male

Dorsal (above)
dark spot
narrow black cell end bar
golden orange
clear golden orange

Ventral (below)
dark base encloses yellow spot
yellow with darker spots

283

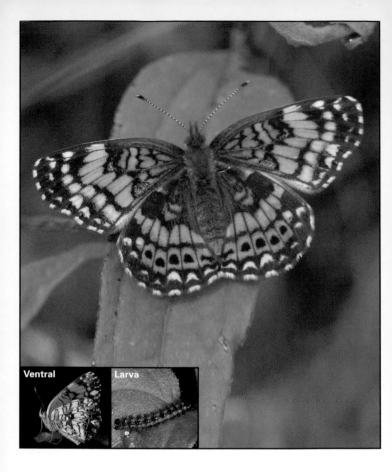

Ventral

Larva

Comments: Widespread and common throughout much of the central U.S., the small, ornately patterned Gorgone Checkerspot reaches the easternmost extension of its range in Georgia, where it is a local and uncommon resident. It frequents open deciduous woodlands and adjacent disturbed areas including utility easements and logged sites. Adults have a low, erratic flight and frequently stop to nectar at available flowers where their distinctive markings can be closely observed. An excellent colonizer, adults frequently wander far to establish new populations. Young larvae feed gregariously on host. Late instar larvae overwinter.

Gorgone Checkerspot
Chlosyne gorgone

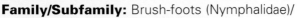

Family/Subfamily: Brush-foots (Nymphalidae)/
True Brush-foots (Nymphalinae)

Wingspan: 1.1–1.4" (2.8–3.6 cm)

Above: tawny orange with black bands and spots

Below: hindwing has a distinct zigzag pattern of white
chevrons between darker bands

Sexes: similar

Egg: pale green, laid in clusters on host leaves

Larva: yellow orange with black longitudinal stripes,
black branching spines and a black head

Larval Host Plants: various composites including Great
Ragweed and sunflowers

Habitat: open woodlands, stream corridors, forest
edges, and adjacent dry, open, grassy areas, utility
easements and previously burned sites

Broods: multiple generations

Abundance: locally rare to occasional

Compare: Silvery Checkerspot (pg. 315) is larger, its dorsal hindwing has white-centered black spots and its
ventral hindwing has a dark marginal patch, an incomplete row of silvery white crescents along the margin,
and lacks zig-zag pattern.

Resident

Jan. Feb. Mar. Apr. May June July Aug. Sept. Oct. Nov. Dec.

Dorsal (above)
orange with black
bands and spots

pale orange chevrons
in black border

Ventral (below)
scalloped zig-zag
pattern

285

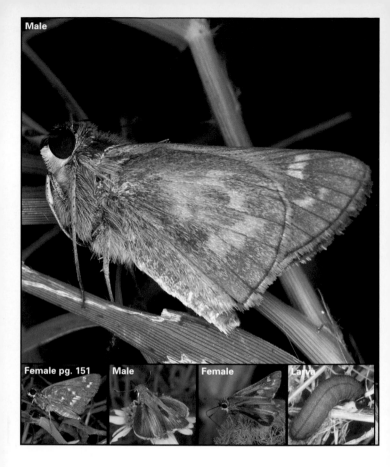

Male

Female pg. 151 | Male | Female | Larva

Comments: The Sachem shares its affinity for open, disturbed sites with the Whirlabout and Fiery Skipper with which it often flies. Adults have a quick, darting flight that is usually low to the ground. All three species are somewhat nervous butterflies, but readily congregate at available flowers. Together, they often form a circus of activity with several pausing briefly to perch or nectar before one flies up and disturbs the others, only to alight again moments later.

Sachem
Atalopedes campestris

Family/Subfamily: Skippers (Hesperiidae)/ Banded Skippers (Hesperiinae)

Wingspan: 1.0–1.5" (2.5–3.8 cm)

Above: elongated wings; male is golden orange with brown borders and large, black stigma; female is dark brown with golden markings in wing centers; forewing has black median spot and several semitransparent spots

Below: variable; hindwing golden brown in male, brown in female with pale postmedian patch or band of spots

Sexes: dissimilar; female darker with semitransparent forewing spots and reduced orange markings

Egg: white, laid singly on host leaves

Larva: greenish brown with thin, dark dorsal stripe and black head

Larval Host Plants: various grasses including Bermuda Grass and crabgrass

Habitat: open, disturbed areas including old fields, pastures, roadsides, parks, lawns and gardens

Broods: multiple generations

Abundance: occasional to common

Compare: Fiery Skipper (pg. 273) and Whirlabout (pg. 275) have dark spots on the ventral hindwing.

Visitor Stray

Jan. Feb. Mar. Apr. May June July Aug. Sept. Oct. Nov. Dec.

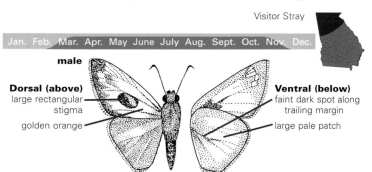

male

Dorsal (above)
large rectangular stigma

golden orange

Ventral (below)
faint dark spot along trailing margin

large pale patch

287

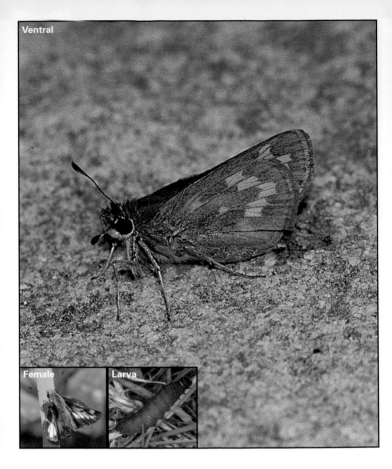

Ventral

Female

Larva

Comments: Although widespread throughout the Northeast, the range of this lovely tawny orange skipper extends southward in a narrow band through the Appalachian Mountains to the northern border of Georgia. As a result, its occurrence within the state is spotty and highly localized. Producing only one generation each year, the Indian Skipper on the wing in late spring and early summer. Both sexes readily visit a variety of early season wildflowers.

Indian Skipper
Hesperia sassacus

Family/Subfamily: Skippers (Hesperiidae)/
Banded Skippers (Hesperiinae)

Wingspan: 1.2–1.4" (3.0–3.6 cm)

Above: bright orange with wide, somewhat jagged, dark
brown borders

Below: hindwing is tawny orange with a pale golden
orange spot band through center; middle spot displaced outward toward margin

Sexes: similar, although female has broader dark borders,
larger, paler yellow orange spot bands and reduced
orange scaling

Egg: whitish green, laid singly on host leaves or stems

Larva: dark brown, often with lighter mottling and a
round black head

Larval Host Plants: various grasses including Little
Bluestem, panic grasses, Poverty Oatgrass, bluegrass
and Red Fescue

Habitat: woodland clearings and margins, pastures, old
brushy fields and forest meadows

Broods: single generation

Abundance: rare

Compare: Female Sachem (pg. 151) has longer, more
pointed forewings and glassy forewing spots.

Resident

Jan. Feb. Mar. Apr. May June July Aug. Sept. Oct. Nov. Dec.

male

Dorsal (above)
dark, sharply
defined, jagged
borders

Ventral (below)
pale spot band with
center spot offset
toward outer margin

291

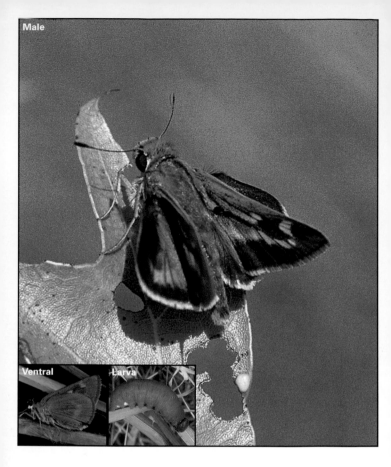

Male

Ventral

Larva

Comments: This fairly large golden orange skipper is always considered a good find. Rare and recluse throughout its fragmented southeastern range, it typically occurs in spotty and highly localized colonies. Like most skippers, it has a quick darting flight and is difficult to observe unless perched or feeding. Due to its elusive nature, little detailed information is known about the species' life history, behavior and ecology.

Meske's Skipper
Hesperia meskei

Family/Subfamily: Skippers (Hesperiidae)/
Banded Skippers (Hesperiinae)

Wingspan: 1.2–1.6" (3.0–4.1 cm)

Above: dark brown with tawny orange scaling toward
bases and orange spot bands

Below: hindwing is bright golden orange with a pale spot
band, often very faint

Sexes: similar, although female is darker with broader
wings, large, pale yellow orange spot bands and
reduced basal orange scaling

Egg: currently undocumented

Larva: green brown; round black head

Larval Host Plants: various grasses including
Arrowfeather Threeawn and Little Bluestem

Habitat: open woodlands, forest clearings and margins,
and adjacent open areas

Broods: two generations

Abundance: rare and local

Compare: Indian Skipper (pg. 291) is smaller with more
extensive orange scaling on the wings above, and
more well-defined ventral hindwing spot band.

Resident

Jan. Feb. Mar. Apr. May June July Aug. Sept. Oct. Nov. Dec.

male

Dorsal (above)
orange spot bands
tawny toward base

Ventral (below)
hindwing yellow
orange
faint spot band

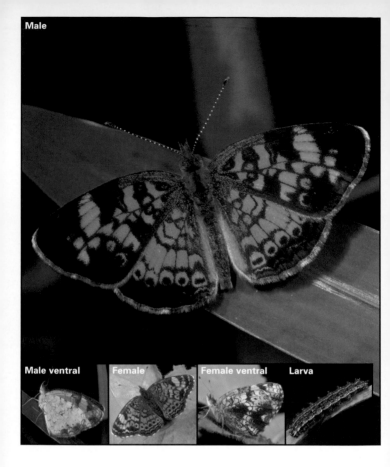

Male

Male ventral | Female | Female ventral | Larva

Comments: The lovely tawny-orange Pearl Crescent is our most widespread and abundant crescent. It is seasonally variable, and spring and fall individuals are darker and more heavily patterned on the ventral hindwings. It is an opportunistic breeder, continually producing new generations as long as favorable conditions allow. It has a rapid, erratic flight. Males perch on low vegetation with wings outstretched and frequently patrol for females. Freshly emerged males often gather at moist ground.

Pearl Crescent
Phyciodes tharos

Family/Subfamily: Brush-foots (Nymphalidae)/
True Brush-foots (Nymphalinae)

Wingspan: 1.25–1.60" (3.2–4.1 cm)

Above: orange with dark bands, spots and wing borders

Below: seasonally variable; light brownish orange with
brown markings; winter-form has increased dark coloration and pattern elements

Sexes: similar, although female is paler orange with
increased black markings

Egg: green, laid in clusters on the underside of host
leaves

Larva: dark brown to charcoal with lateral cream stripes
and numerous short, branched spines

Larval Host Plants: various asters including Frost
Aster, Smooth Blue Aster and Bushy Aster

Habitat: open, sunny locations including roadsides, old
fields, utility easements, forest edges and gardens

Broods: multiple generations

Abundance: occasional to common

Compare: Phaon Crescent (pg. 271) has a pale yellow
median forewing band and lighter ventral hindwing coloration.

Resident

Jan. Feb. Mar. Apr. May June July Aug. Sept. Oct. Nov. Dec.

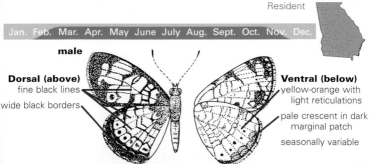

male

Dorsal (above)
fine black lines
wide black borders

Ventral (below)
yellow-orange with
light reticulations

pale crescent in dark
marginal patch

seasonally variable

295

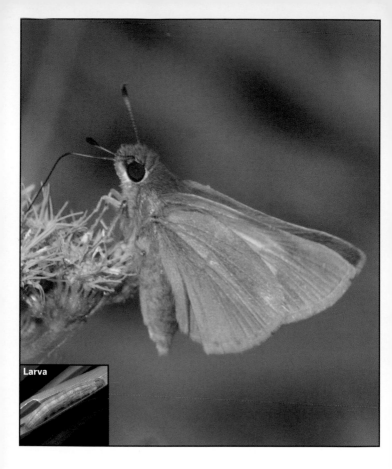

Larva

Comments: This southeastern skipper is confined to the Atlantic seaboard and Gulf Coast from New Jersey to Texas. Rare and extremely localized, it is an inhabitant of coastal saltwater marshes but may occasionally be found in inland wetlands. Adults visit a variety of mois-ture-loving flowers. It remains one of our most poorly known and studied butterflies.

Aaron's Skipper
Poanes aaroni

Family/Subfamily: Skippers (Hesperiidae)/
Banded Skippers (Hesperiinae)

Wingspan: 1.3–1.7" (3.3–4.3 cm)

Above: clear golden orange with dark brown borders and
a thin, faint black stigma

Below: hindwing is dull orange brown with a narrow pale
ray in the center

Sexes: dissimilar; female is darker with more rounded
wings and has reduced golden orange scaling

Egg: white, laid singly on host leaves

Larva: pale brown with dark longitudinal stripes; reddish
brown head

Larval Host Plants: in association with Smooth
Cordgrass

Habitat: coastal salt marshes, some inland freshwater
marshes

Broods: two generations

Abundance: rare to occasional

Compare: Broad-winged Skipper (pg. 317) is larger and
has a broader, more distinct pale hindwing ray below.

Resident

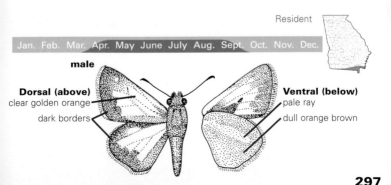

Jan. Feb. Mar. Apr. May June July Aug. Sept. Oct. Nov. Dec.

male

Dorsal (above)
clear golden orange
dark borders

Ventral (below)
pale ray
dull orange brown

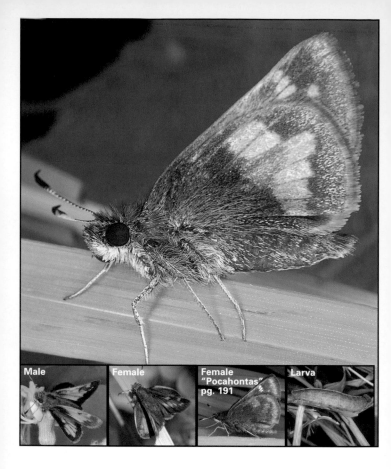

Male

Female

Female "Pocahontas" pg. 191

Larva

Comments: This small woodland skipper has a single early summer flight. Males perch on sunlit leaves along forest margins and aggressively dart out at other passing butterflies. Although common throughout the northeast, its range just enters the extreme northern mountains of Georgia. The female produces two distinct forms. The lighter form closely resembles the male and the darker form "Pocahontas" is superficially similar to Zabulon Skipper females. Larvae construct individual leaf shelters on the host. Larvae overwinter and complete development the following spring.

Hobomok Skipper
Poanes hobomok

Family/Subfamily: Skippers (Hesperiidae)/
Banded Skippers (Hesperiinae)

Wingspan: 1.4–1.6" (3.6–4.1 cm)

Above: golden orange with irregular dark brown borders
and a narrow black cell-end bar on the forewing

Below: purplish brown with a broad yellow orange patch
through the hindwing

Sexes: dissimilar; female has two forms. Normal form
resembles male but has reduced orange scaling above.
"Pocahontas" form is dark brown above with pale
forewing spots; hindwing is purplish brown below with
faint band and violet gray frosting along outer margin.

Egg: white, laid singly on host leaves

Larva: brown green with numerous short, light-colored
hairs; round, brown head

Larval Host Plants: various grasses including Little
Bluestem, panic grasses, Poverty Oatgrass, bluegrass
and Rice Cutgrass

Habitat: open woodlands, forest edges, clearings and
trails, roadsides and along forested stream margins

Broods: single generation

Abundance: occasional to common

Compare: Zabulon (pg. 283) and Peck's (pg. 129)
Skippers have yellow basal scaling on ventral hindwing.

Resident

Jan. Feb. Mar. Apr. May June July Aug. Sept. Oct. Nov. Dec.

male

Dorsal (above)
narrow cell-end bar
no stigma
irregular dark brown
borders

Ventral (below)
purplish brown
broad yellow orange
patch

299

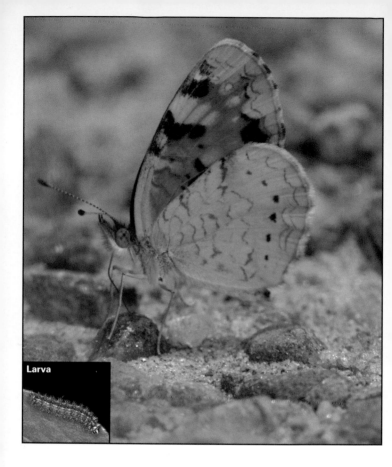

Larva

Comments: The Tawny Crescent is a rare resident that has severely declined in recent years in much of its eastern range. As a result, it is of conservation concern and strongly in need of surveys to determine the location and number of colonies. Due to is close resemblance to other crescents, it is possible that some populations have been overlooked. Highly restricted within the Appalachians, it barely enters the northeastern tip of Georgia. Adults have a quick, somewhat erratic flight and frequently alight on low vegetation with wings outstretched. Males occasionally visit puddles to sip moisture. Later instar larvae overwinter.

Tawny Crescent
Phyciodes batesii

Family/Subfamily: Brush-foots (Nymphalidae)/
True Brush-foots (Nymphalinae)

Wingspan: 1.30–1.75" (3.3–4.3 cm)

Above: tawny orange with heavy black bands, spots and
broad wing borders

Below: hindwing is golden yellow brown with very fine
brown markings and a postmedian row of small dark
spots

Sexes: similar

Egg: pale green, laid in clusters on the underside of host
leaves

Larva: pinkish brown with a dark dorsal band, a lateral
yellow stripe and numerous short, light brown spines

Larval Host Plants: various asters including Waxyleaf
Aster

Habitat: woodland openings, pastures and hillsides

Broods: single generation

Abundance: locally rare to uncommon

Compare: Pearl Crescent (pg. 295) is has more extensive open orange areas on wings above and has a
distinct dark marginal patch on the ventral hindwing.

Resident

Jan. Feb. Mar. Apr. May June July Aug. Sept. Oct. Nov. Dec.

Dorsal (above)

Ventral (below)
lacks dark patch
below apex

broad, straight dark
band

fine brown markings

row of small dark
spots

301

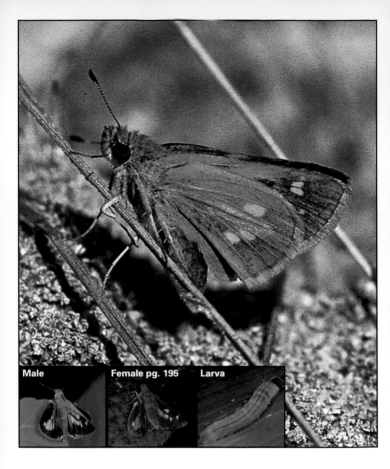

Male | **Female pg. 195** | **Larva**

Comments: The Yehl Skipper is rare to uncommon large
butterfly of southeastern forested swamps or moist
woodlands. It is most frequently encountered in sunlit
clearings, margins or roadsides. The adults are very
wary and often difficult to closely approach. They visit
a variety of moisture-loving flowers. Little detailed
information is known about the biology and behavior of
this reclusive species.

Yehl Skipper
Poanes yehl

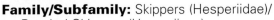

Family/Subfamily: Skippers (Hesperiidae)/
Banded Skippers (Hesperiinae)

Wingspan: 1.30–1.75" (3.3–4.3 cm)

Above: golden orange with broad dark brown borders;
forewing has long, narrow black stigma; female is
overall brownish

Below: hindwing is yellow orange with a pale band of
spots (usually three prominent spots)

Sexes: dissimilar; female has pale forewing spots and
reduced golden orange scaling on the wing bases
above; ventral hindwing is brown with pale spot band

Egg: currently undocumented

Larva: green brown with a dark dorsal stripe; dark brown
head

Larval Host Plants: currently undocumented

Habitat: forested swamps and associated clearings and
margins

Broods: two generations

Abundance: rare to occasional to abundant

Compare: Broad-winged Skipper (pg. 317) has broad
pale ray through the spot band on the hindwing below.

Resident

Jan. Feb. Mar. Apr. May June July Aug. Sept. Oct. Nov. Dec.

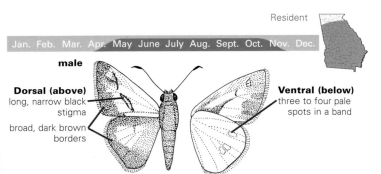

male

Dorsal (above)
long, narrow black
stigma

broad, dark brown
borders

Ventral (below)
three to four pale
spots in a band

303

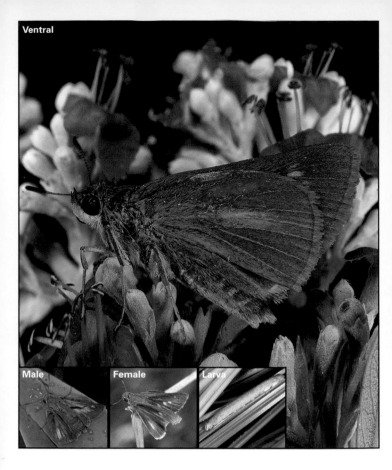

Ventral

Male

Female

Larva

Comments: Another large skipper of open swamps and marshes, this lovely tawny orange species has a distinctive pale ray through the ventral hindwing. Although widespread geographically throughout the East, the Dion Skipper is generally quite localized and uncommon. Adults are somewhat sluggish fliers through wetland vegetation but can move very quickly if disturbed. Males readily perch on the tops of sedges or grasses but tend to be wary and difficult to closely approach. They do not wander far from their wetland haunts. Larvae overwinter.

Dion Skipper
Euphyes dion

Family/Subfamily: Skippers (Hesperiidae)/ Banded Skippers (Hesperiinae)

Wingspan: 1.4–1.7" (3.6–4.3 cm)

Above: forewing is orange with broad, dark brown borders and a prominent black forewing stigma; hindwing is faint orange with a dark brown border and distinctly brighter elongated orange spot

Below: hindwing is tawny orange with faint light ray through the center

Sexes: dissimilar; female is primarily dark brown dorsally with yellow orange forewing spots and prominent single elongated orange hindwing spot

Egg: light green, laid singly on host leaves

Larva: blue-green with darker green dorsal line; white head marked with a black forehead spot bordered by orange brown vertical lines

Larval Host Plants: various sedges including Woolgrass and Shoreline Sedge

Habitat: open wetlands, marshes and swamps

Broods: two generations

Abundance: rare to occasional

Compare: Duke's Skipper (pg. 311) lacks bright orange scaling above, has more rounded wings and prefers more shaded habitats.

Resident

Jan. Feb. Mar. Apr. May June July Aug. Sept. Oct. Nov. Dec.

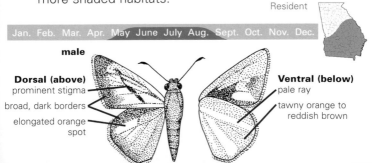

male

Dorsal (above)
prominent stigma
broad, dark borders
elongated orange spot

Ventral (below)
pale ray
tawny orange to reddish brown

305

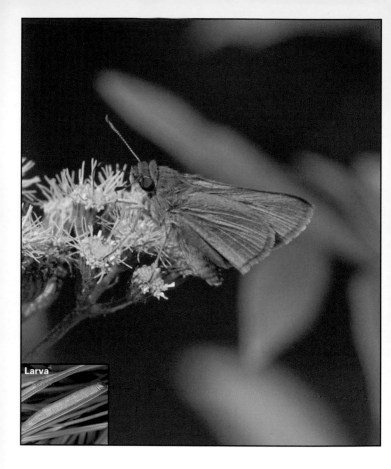

Larva

Comments: Berry's Skipper is easily one of our rarest butterflies. Limited entirely to the Southeast from southern South Carolina to the Florida panhandle, it is restricted to wetlands and their associated margins. Occurring in spotty and highly localized colonies, it is seldom encountered in large numbers. Due to its reclusive nature, little is known about the species' biology or behavior.

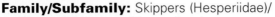

Berry's Skipper
Euphyes berryi

Family/Subfamily: Skippers (Hesperiidae)/
Banded Skippers (Hesperiinae)

Wingspan: 1.4–1.8" (3.6–4.6 cm)

Above: orange with broad, dark brown borders and a
prominent black stigma

Below: hindwing is tawny orange with light veins

Sexes: dissimilar; female is primarily dark brown with a
few yellow orange spots, including one in the forewing
cell

Egg: currently undocumented

Larva: pale green with a dark dorsal stripe; reddish
brown head bears a black spot on forehead surrounded by white

Larval Host Plants: various sedges

Habitat: swamps, wetland margins including pond
edges and along canals

Broods: two generations

Abundance: very rare and localized

Compare: Dion Skipper (pg. 305) has pale ray through
the hindwing below.

Resident

| Jan. | Feb. | Mar. | Apr. | May | June | July | Aug. | Sept. | Oct. | Nov. | Dec. |

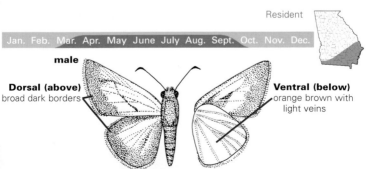

male

Dorsal (above)
broad dark borders

Ventral (below)
orange brown with
light veins

307

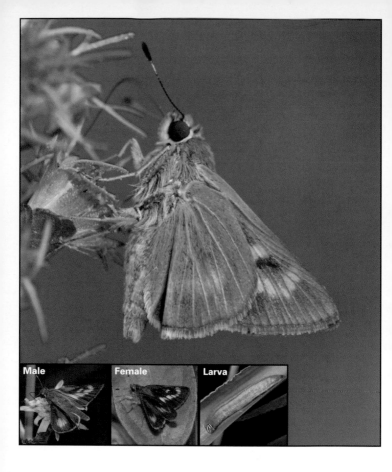

Male

Female

Larva

Comments: The Byssus Skipper is a butterfly of
wooded swamps and freshwater or brackish coastal
marsh edges. Local and uncommon throughout much
of its fragmented range, it may occasionally be found
alongside the similar but much larger Rare Skipper in
the southeastern corner of the state. Adults have a
strong, darting flight but readily feed at available wildflowers. The larvae pupate within a dense cocoon of
silk and leaves.

Byssus Skipper
Problema byssus

Family/Subfamily: Skippers (Hesperiidae)/
Banded Skippers (Hesperiinae)

Wingspan: 1.4–1.8" (3.6–4.6 cm)

Above: bright orange with dark brown black borders,
dark veins and a black bar at the end of the forewing
cell; forewings pointed

Below: golden orange to yellow brown with a band of
paler yellow spots

Sexes: similar, although female has broader dark brown
borders and reduced golden orange scaling above

Egg: white, laid singly on the upper surface of host
leaves

Larva: bluish green with short white hairs and a light reddish brown head marked with pale yellow vertical
stripes

Larval Host Plants: various grasses including Big
Bluestem and Eastern Gammagrass

Habitat: forested wetlands and coastal marshes and
their margins

Broods: two generations

Abundance: rare to occasional

Compare: Rare Skipper (pg. 321) lacks faint ventral spot
band.

Resident

Jan. Feb. Mar. Apr. May June July Aug. Sept. Oct. Nov. Dec.

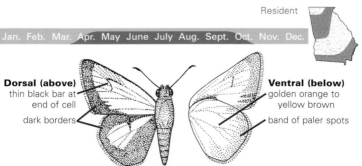

Dorsal (above)
thin black bar at
end of cell

dark borders

Ventral (below)
golden orange to
yellow brown

band of paler spots

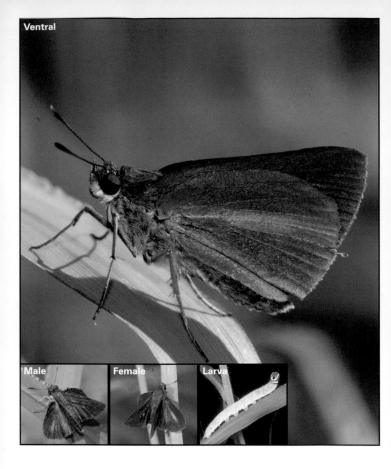

Comments: A butterfly of contrasting color, it is a rich tawny orange below compared to a much darker sooty black dorsal appearance. Duke's Skipper is a denizen of shaded southern swamps and marshes, but may occasionally be encountered along wet roadside ditches if sedges are present. Typically rare and localized, it can be a difficult species to locate. Larvae overwinter. Much remains to be learned about its life history, ecology and behavior.

Duke's Skipper
Euphyes dukesi

Family/Subfamily: Skippers (Hesperiidae)/
Banded Skippers (Hesperiinae)

Wingspan: 1.50–1.75" (3.8–4.4 cm)

Above: dark sooty brownish black with faint tawny
orange scaling along base of costal forewing margin;
wings are somewhat rounded

Below: rich brownish orange with black forewing base
and a pale ray through the hindwing

Sexes: similar, although female has small white forewing
spots

Egg: laid singly on the underside of host leaves

Larva: pale green; reddish brown head with a black spot
on the forehead surrounded by white

Larval Host Plants: various sedges, including Shoreline
Sedge

Habitat: shaded wooded swamp, marshes and moist
roadside ditches

Broods: two generations

Abundance: rare to occasional

Compare: Dion Skipper (pg. 305) has bright orange scaling above with more pointed forewings and prefers
more open, sunlit habitats.

Resident

Jan. Feb. Mar. Apr. May June July Aug. Sept. Oct. Nov. Dec.

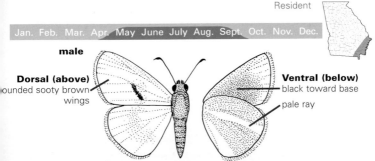

male

Dorsal (above)
rounded sooty brown
wings

Ventral (below)
black toward base

pale ray

311

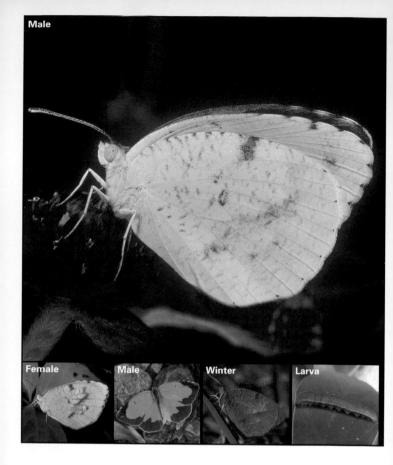

Male

Female Male Winter Larva

Comments: Much debate centers on the origin of the
butterfly's common name. One interpretation points to
its narrow black forewing spot, which to many
observers resembles a closed eye. Others suggest that
behavior is responsible. Late-season adults overwinter
in reproductive diapause. They are sedentary and seldom seen, but often become active on mild days to
nectar before disappearing again. The Sleepy Orange is
a frequent garden visitor, and is most abundant in late
summer and fall. It typically rests and feeds with its
wings closed; orange color is seen primarily in flight or
when the butterfly is basking in the sun.

Sleepy Orange
Eurema nicippe

Family/Subfamily: Whites and Sulphurs (Pieridae)/ Sulphurs (Coliadinae)

Wingspan: 1.3–2.0" (3.3–5.1 cm)

Above: bright orange with broad irregular black wing borders; forewing cell bears small, elongated black spot

Below: hindwings seasonally variable; butter-yellow with brown markings in summer-form and tan to reddish brown with darker pattern elements in winter-form

Sexes: similar, although female is larger and less vibrant with heavier ventral hindwing pattern

Egg: white, laid singly on host leaves

Larva: green with thin, cream lateral stripe and numerous short hairs

Larval Host Plants: various wild sennas including Sicklepod Senna, Wild Senna, Maryland Senna and Coffee Senna

Habitat: open, disturbed sites including roadsides, vacant fields, agricultural land, parks and gardens

Broods: multiple generations

Abundance: common

Compare: Orange Sulphur (pg. 327) has rounded black cell spot on dorsal forewing, regular wing borders and distinct, red-rimmed silver spot on ventral hindwing.

Resident Visitor

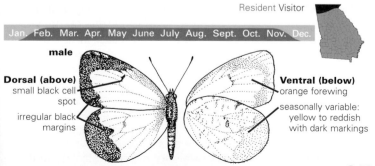

Jan. Feb. Mar. Apr. May June July Aug. Sept. Oct. Nov. Dec.

male

Dorsal (above)
small black cell spot

irregular black margins

Ventral (below)
orange forewing

seasonally variable: yellow to reddish with dark markings

313

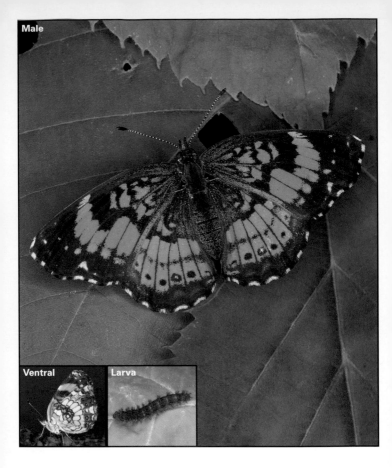

Male

Ventral

Larva

Comments: This large checkerspot is a spotty but often common Georgia resident, primarily limited to northern portions of the state. It is most frequently encountered in moist woodland openings or along forested streams in close proximity to its larval hosts. The Silvery Checkerspot tends to fluctuate considerably in abundance from year to year, being locally common at times or nearly absent. Adults are often seen nectaring at flowers or while perched on low vegetation. They have s slow, gliding flight and maneuver close to the ground in open areas or along woodland roads. Males often gather at damp soil or animal dung.

Silvery Checkerspot
Chlosyne nycteis

Family/Subfamily: Brush-foots (Nymphalidae)/ True Brush-foots (Nymphalinae)

Wingspan: 1.4–2.0" (3.6–5.1 cm)

Above: tawny orange with black bands and wide black borders; hindwing has a submarginal row of white-centered, somewhat square black spots

Below: hindwing is pale yellow brown with a dark marginal patch and incomplete marginal row of silvery white crescents

Sexes: similar

Egg: cream, laid in large clusters on underside of leaves

Larva: dark brownish black; wide yellow orange lateral band and several rows of black spines; black head

Larval Host Plants: various composites including Wing-stem, Gravelweed, White Crownbeard, asters, sunflowers, Cut-leaf Coneflower and Sneezeweed

Habitat: moist woodland openings, forest margins, stream corridors, semi-open areas near moist deciduous forest, and mesic fields

Broods: multiple generations

Abundance: uncommon to common

Compare: Gorgone Checkerspot (pg. 285) has a distinctly zigzag pattern on ventral hindwing.

Resident

Jan. Feb. Mar. Apr. May June July Aug. Sept. Oct. Nov. Dec.

Dorsal (above)
submarginal row of white-centered black spots

Ventral (below)
incomplete row of silvery white marginal crescents

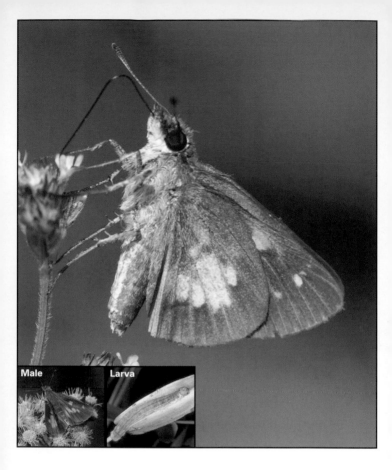

Male

Larva

Comments: This is a large, somewhat distinctive skipper often common in freshwater and brackish marshes along costal portions of the Atlantic Coast and Gulf Coast. Living up to its name, the species has noticeably rounded, somewhat wide wings. Although often locally abundant, much remains to be learned about the life history and ecology of this attractive but poorly known species. Adults are readily encountered at the blossoms of numerous wetland flowers.

Broad-winged Skipper
Poanes viator

Family/Subfamily: Skippers (Hesperiidae)/
Banded Skippers (Hesperiinae)

Wingspan: 1.3–2.1" (3.3–5.3 cm)

Above: tawny orange with broad dark brown borders;
forewing has rounded apex; hindwing has dark brown
scaling along veins; male lacks stigma

Below: hindwing is tawny orange with distinct broad
pale ray through pale spot band

Sexes: similar, although female has cream white spots
on the forewing above

Egg: grayish, laid singly on the underside of host leaves

Larva: pale brown with an overall velvety appearance;
reddish brown head

Larval Host Plants: Giant Cutgrass, Annual Wild Rice
and Common Reed, also sedges

Habitat: forested swamps and associated clearings and
margins

Broods: two generations

Abundance: occasional to common

Compare: Yehl Skipper (pg. 303) lacks distinct broad
pale ray through spot band on hindwing below.

Resident

Jan. Feb. Mar. Apr. May June July Aug. Sept. Oct. Nov. Dec.

male

Dorsal (above)
squarish yellow
orange spots
lacks stigma
broad dark borders

Ventral (below)
broad pale ray
pale spot band

317

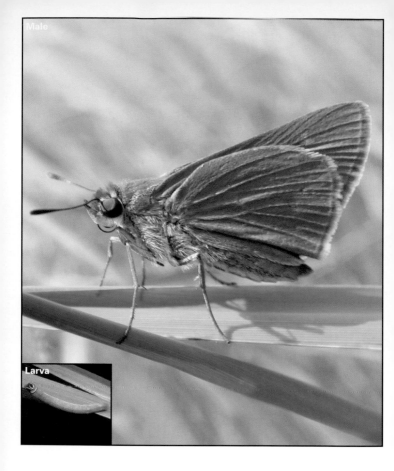

Male

Larva

Comments: This is a large southern skipper restricted primarily to Florida. It just barely enters our area in the extreme southeastern portion of the state. As its name implies, the Palmetto Skipper inhabits scrubby woodland areas that support palmettos. It tends to be local and uncommon. Adults have a strong, rapid flight but are often encountered feeding at available blossoms. They are particularly fond of thistles.

Palmetto Skipper
Euphyes arpa

Family/Subfamily: Skippers (Hesperiidae)/
Banded Skippers (Hesperiinae)

Wingspan: 1.6–1.9" (4.1–4.8 cm)

Above: male is bright golden-orange with dark brown
borders, forewing bears a narrow black stigma; female
is primarily dark brown with pale yellow-orange
forewing spots; head and thorax yellow orange

Below: hindwing is unmarked golden orange

Sexes: dissimilar; female is primarily dark brown above
with pale forewing spots

Egg: light green, laid singly on host leaves

Larva: green with a black and white collar; white head
marked by tan stripes and a black spot on the forehead

Larval Host Plants: Saw Palmetto

Habitat: pinelands and scrub with palmetto

Broods: two generations

Abundance: uncommon; local

Compare: Unlikely to be confused with any other skipper based on habitat.

Resident

Jan. Feb. Mar. Apr. May June July Aug. Sept. Oct. Nov. Dec.

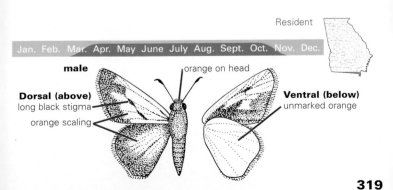

male

orange on head

Dorsal (above)
long black stigma

orange scaling

Ventral (below)
unmarked orange

319

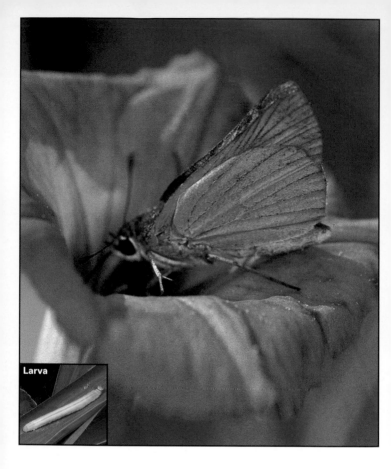

Larva

Comments: The Rare Skipper is a large golden orange butterfly entirely restricted to brackish coastal marshes. It occurs in small, highly localized and spotty colonies, but may be fairly common when encountered. A great many of its typical haunts are somewhat inaccessible to humans. Adults are best found and observed feeding at the numerous wildflowers growing along the marsh edges. Little detailed information is known about the life history, ecology and behavior of this skipper.

Rare Skipper
Problema bulenta

Family/Subfamily: Skippers (Hesperiidae)/
Banded Skippers (Hesperiinae)

Wingspan: 1.5–2.1" (3.8–5.3 cm)

Above: bright orange with broad, dark brown borders
and a black bar at the end of the forewing cell;
forewings pointed

Below: unmarked golden orange; forewing has distinct
black cell-end bar often visible above hindwing

Sexes: similar, although female has brown wing bases
and reduced golden orange scaling

Egg: currently undocumented

Larva: pale green with a dark dorsal stripe; reddish
brown head with cream markings

Larval Host Plants: Giant Cutgrass and Annual Wild
Rice

Habitat: brackish coastal marshes

Broods: two generations

Abundance: rare to occasional

Compare: Byssus Skipper (pg. 309) is smaller and has a
faint spot band on the wings below.

Resident

Jan. Feb. Mar. Apr. May June July Aug. Sept. Oct. Nov. Dec.

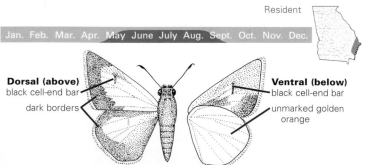

Dorsal (above)
black cell-end bar

dark borders

Ventral (below)
black cell-end bar

unmarked golden
orange

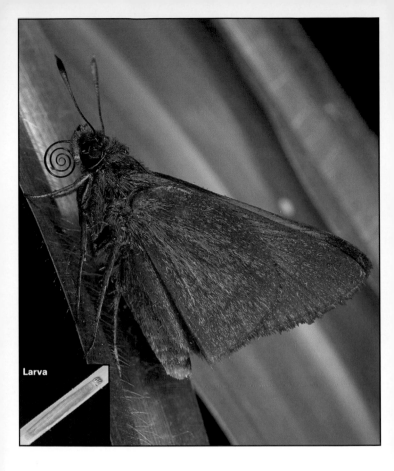

Larva

Comments: The Palatka Skipper, also called the Sawgrass Skipper, is generally found in close proximity to its larval host. The large adults have a strong, rapid flight and frequently visit available flowers. Males perch on low vegetation and readily investigate passing objects. The larvae construct individual shelters on the host by tying leaves together with silk.

Palatka Skipper
Euphyes pilatka

Family/Subfamily: Skippers (Hesperiidae)/
Banded Skippers (Hesperiinae)

Wingspan: 1.7–2.1" (4.3–5.3 cm)

Above: male is tawny orange with dark brown borders
and narrow black forewing stigma; female is browner
with reduced orange markings

Below: brown; forewing dark brown toward base and
along trailing edge

Sexes: dissimilar; female is primarily brown with an
orange spot band on the forewing

Egg: light green, laid singly on host leaves

Larva: green with fine black dots; head is whitish with
three black stripes

Larval Host Plants: Sawgrass

Habitat: wetlands, coastal freshwater and brackish
marshes

Broods: two generations

Abundance: occasional to common

Compare: Dion Skipper (pg. 305) has a pale ray through
the center of the ventral hindwing.

Resident

Jan. Feb. Mar. Apr. May June July Aug. Sept. Oct. Nov. Dec.

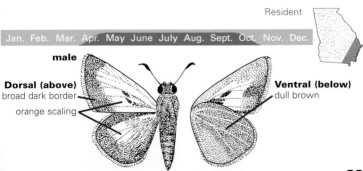

male

Dorsal (above)
broad dark border
orange scaling

Ventral (below)
dull brown

323

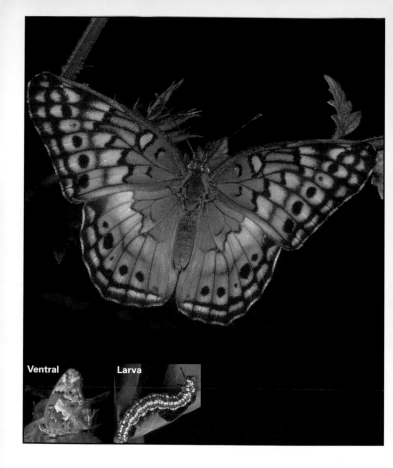

Ventral

Larva

Comments: The Variegated Fritillary shares its affinity for open, sunny habitats with the similar-looking Gulf Fritillary but is generally less common and local in occurrence. Adults have a low, erratic flight but regularly stop to nectar at available flowers. It is an infrequent garden visitor. Although a resident of the Deep South, it regularly expands its range northward each summer and occasionally even reaches southern Canada.

Variegated Fritillary
Euptoieta claudia

Family/Subfamily: Brush-foots (Nymphalidae)/
Longwing Butterflies (Heliconiinae)

Wingspan: 1.75–2.25" (4.4–5.7 cm)

Above: pale brownish orange with dark markings, narrow light median band and darker reddish orange base

Below: overall brown; forewing has basal orange scaling; hindwing mottled with tan, cream and dark brown; hindwing lacks silvery spots

Sexes: similar, although female is larger and has broader, more rounded wings

Egg: tiny cream eggs laid singly on host leaves and tendrils

Larva: reddish orange with black-spotted white stripes and black spines

Larval Host Plants: various violets and passion flower vines

Habitat: open, sunny sites including roadsides, pastures, old fields and utility easements

Broods: multiple generations

Abundance: occasional to locally abundant

Compare: Gulf Fritillary (pg. 343) is brighter orange with more elongated wings and silvery ventral spots.

Resident Visitor

Jan. Feb. Mar. Apr. May June July Aug. Sept. Oct. Nov. Dec.

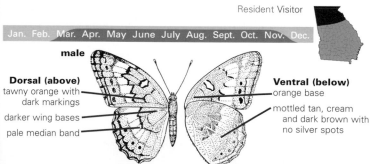

male

Dorsal (above)
tawny orange with dark markings

darker wing bases

pale median band

Ventral (below)
orange base

mottled tan, cream and dark brown with no silver spots

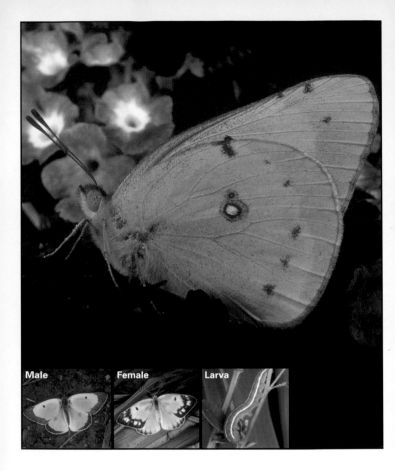

Male Female Larva

Comments: The Orange Sulphur can be found in virtually any open landscape and is particularly abundant in
and around cultivated alfalfa fields, where it occasionally can become a serious pest. Because of this strong
preference, it is often called the Alfalfa Butterfly. It is a
prolific colonizer. Adults have a rapid, erratic flight.
Butterflies produced very early or late in the season
are generally smaller and darker. This butterfly typically
rests and feeds with its wings closed, so its orange
color is seen primarily in flight or when the butterfly is
basking in the sun.

Orange Sulphur
Colias eurytheme

Family/Subfamily: Whites and Sulphurs (Pieridae)/ Sulphurs (Coliadinae)

Wingspan: 1.6–2.4" (4.1–6.1 cm)

Above: bright yellow orange with black wing borders and black forewing cell spot; hindwing has central orange spot

Below: yellow with row of dark submarginal spots; hindwing has one or two central red-rimmed silvery spots

Sexes: similar, although female has yellow spots in broader black wing borders and are less vibrant; female is occasionally white

Egg: white, laid singly on host leaves

Larva: green with thin, cream lateral stripe and numerous short hairs

Larval Host Plants: Alfalfa, White Sweet Clover, White Clover and vetches

Habitat: open, sunny sites including roadsides, old fields, alfalfa fields, pastures and home gardens

Broods: multiple generations

Abundance: occasional to abundant

Compare: Southern Dogface (pg. 385) is larger, has pointed forewings and wide, scalloped forewing borders. Clouded Sulphur (pg. 387) lacks dorsal orange scaling.

Resident

Jan. Feb. Mar. Apr. May June July Aug. Sept. Oct. Nov. Dec.

Dorsal (above)
black cell spot
smooth black borders
bright yellow orange
central orange spot

Ventral (below)
red-rimmed silvery spots
dark submarginal spots

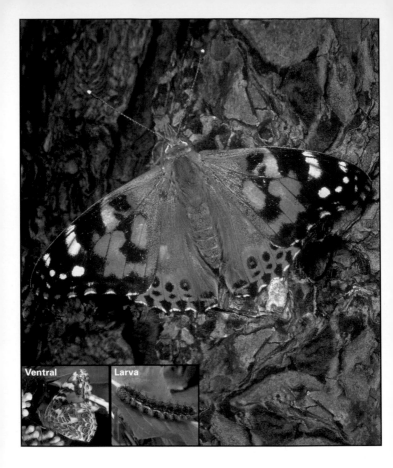

Ventral

Larva

Comments: Unable to survive freezing temperatures, the Painted Lady typically overwinters in Mexico and annually colonizes much of North American continent each summer. Its occurrence in the Southeast is sporadic with populations varying considerably in abundance from year to year. It can be found in just about any open, disturbed landscape where its weedy larval hosts abound. The adults have a rapid, erratic flight usually close to the ground but frequently stop to perch or nectar. The larvae construct individual shelters of loose webbing on the host.

Painted Lady
Vanessa cardui

Family/Subfamily: Brush-foots (Nymphalidae)/
True Brush-foots (Nymphalinae)

Wingspan: 1.75–2.40" (4.4–6.1 cm)

Above: pinkish orange with dark markings and small
white spots near tip of forewing

Below: brown with cream patches in ornate cobweb pattern; hindwing has row of four small eyespots and
marginal band of lavender spots

Sexes: similar

Egg: small pale green eggs laid singly on host leaves

Larva: variable; greenish yellow with black mottling to
charcoal with cream mottling and several rows of light-
colored, branched spines

Larval Host Plants: wide variety of plants in several
families including thistles and mallows; also Hollyhock

Habitat: open, disturbed sites including roadsides, old
fields, fallow agricultural land, pastures, utility easements and gardens

Broods: multiple generations

Abundance: uncommon to common

Compare: American Painted Lady (pg. 331) is overall
more orange, has a more extended forewing apex and
two large ventral hindwing eyespots.

Visitor

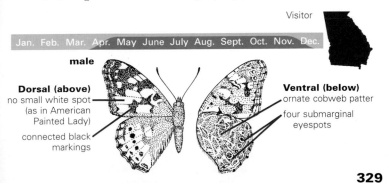

Jan. Feb. Mar. Apr. May June July Aug. Sept. Oct. Nov. Dec.

male

Dorsal (above)
no small white spot
(as in American
Painted Lady)

connected black
markings

Ventral (below)
ornate cobweb patter

four submarginal
eyespots

329

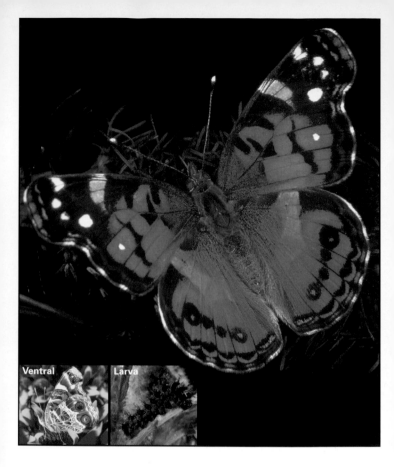

Ventral

Larva

Comments: Considered a common butterfly, the
American Painted Lady is often overlooked despite its
attractiveness. The intricately detailed, agate-like
design on the underside of the wings is a sharp contrast to the bold orange and black pattern above.
Nervous and wary, it is difficult to approach and a challenge to closely observe. When disturbed, it takes off
in a low, erratic flight but often returns to a nearby
location just a few moments later. The larvae construct
individual shelters on the host by spinning together
leaves and flowerheads with silk. Inside, the larvae
safely rest when not actively feeding.

American Painted Lady
Vanessa virginiensis

Family/Subfamily: Brush-foots (Nymphalidae)/
True Brush-foots (Nymphalinae)

Wingspan: 1.75–2.40" (4.4–6.1 cm)

Above: orange with dark marks and borders; forewing has
small white spots near extended and squared-off apex

Below: brown with ornate, cream cobweb pattern; hindwing has two large eyespots and narrow lavender
marginal band

Sexes: similar; females with broader wings

Egg: small pale green eggs laid singly on upper surface
of host leaves

Larva: variable; greenish yellow with narrow black bands
to black with cream bands and numerous red-based,
branched spines; pair of prominent white spots on
each segment

Larval Host Plants: Purple Cudweed, Wandering
Cudweed, Narrow-leaved Cudweed, Sweet
Everlasting, pussy-toes and others

Habitat: open, disturbed sites including roadsides, old
fields, pastures, utility easements and gardens

Broods: multiple generations

Abundance: common to abundant

Compare: Painted Lady (pg. 329) is pinker and has a row
of four small ventral hindwing eyespots.

Resident Visitor

Jan. Feb. Mar. Apr. May June July Aug. Sept. Oct. Nov. Dec.

Dorsal (above)
apex extended and
squared off

small white spot

disconnected black
markings

some blue in one or
more eyespots

Ventral (below)
small white spot

ornate cobweb pattern

two large eyespots

331

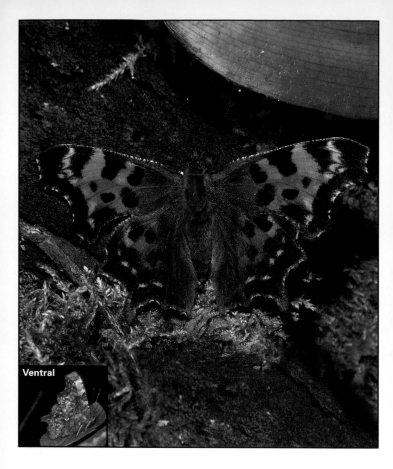

Ventral

Comments: A butterfly of boreal forests, the Green Comma extends southward through the Appalachians into the northeastern tip of Georgia. This uncommon, somewhat reclusive species is named for the green spots on the ventral wing margins. It overwinters as an adult, hibernating in log piles, tree hollows or even in manmade structures. The long-lived adults become active again in early spring to mate and reproduce. It has an erratic, darting flight and frequently perches on the ground, logs or rocks. It is often quite wary and difficult to closely approach. Seldom visits flowers; feeds instead at rotting fruit, dung, carrion and tree sap.

Green Comma
Polygonia faunus

Family/Subfamily: Brush-foots (Nymphalidae)/ True Brush-foots (Nymphalinae)

Wingspan: 1.9–2.4" (4.8–6.1 cm)

Above: tawny orange with irregular wing edge, heavy black borders and spots; hindwing has a row of small yellow orange spots in border and a short, stubby tail; forewing apex is extended and squared off

Below: mottled brown with dark striations, small green spots along margin and silver comma in center of hindwing; darker toward base; dead leaf appearance

Sexes: similar

Egg: green, laid singly on host leaves

Larva: variable; yellow brown to rust with transverse black and yellow bands and spots, two wavy orange lateral lines and white and orange branched spines

Larval Host Plants: gooseberry, willows and birch

Habitat: higher elevation deciduous and mixed forests, riparian woodlands, woodland roads, forest edges and adjacent open brushy areas

Broods: singe generation

Abundance: rare to occasional

Compare: Eastern Comma (pg. 335) has less jagged wing margins and lacks submarginal green spots on wings below.

Resident

Jan. Feb. Mar. Apr. May June July Aug. Sept. Oct. Nov. Dec.

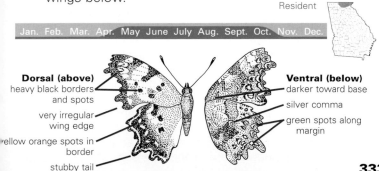

Dorsal (above)
heavy black borders and spots
very irregular wing edge
yellow orange spots in border
stubby tail

Ventral (below)
darker toward base
silver comma
green spots along margin

333

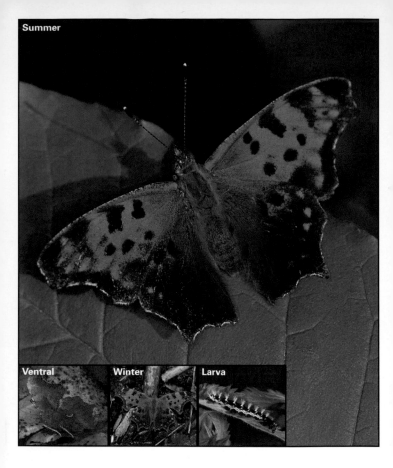

Summer

Ventral Winter Larva

Comments: The Eastern Comma survives the winter as an adult, hibernating in log piles, tree hollows or even within manmade structures. Once warm weather returns, they become active and reproduce, with the resulting generation flying in early summer. A woodland butterfly, it inhabits riparian forests, clearings and adjacent open, brushy areas. Adults have a rapid, erratic flight and frequently perch on overhanging branches or tree trunks. They are quite wary and difficult to closely approach. It seldom visits flowers, feeding instead at rotting fruit, dung, carrion and tree sap.

Eastern Comma
Polygonia comma

Family/Subfamily: Brush-foots (Nymphalidae)/ True Brush-foots (Nymphalinae)

Wingspan: 2.0–2.4" (5.1–6.1 cm)

Above: tawny orange with black borders and spots, irregular wing edge; forewing apex is extended and squared off; hindwing has single distinct tail; summer-form hindwing is primarily black; winter-form has increased orange

Below: seasonally variable; dead leaf appearance; summer-form is heavily mottled light and dark brown; winter-form is uniform brown with fine striations; hindwing has a single distinct curved silvery spot in center

Sexes: similar

Egg: green, laid singly or in small stacks on host leaves

Larva: variable; black to greenish brown with a white lateral band and several rows of white, branched spines

Larval Host Plants: Canadian Wood Nettle, American Elm, False Nettle, Common Hop and nettles

Habitat: deciduous forests, riparian woodlands, forest roads and edges and adjacent open brushy areas

Broods: two generations

Abundance: occasional to common

Compare: Question Mark (pg. 341) is larger and has silver spots in the center of ventral hindwing shaped like a question mark.

Resident

Jan. Feb. Mar. Apr. May June July Aug. Sept. Oct. Nov. Dec.

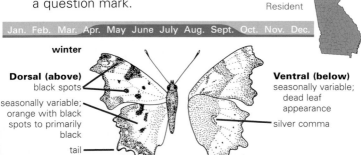

winter

Dorsal (above)
black spots

seasonally variable; orange with black spots to primarily black

tail

Ventral (below)
seasonally variable; dead leaf appearance

silver comma

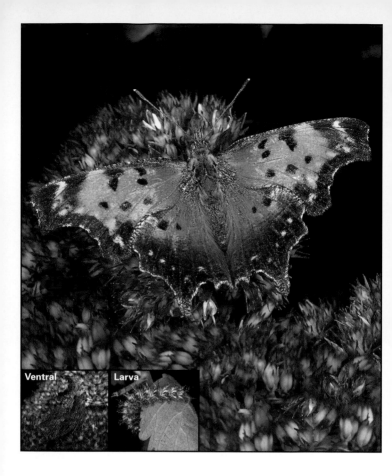

Ventral

Larva

Comments: This woodland butterfly is aptly named for its dull gray, highly striated underwings that closely resemble tree bark. Infrequent and somewhat reclusive, the Gray Common occurs in small, highly localized colonies. It is most often encountered as a single, isolated individual along woodland trails, clearings or roadsides. Adults have an erratic, darting flight and frequently perch tree trunks or on overhanging branches. They are quite wary and difficult to closely approach. Both sexes seldom visit flowers, but prefer to feed at rotting fruit, dung, carrion and tree sap.

Gray Comma
Polygonia progne

Family/Subfamily: Brush-foots (Nymphalidae)/
True Brush-foots (Nymphalinae)

Wingspan: 2.1–2.4" (5.3–6.1 cm)

Above: tawny orange with heavy black borders and
spots, highly irregular wing edge; forewing apex is
extended and squared off; hindwing bears a single
short, stubby tail; hindwing border encloses a row of
small yellow orange spots

Below: dull gray with fine striations and a narrow silver
comma in center of hindwing; darker toward base

Sexes: similar

Egg: green, laid singly on host leaves

Larva: variable; yellow brown with transverse black lines
between segments, dark botches and dashes, and
several rows of pale yellow and black branched spines

Larval Host Plants: Appalachian Gooseberry, Wild
Azalea and perhaps Paper Birch

Habitat: deciduous woodlands, clearings, woodland
roads, forest edges and adjacent open brushy areas

Broods: two generations

Abundance: rare to occasional

Compare: Green Comma (pg. 333) has distinct row of
green spots on ventral hindwing margin.

Stray

Jan. Feb. Mar. Apr. May June July Aug. Sept. Oct. Nov. Dec.

Dorsal (above)
irregular wing edge

yellowish orange
spots in dark
border

Ventral (below)
fine gray brown
striations

two-toned appearance

silver comma

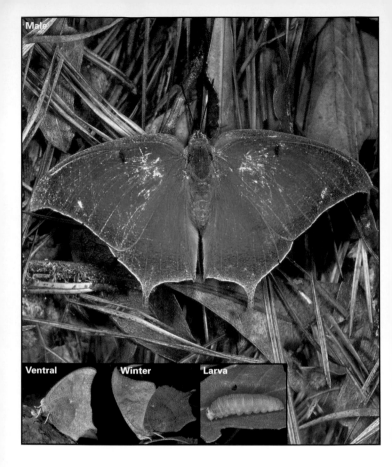

Male

Ventral   Winter   Larva

Comments: The distinctive Goatweed Butterfly is named for one of its primary larval hosts. Although brilliant reddish orange dorsally, the leaf-like pattern of its ventral wings provides superb camouflage when it is at rest. Distinct seasonal forms vary in wing shape and to a lesser extent in ground color. Individuals produced late in the season survive the cold winter in reproductive diapause. It has a strong, darting flight and perches with wings closed on treetrunks, branches or on the ground. They can be quite a challenge to find, let alone closely approach. It prefers rotting fruit and sap flows. Orange color is seen primarily in flight or when basking.

Goatweed Butterfly
Anaea andria

Family/Subfamily: Brush-foots (Nymphalidae)/
Leafwings (Charaxinae)

Wingspan: 2.25–3.00" (5.7–7.6 cm)

Above: pointed forewings and hindwing tail; male is
bright reddish orange; female is lighter orange with
dark markings and pale band along wing margins

Below: seasonally variable; brownish gray resembling a
dead leaf; winter-form is more heavily patterned, has
longer hindwing tails and a more pronounced hooked
forewing apex

Sexes: similar, although female is lighter with more
extensive dorsal markings

Egg: gray-green, laid singly on host leaves

Larva: gray-green with light head and numerous tiny light
spots

Larval Host Plants: Goatweed and Silver Croton

Habitat: dry pinelands, woodland edges and adjacent
open areas

Broods: two generations

Abundance: uncommon to occasional; localized

Compare: Question Mark (pg. 341) has irregular wing
edges, an extended and squared-off forewing apex
and black dorsal forewing spots.

Visitor Stray

Jan. Feb. Mar. Apr. May June July Aug. Sept. Oct. Nov. Dec.

male

Dorsal (above)
hooked apex

orange wings

tail

Ventral (below)
dead leaf appearance

Summer

Ventral

Winter

Larva

Comments: The Question Mark's dark markings, irregular wing edges and cryptically colored undersides help the butterfly resemble a dead leaf when resting. Its name comes from the silvery marks on the ventral hindwing that resemble a rudimentary question mark. Adults have a strong, rapid flight but frequently alight on overhanging branches, tree trunks or leaf litter. Wary and nervous, they are often difficult to closely approach. Males readily establish territories and aggressively investigate any passing objects. Both sexes visit rotting fruit, dung, carrion and tree sap.

Question Mark
Polygonia interrogationis

Family/Subfamily: Brush-foots (Nymphalidae)/
True Brush-foots (Nymphalinae)

Wingspan: 2.25–3.00" (5.7–7.6 cm)

Above: orange with black spots, narrow lavender borders and irregular, jagged edges; seasonally variable; summer-form hindwing is primarily black; winter-form has increased orange on hindwing

Below: seasonally variable; pinkish brown dead leaf appearance; hindwing has two, small median silvery spots that form a question mark

Sexes: similar

Egg: green, laid singly or in small groups on top of each other on host leaves

Larva: gray to black with orange and cream stripes and spots and several rows of branched spines

Larval Host Plants: Sugarberry, American Elm, Winged Elm, also False Nettle and Stinging Nettle

Habitat: deciduous forests, moist woodlands, forest edges and adjacent open areas

Broods: two generations

Abundance: occasional to common

Compare: Eastern Comma (pg. 335) is smaller and has comma-shaped spot on ventral hindwing.

Resident

Jan. Feb. Mar. Apr. May June July Aug. Sept. Oct. Nov. Dec.

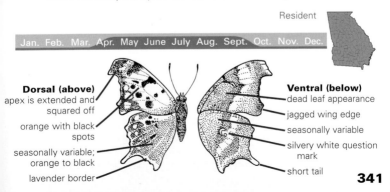

Dorsal (above)
apex is extended and squared off

orange with black spots

seasonally variable; orange to black

lavender border

Ventral (below)
dead leaf appearance

jagged wing edge

seasonally variable

silvery white question mark

short tail

341

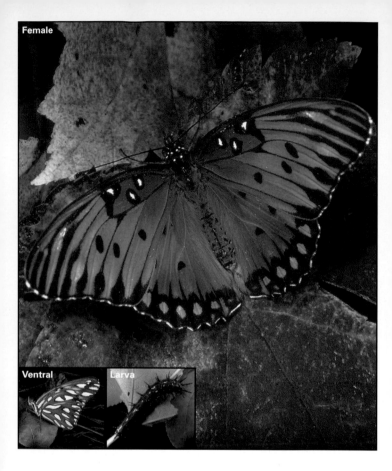

Female

Ventral

Larva

Comments: The underside of the Gulf Fritillary's hindwings are beautifully decorated with numerous silvery,
mercury-like patches that quickly distinguish it from
the equally common Monarch. In mild years, it may be
able to survive the winter in southern portions of the
state, but is typically a seasonal colonist. Exceedingly
fond of flowers, it is often a regular garden visitor.
Adults have a low, rapid flight. It is one of several
migratory species in the Southeast. During the fall,
adults move southward in large numbers into the
Florida peninsula to escape harsh winter temperatures.

Gulf Fritillary
Agraulis vanillae

Family/Subfamily: Brush-foots (Nymphalidae)/ Longwing Butterflies (Heliconiinae)

Wingspan: 2.5–3.0" (6.4–7.6 cm)

Above: bright orange elongated wings with black markings and three small, black-rimmed white spots in forewing cell; hindwing has chain-like black border

Below: brown with elongated silvery spots

Sexes: similar, although female is paler above with increased black markings

Egg: yellow eggs laid singly on host leaves

Larva: orange with greenish black stripes and black, branched spines

Larval Host Plants: various passion flower vines including Maypop, Corky-Stemmed Passion Flower, Yellow Passion Flower and Incense Passion Flower

Habitat: open, disturbed sites including roadsides, old fields, utility easements, parks and gardens

Broods: multiple generations

Abundance: occasion to abundant

Compare: The Gulf Fritillary's distinct ventral silver spots quickly distinguish it from the Variegated Fritillary (pg. 325) and Monarch (pg. 353).

Resident Visitor

Jan. Feb. Mar. Apr. May June July Aug. Sept. Oct. Nov. Dec.

male

Dorsal (above)
elongated wings

black-rimmed white spots

chain-like black border

Ventral (below)
orange forewing base

elongated silvery spots

343

Male

Ventral

Larva

Comments: The colorful Viceroy is usually found in or near wetland areas in close proximity to its larval hosts. Males perch on overhanging branches and occasionally dart out to investigate passing objects or to take periodic exploratory flights. Both sexes tend to be somewhat wary and difficult to closely approach. Although once thought to be a palatable mimic of the distasteful Monarch, studies have shown that both species are actually toxic to certain predators. Individuals occurring in the southern portion of the state may occasionally resemble the darker, more mahogany brown Florida subspecies.

Viceroy
Limenitis archippus

Family/Subfamily: Brush-foots (Nymphalidae)/ Admirals and Relatives (Limenitidinae)

Wingspan: 2.6–3.2" (6.6–8.1 cm)

Above: orange with black markings, veins and broad wing borders; borders contain central row of small, white spots; forewing has black postmedian band and white spots; hindwing has distinct thin, black post-median line

Below: as above with lighter orange coloration and increased white markings

Sexes: similar

Egg: gray-green, laid singly on tip of host leaves

Larva: mottled green, brown and cream with two long, knobby horns on thorax

Larval Host Plants: various willows including Black Willow, Carolina Willow, Weeping Willow

Habitat: pond edges, wetlands, roadside ditches and moist areas supporting willows

Broods: multiple generations

Abundance: occasional to common

Compare: Monarch (pg. 353) is larger and lacks black postmedian hindwing line. Gulf Fritillary (pg. 343) is brighter orange with elongated wings and distinct silver ventral spots.

Resident

Jan. Feb. Mar. Apr. May June July Aug. Sept. Oct. Nov. Dec.

Dorsal (above)
white spots
thin black line
white spots in black border

Ventral (below)
orange with black bands containing white spots

345

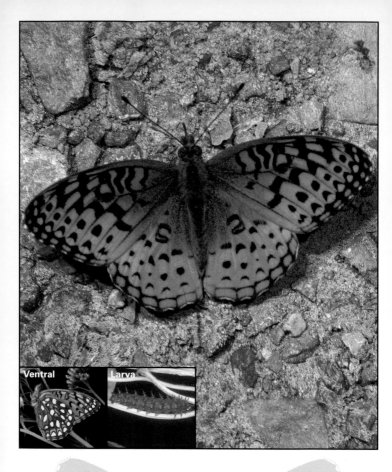

Ventral

Larva

Comments: This widespread northern species extends southward through the Appalachian Mountains and just barely enters the northern tip of Georgia. The species tends to be considerably rarer and more highly localized than its common relative, the Great Spangled Fritillary with which it is often confused. Adults have a swift flight but may readily be encountered nectaring on a variety of colorful wildflowers. Males patrol for females along woodland margins, roadsides and in other open areas.

Aphrodite Fritillary
Speyeria aphrodite

Family/Subfamily: Brush-foots (Nymphalidae)/ Longwing Butterflies (Heliconiinae)

Wingspan: 2.7–3.3" (6.9–8.4 cm)

Above: bright orange with heavy black lines and spots

Below: variable; hindwing is dark orange brown to reddish brown with numerous large metallic silver spots and a narrow yellowish submarginal band

Sexes: similar, although female is larger with darker brown wing bases, more pronounced black markings and paler golden orange wings

Egg: tiny cream eggs laid singly and somewhat haphazardly near host leaves

Larva: velvety black with several rows of black spines; lateral two rows of spines reddish brown with black tips

Larval Host Plants: various violets

Habitat: open woodlands, fields, moist meadows, pastures, woodland edges and roadsides

Broods: single generation

Abundance: rare to occasional

Compare: Great Spangled Fritillary (pg. 351) is slightly larger and has wide yellowish submarginal band on the hindwing below.

Resident

Jan. Feb. Mar. Apr. May June July Aug. Sept. Oct. Nov. Dec.

Dorsal (above)
bright orange with heavy black lines and spots

Ventral (below)
large metallic silver spots

reddish brown base

narrow yellowish submarginal band

347

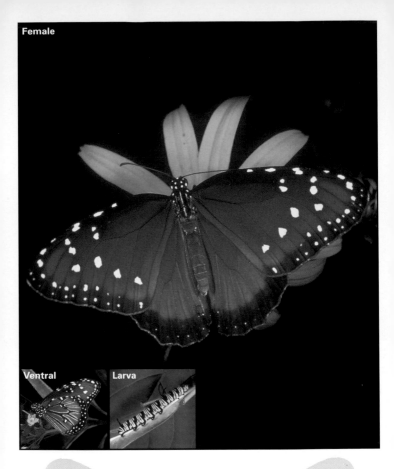

Female

Ventral

Larva

Comments: The Queen is a year-round resident of Florida and extreme southern portions of the Gulf States. In favorable years, it may occasionally expand its range northward, periodically straying or even temporarily colonizing. Adults have a slow, soaring flight and are fond of flowers. As a result, it may be a frequent garden visitor. The larvae feed on plants in the Milkweed Family from which they sequester toxic chemicals that render them and the resulting adults distasteful to certain predators. Their rich mahogany and black coloration advertises this unpalatability. It does not undertake massive annual migrations.

Queen
Danaus gilippus

Family/Subfamily: Brush-foots (Nymphalidae)/ Milkweed Butterflies (Danainae)

Wingspan: 3.0–3.5" (7.6–8.9 cm)

Above: mahogany with black wing borders and small white forewing spots; male has a single black post-median androconial scent patch on the hindwing

Below: reddish brown; forewing as above; hindwing has black veins and small white spots in black border

Sexes: similar; female lacks black scent patch

Egg: white, laid singly on host leaves

Larva: black with transverse cream stripes and yellow spots; body has three pairs of long, black filaments

Larval Host Plants: various milkweed family plants including Mexican Milkweed, White Swamp Milkweed, Sandhill Milkweed and Swamp Milkweed

Habitat: savannas, pastures, pinelands, roadsides, old fields, utility easements, coastal areas and gardens

Broods: multiple generations

Abundance: occasional

Compare: Monarch (pg. 353) is larger, brighter orange and has black wing veins above. Gulf Fritillary (pg. 343) has elongated wings and prominent silver ventral spots.

Visitor Stray

Jan. Feb. Mar. Apr. May June July Aug. Sept. Oct. Nov. Dec.

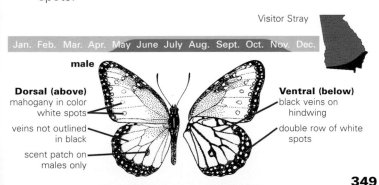

male

Dorsal (above)
mahogany in color
white spots

veins not outlined in black

scent patch on males only

Ventral (below)
black veins on hindwing

double row of white spots

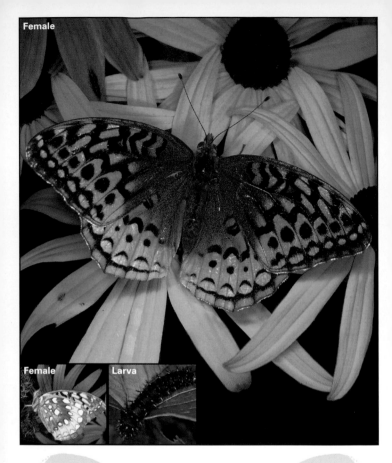

Female

Female   Larva

Comments: This large, conspicuous fritillary may be common in northern Georgia. Adults have a strong, directed flight but frequently pause to nectar at colorful wildflowers, being particularly fond of milkweed, Joe-pye Weed and thistles. It is not unusual to see several individuals at a single flower. It has a single, protracted summer flight with males typically emerging several weeks before females. Although females may be on the wing in early July, they do not begin laying eggs until later in the summer and often fly until late September. Newly hatched larvae overwinter and complete development the following spring.

Great Spangled Fritillary
Speyeria cybele

Family/Subfamily: Brush-foots (Nymphalidae)/ Longwing Butterflies (Heliconiinae)

Wingspan: 2.9–3.8" (7.1–9.7 cm)

Above: bright orange with heavy black lines and spots

Below: variable; hindwing is dark orange brown to brown with numerous large metallic silver spots and a broad yellowish submarginal band

Sexes: similar, although female is larger with darker brown wing bases, more pronounced black markings and paler golden orange to pale yellowish wings

Egg: tiny cream eggs laid singly and somewhat haphazardly on or host leaves

Larva: velvety black with several rows of reddish orange-based black spines

Larval Host Plants: various violets

Habitat: open, sunny sites including roadsides, pastures, old fields, wet meadows and utility easements close to rich woodlands; also sunlit forested roadsides

Broods: single generation

Abundance: occasional to common

Compare: Aphrodite Fritillary (pg. 347) is smaller, less common and has a narrow yellowish submarginal band on the ventral hindwing.

Resident

Jan. Feb. Mar. Apr. May June July Aug. Sept. Oct. Nov. Dec.

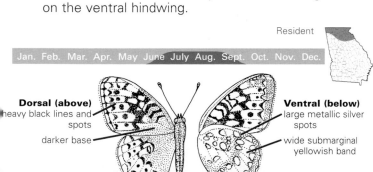

Dorsal (above)
heavy black lines and spots
darker base

Ventral (below)
large metallic silver spots
wide submarginal yellowish band

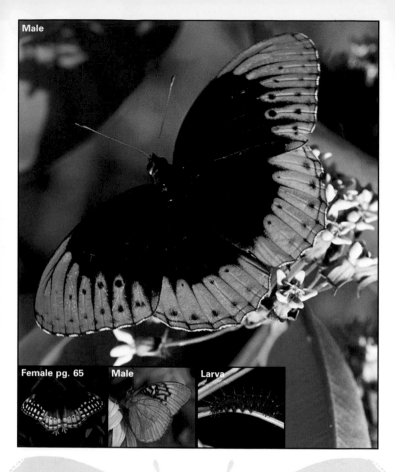

Male

Female pg. 65   Male   Larva

Comments: The Diana Fritillary is a showstopper! Strikingly sexually dimorphic, the blue and black female mimics the toxic Pipevine Swallowtail to presumably gain protection from predators. Although often spotty and localized, it can be fairly numerous when encountered. Adults have a strong, directed flight but readily stop to nectar at colorful wildflowers, being particularly fond of milkweeds, Joe-pye Weed and thistles. As with other fritillaries, males typically emerge several weeks before females. Young larvae overwinter and complete development the following spring.

Diana Fritillary
Speyeria diana

Family/Subfamily: Brush-foots (Nymphalidae)/ Longwing Butterflies (Heliconiinae)

Wingspan: 3.5–4.4" (8.9–11.2 cm)

Above: male is dark unmarked blackish brown with bright orange on the outer third; female is black basally with white and iridescent blue spots on outer half

Below: forewing is orange with heavy black markings toward base; male hindwing is brownish orange with two rows of small narrow silver dashes; female hindwing is chocolate brown

Sexes: dissimilar; female is black basally with white and iridescent blue spots on outer half; ventral hindwing is chocolate brown

Egg: tiny cream eggs laid singly and somewhat haphazardly near host leaves

Larva: velvety black with several rows of reddish orange based black spines

Larval Host Plants: various woodland violets

Habitat: rich, moist deciduous mountain woodlands, stream corridors, forested roads, clearings and adjacent open areas

Broods: single generation

Abundance: rare to locally common

Compare: unique

Resident

Jan. Feb. Mar. Apr. May June July Aug. Sept. Oct. Nov. Dec.

male

Dorsal (above)
black
orange
(female primarily black and blue)

Ventral (below)
black markings toward base

lacks prominent silvery hindwing spots characteristic of other fritillaries

355

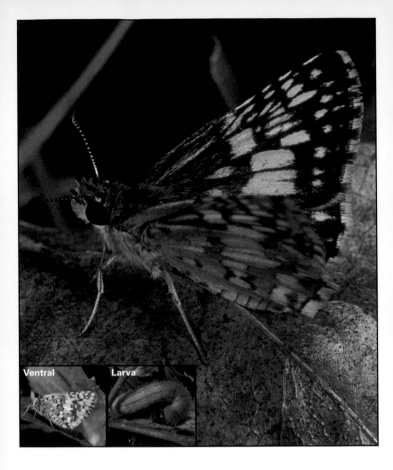

Ventral

Larva

Comments: New data suggests that the once abundant Common Checkered-Skipper has been almost entirely displaced by the White Checkered-Skipper's recent expansion into the Deep South. This trend is continuing northward along the coast into South Carolina. Virtually identical in appearance and behavior, the two sibling species can be reliably differentiated only through dissection. Adults have a rapid, darting flight. While at rest, they generally hold their wings open, allowing a glimpse of the butterfly's distinctive checkerboard pattern.

Common/White Checkered-Skipper
Pyrgus communis/Pyrgus albescens

Family/Subfamily: Skippers (Hesperiidae)/
Spread-wing Skippers (Pyrginae)

Wingspan: 0.75–1.25" (1.9–3.2 cm)

Above: male is black with numerous small, white spots
and some bluish white scaling on base of wings and
thorax; female is dark brown with reduced white scaling

Below: white with tan to brown irregular bands and
spots

Sexes: similar, although female has reduced white
markings

Egg: pale green, laid singly on host leaves

Larva: gray-green with dark dorsal stripe, light side
stripes and black head

Larval Host Plants: various mallow family plants
including Indian Hemp, Broomweed, Poppy Mallow
and False Mallow

Habitat: open, disturbed sites including roadsides, old
fields, utility easements and fallow agricultural land

Broods: multiple generations

Abundance: common

Compare: Tropical Checkered-Skipper (pg. 359) male has
increased bluish white scaling on wings above and
both sexes have more diffuse or smudged ventral
bands.

Resident

| Jan. | Feb. | Mar. | Apr. | May | June | July | Aug. | Sept. | Oct. | Nov. | Dec. |

Dorsal (above)
fringe checkered to
apex

generally black and
white above

marginal spots much
smaller than those
in submarginal row

Ventral (below)
clear distinct bands

paler below

357

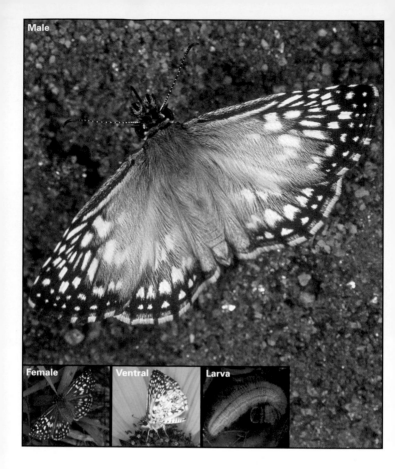

Male

Female | Ventral | Larva

Comments: The Tropical Checkered-Skipper is a common butterfly throughout Florida and along the extreme Gulf Coast, barely crossing the border into Georgia. Like its more widespread relatives, it can be encountered in a variety of open, disturbed sites, where it is particularly abundant in late summer and early fall. Adults have a fast, erratic flight and buzz rapidly among low vegetation, pausing occasionally to nectar or perch with their wings outstretched. The light green larvae construct individual shelters on the host by tying two or more leaves together with silk.

Tropical Checkered-Skipper
Pyrgus oileus

Family/Subfamily: Skippers (Hesperiidae)/
Spread-wing Skippers (Pyrginae)

Wingspan: 0.90–1.35" (2.3–3.4 cm)

Above: male is dark blackish brown with numerous small, white spots and extensive bluish gray hair-like scales on base of wings and thorax; female is dark brown with reduced white scaling

Below: powdery white with tan to brown irregular, somewhat diffuse or smudged bands

Sexes: similar, although female darker with reduced white markings

Egg: pale green, laid singly on host leaves

Larva: yellow-green with thin green dorsal stripe, light side stripes and black head; body is covered with numerous small, light-colored hairs

Larval Host Plants: various mallows including Indian Hemp, Broomweed, Poppy Mallow and False Mallow

Habitat: open, disturbed sites including roadsides, old fields, utility easements and fallow agricultural land

Broods: multiple generations

Abundance: rare

Compare: Common/White Checkered-Skipper (pg. 357) male has reduced bluish white dorsal scaling; both sexes have well-defined ventral bands.

Resident

| Jan. | Feb. | Mar. | Apr. | May | June | July | Aug. | Sept. | Oct. | Nov. | Dec. |

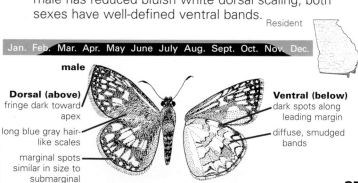

male

Dorsal (above)
fringe dark toward apex

long blue gray hair-like scales

marginal spots similar in size to submarginal spots

Ventral (below)
dark spots along leading margin

diffuse, smudged bands

359

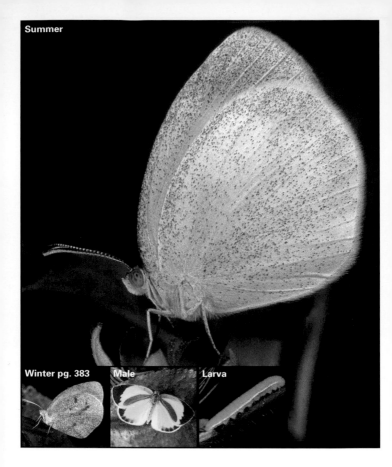

Summer

Winter pg. 383

Male

Larva

Comments: The Barred Sulphur is a common butterfly of open, weedy sites throughout the Deep South, where it is particularly abundant in the late summer and early fall. Adults have a quick, dancing flight and typically bob among low vegetation. It displays dramatic seasonal variation in color and behavior. Individuals produced during the summer are short-lived, reproductively active and almost pure white on the ventral wings. Winter-forms have highly pigmented and patterned ventral hindwings and overwinter in reproductive diapause. It typically rests and feeds with its wings closed.

Barred Sulphur
Eurema daira

Family/Subfamily: Whites and Sulphurs (Pieridae)/ Sulphurs (Coliadinae)

Wingspan: 1.0–1.8" (2.5–4.6 cm)

Above: seasonally variable; winter-form bright yellow; summer-form whitish; all have black wing tips and a black bar along the trailing edge of forewing; forewing bar is diffuse or absent in female; wide black hindwing border is reduced to a small patch in winter-form

Below: seasonally variable; hindwings light gray to pure white in summer-form; tan to reddish brown with numerous pattern elements in winter-form

Sexes: similar, although black markings paler and less extensive in female

Egg: white, laid singly on host leaves

Larva: green with thin, lateral cream stripe

Larval Host Plants: Joint Vetch and other Fabaceae

Habitat: open, disturbed sites including roadsides, pastures, utility easements, vacant fields, pond margins

Broods: multiple generations

Abundance: rare to common

Compare: Dainty Sulphur (pg. 379) is much smaller; lacks white ventral hindwings. Little Sulphur (pg. 381) lacks black dorsal forewing bar.

Resident Visitor Stray

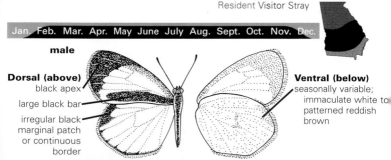

Jan. Feb. Mar. Apr. May June July Aug. Sept. Oct. Nov. Dec.

male

Dorsal (above)
black apex
large black bar
irregular black marginal patch or continuous border

Ventral (below)
seasonally variable; immaculate white to patterned reddish brown

361

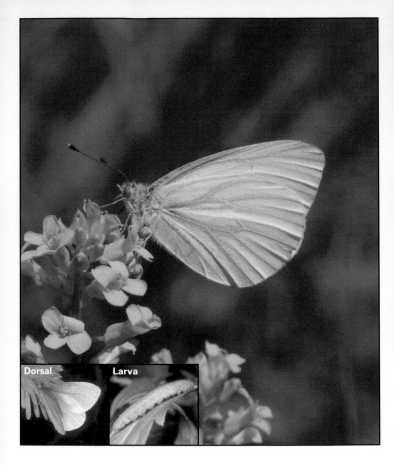

Dorsal

Larva

Comments: The West Virginia White is strictly an early
spring butterfly of moist, shady mountain woodlands.
Although widespread throughout the Appalachian
region, it tends to occur in highly localized populations
in close association with patches of its larval host. It is
a poor pioneer species, reluctant to cross large open
expanses to colonize nearby scattered patches of
woodland or second growth forest. Adults have a low,
weak flight and maneuver slowly along the forest floor
stopping occasionally to nectar on a variety of early
season wildflowers. Males frequently puddle at damp
ground along woodland trails or forested roads.

West Virginia White
Pieris virginiensis

Family/Subfamily: Whites and Sulphurs (Pieridae)/ Whites (Pierinae)

Wingspan: 1.2–1.6" (3.0–4.1 cm)

Above: unmarked white to smoky white with black scaling along costal margin and wing bases

Below: hindwings white with brown gray scaling along veins

Sexes: similar, although female typically appears more smoky gray on the wings above

Egg: greenish white, laid singly on underside of leaves

Larva: gray green with longitudinal yellow orange stripes and covered with small black dots

Larval Host Plants: toothwort, rockcress, Garlic Mustard and bittercress

Habitat: rich, moist deciduous woodlands, forest edges, and adjacent meadows or open areas

Broods: single generation

Abundance: rare to occasional; often quite localized

Compare: The Cabbage White (pg. 369) is similar in size but has charcoal wing tips, one or two postmedian black spots on the dorsal forewing and lacks brown gray scaling along the veins on the ventral hindwing.

Resident

| Jan. | Feb. | Mar. | Apr. | May | June | July | Aug. | Sept. | Oct. | Nov. | Dec. |

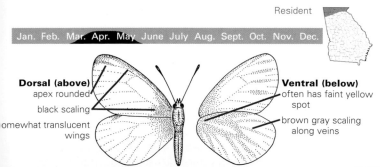

Dorsal (above)
apex rounded
black scaling
somewhat translucent wings

Ventral (below)
often has faint yellow spot
brown gray scaling along veins

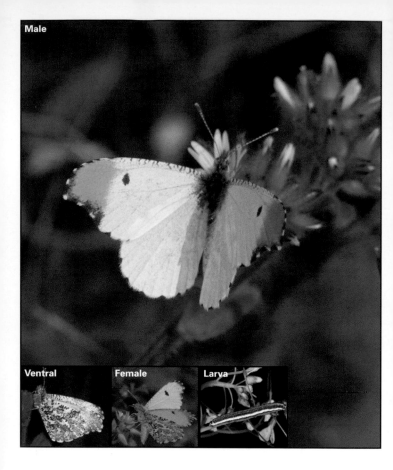

Male

Ventral

Female

Larva

Comments: This small, delicate butterfly provides a welcome hint of approaching spring by appearing during the cool, unpredictable early spring weather. Aptly named, the Falcate Orangetip may be quickly identified by its characteristic hooked forewings. Although considered a forest species, it avoids dense shade and is typically associated with open, thinly wooded habitats and adjacent clearings. Adults have a quick flight and maneuver adeptly close to the ground with a zigzag motion. Both sexes visit a variety of early spring flowers and readily nectar on the blossoms of their larval hosts.

Falcate Orangetip
Anthocharis midea

Family/Subfamily: Whites and Sulphurs (Pieridae)/ Whites (Pierinae)

Wingspan: 1.25–1.75" (3.2–4.4 cm)

Above: white; forewing has a small black cell spot and distinctive hooked (falcate) tip; male has orange tips on forewings; female has white forewing tips

Below: hindwings white; heavily marbled with gray

Sexes: dissimilar; male has orange forewing tips

Egg: orange, laid singly on leaves, stems or flower buds

Larva: blue-green with a narrow yellow orange dorsal stripe, bright white lateral stripe and small black dots

Larval Host Plants: herbaceous plants in mustard family, including rockcress, Field Peppergrass, Cut-leaf Toothwort, bittercress, Shepherd's Purse and Garlic Mustard

Habitat: lowland forested stream corridors, hilltops, roadsides, open deciduous forests and pine-oak woodlands, and associated margins and clearings

Broods: single generation

Abundance: uncommon to common, often localized

Compare: West Virginia White (pg. 363) lacks black forewing cell spot, falcate wing tips and heavily marbled ventral hindwing.

Resident

Jan. Feb. Mar. Apr. May June July Aug. Sept. Oct. Nov. Dec.

male

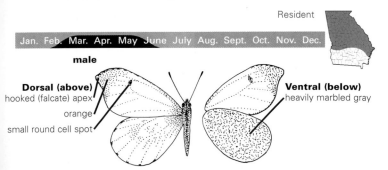

Dorsal (above)
hooked (falcate) apex
orange
small round cell spot

Ventral (below)
heavily marbled gray

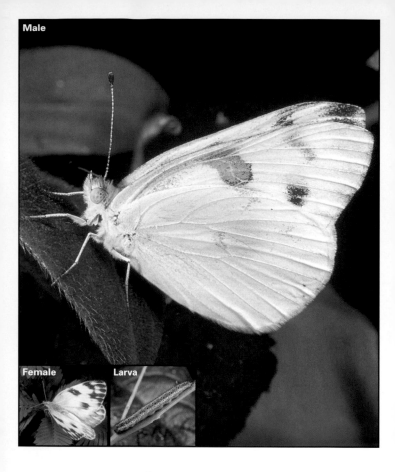

Male

Female

Larva

Comments: A butterfly of dry, weedy sites, the Checkered White is a wide-ranging species but often only locally abundant. Adults have a fast, erratic flight and can be difficult to approach. The sexes differ dramatically and can be easily told apart even from a distance. Adults produced in early spring or late fall, under cooler conditions and shorter days, are typically smaller, darker and more heavily patterned. It readily stops to nectar on low flowers and is especially fond of the blossoms of its larval hosts.

Checkered White
Pontia protodice

Family/Subfamily: Whites and Sulphurs (Pieridae)/ Whites (Pierinae)

Wingspan: 1.25–2.00" (3.2–5.1 cm)

Above: male is white with charcoal markings on forewing and immaculate hindwing; female is grayish white with extensive black or grayish brown checkered markings on both wings

Below: hindwings white with grayish markings and yellow-green scaling along the veins; seasonally variable; cool season individuals are more heavily patterned

Sexes: similar, although female has more extensive black markings

Egg: yellow, laid singly on host leaves or flowers

Larva: gray; longitudinal yellow-orange stripe, black dots

Larval Host Plants: Virginia Peppergrass, Common Pepperweed, Garden Yellowrocket, Shepherd's Purse

Habitat: open, disturbed sites including roadsides, pastures, utility easements, vacant fields, agricultural land

Broods: multiple generations

Abundance: occasional to common

Compare: Cabbage White (pg. 369) has charcoal wing tips and single or double dorsal forewing spots. Great Southern White (pg. 371) has scalloped black forewing border.

Resident Visitor

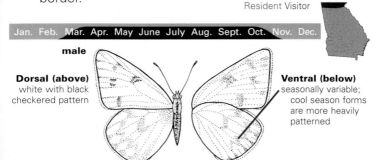

Jan. Feb. Mar. Apr. May June July Aug. Sept. Oct. Nov. Dec.

male

Dorsal (above)
white with black checkered pattern

Ventral (below)
seasonally variable; cool season forms are more heavily patterned

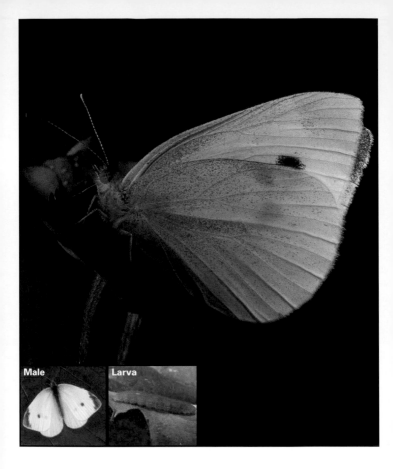

Male

Larva

Comments: Accidentally introduced into the U.S. from Europe in 1860, the Cabbage White (or European Cabbage Butterfly) quickly radiated across much of North America. It is one of the few butterfly species that is considered to be a serious agricultural and garden pest. Adults have a slow, somewhat awkward flight and are easy to observe. Although appearing pure white from a distance, upon closer inspection the wings beneath are delicately shaded with yellow.

Cabbage White
Pieris rapae

Family/Subfamily: Whites and Sulphurs (Pieridae)/ Whites (Pierinae)

Wingspan: 1.5–2.0" (3.8–5.1 cm)

Above: male is white with single black postmedian forewing spot and wing tips; female is white with two black postmedian forewing spots

Below: forewing white with two black spots and yellow tips; hindwing immaculate whitish yellow

Sexes: similar, although female has two black spots on forewing

Egg: white, laid singly on host leaves and flowers

Larva: green with small lateral yellow dashes and numerous short hairs

Larval Host Plants: cultivated and wild members of the Mustard Family including Virginia Peppergrass, Wild Mustard, Wild Radish, broccoli, cabbage, turnip, cauliflower and radish

Habitat: open, disturbed sites including roadsides, old fields, utility easement, agricultural land and gardens

Broods: multiple generations

Abundance: occasional to abundant

Compare: Checkered White (pg. 367) lacks black tip on forewing. Great Southern White (pg. 371) is larger and has scalloped black forewing borders.

Resident

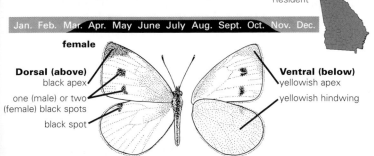

Jan. Feb. Mar. Apr. May June July Aug. Sept. Oct. Nov. Dec.

female

Dorsal (above)
black apex
one (male) or two (female) black spots
black spot

Ventral (below)
yellowish apex
yellowish hindwing

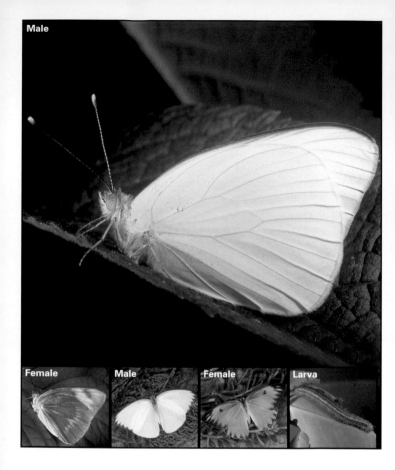

Male

Female | Male | Female | Larva

Comments: The Great Southern White's antennae have distinctive blue tips. While males are always white, females range in color from white to smoky gray. Primarily a coastal species, it inhabits salt marshes and other open, sunny locations where its larval hosts can be found. Although a common species in Florida, it is an infrequent vagrant or temporary colonist northward across the border into Georgia. Adults have a low, generally casual flight but can move swiftly if disturbed. It occasionally experiences tremendous population outbreaks. Extensive northward movements of adults along the coast often follow such explosions in number.

Great Southern White
Ascia monuste

Family/Subfamily: Whites and Sulphurs (Pieridae)/ Whites (Pierinae)

Wingspan: 1.5–2.5" (3.8–6.4 cm)

Above: male is immaculate white with narrow, black scalloped forewing border; female is seasonally variable; dirty white to gray with more pronounced black forewing border and black forewing cell spot

Below: males white with pale yellow hindwings; females dirty white to gray

Sexes: similar, although female has more gray scaling and a single black dorsal forewing spot

Egg: yellow, laid singly or in small groups on host leaves

Larva: yellow with grayish purple longitudinal stripes, black dots and numerous small hairs

Larval Host Plants: Virginia Peppergrass, Saltwort, Sea Rocket and others

Habitat: open sites including roadsides, coastal dunes, salt marshes, vacant fields, agricultural land

Broods: multiple generations

Abundance: rare to uncommon

Compare: Cabbage White (pg. 369) is smaller, lacks black scalloped forewing border and has one (male) or two (female) black postmedian forewing spots.

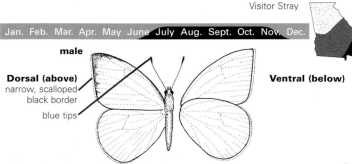

Visitor Stray

Jan. Feb. Mar. Apr. May June July Aug. Sept. Oct. Nov. Dec.

male

Dorsal (above)
narrow, scalloped black border

blue tips

Ventral (below)

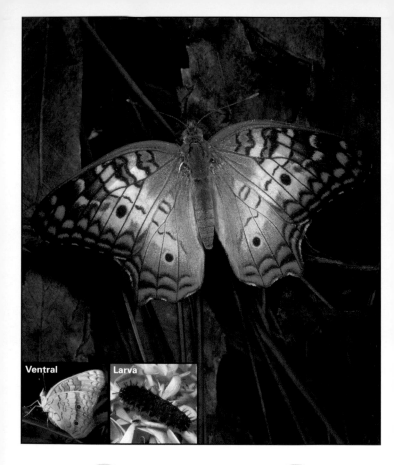

Ventral

Larva

Comments: A year-round resident of southern Florida, the White Peacock annually disperses northward to colonize more of the peninsula, occasionally making its way to coastal portions of Georgia and South Carolina. It occurrence is extremely spotty and varies considerably from year to year. It is most frequently encountered in open, weedy sites along waterways or moist ditches where its larval hosts typically grow. Adults have a fast, erratic flight usually within a few feet of the ground and readily alight on low vegetation with their wings outstretched. They avidly visit available flowers where that can be easily observed.

White Peacock
Anartia jatrophae

Family/Subfamily: Brush-foots (Nymphalidae)/
True Brush-foots (Nymphalinae)

Wingspan: 2.0–2.5" (5.1–6.4 cm)

Above: white with dark brown marking and dull orange
scaling along wing margins; forewing has a single
black spot; hindwing has a short, stubby tail and two
black postmedian spots

Below: as above with paler brown wing margins and
pinkish markings

Sexes: similar, though female is larger and has broader
wings

Egg: green, laid singly on host leaves

Larva: charcoal gray with small silvery white spots and
black, branched spines

Larval Host Plants: Frogfruit and Water Hyssop

Habitat: open, disturbed sites including wet ditches,
roadsides, pond edges, old fields and gardens

Broods: multiple generations

Abundance: rare to uncommon

Compare: unique

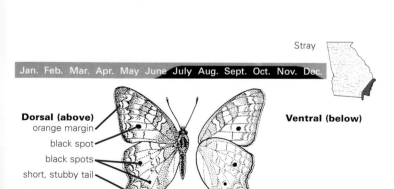

Stray

Jan. Feb. Mar. Apr. May June July Aug. Sept. Oct. Nov. Dec.

Dorsal (above)
orange margin
black spot
black spots
short, stubby tail

Ventral (below)

373

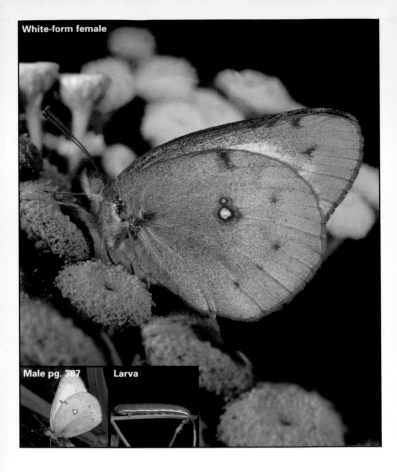

White-form female

Male pg. 387

Larva

Comments: Like its close relative the Orange Sulphur, this aggressive colonizer has likely benefitted from the spread of agriculture. Although often abundant northward, it tends to be an uncommon butterfly in the Deep South. The Clouded Sulphur is generally most abundant in commercial clover or alfalfa fields where it may occasionally become a serious economic pest. The species is sexually dimorphic and seasonally variable. Both yellow and white female forms are common and adults produced under cool, early spring or late fall conditions tend to be smaller and somewhat darker below than those of the summer generations.

Clouded Sulphur
Colias philodice

Family/Subfamily: Whites and Sulphurs (Pieridae)/ Sulphurs (Coliadinae)

Wingspan: 1.90–2.75" (4.8–7.0 cm)

Above: clear lemon yellow with bold, solid black wing borders and a prominent black forewing cell spot; hindwing has a central orange spot

Below: yellow to greenish yellow; row (often faint or occasionally absent) of dark submarginal spots; pink wing fringes; hindwing has central red-rimmed silvery spot and adjacent smaller satellite spot

Sexes: dissimilar; female is less vibrant, often has more black scaling and broader black borders enclosing yellow spots; also has a common white form

Egg: white, laid singly on host leaves

Larva: blue-green with a lateral cream stripe marked in black below and often containing faint red dashes

Larval Host Plants: various weedy herbaceous legumes including Alfalfa, Red Clover, White Clover and White Sweet Clover

Habitat: open, sunny sites including roadsides, fields, alfalfa fields, parks, vacant lots, pastures, gardens

Broods: multiple generations

Abundance: rare to occasional

Compare: White-form females may not be reliably distinguished in the field.

Resident

Jan. Feb. Mar. Apr. May June July Aug. Sept. Oct. Nov. Dec.

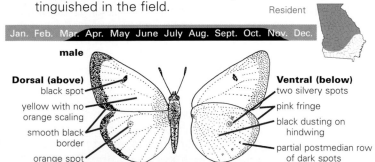

male

Dorsal (above)
black spot
yellow with no orange scaling
smooth black border
orange spot

Ventral (below)
two silvery spots
pink fringe
black dusting on hindwing
partial postmedian row of dark spots

375

Ventral Larva

Comments: Easily our most elegant species, the long-
tailed black-and-white striped Zebra Swallowtail can be
confused with no other resident Eastern butterfly.
Adults have a low, rapid flight and adeptly maneuver
through the understory or among shrubby vegetation.
Seldom found far from stands of its larval host, it is
unlikely to be encountered in highly developed areas
although may occasionally wander into nearby home
gardens. The swallowtail has a proportionately short
proboscis and is thus unable to nectar at many long,
tubular flowers. It instead prefers composites, and is
regularly attracted to white flowers.

Zebra Swallowtail
Eurytides marcellus

Family/Subfamily: Swallowtails (Papilionidae)/ Swallowtails (Papilioninae)

Wingspan: 2.5–4.0" (6.4–10.2 cm)

Above: white with black stripes and long, slender tails; hindwings bear a bright red patch above the eyespot; spring-forms are smaller, lighter and have shorter tails

Below: as above, but with a red stripe through hindwing

Sexes: similar

Egg: light green, laid singly on host leaves or budding branches

Larva: several color forms; may be green, green with light blue and yellow stripes or charcoal with white and yellow stripes

Larval Host Plants: Pawpaw

Habitat: rich woodlands, stream corridors, swamp margins, forest edges and old fields

Broods: multiple generations

Abundance: occasional to common

Compare: unique

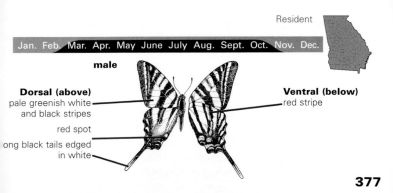

Resident

Jan. Feb. Mar. Apr. May June July Aug. Sept. Oct. Nov. Dec.

male

Dorsal (above)
pale greenish white and black stripes

red spot

ong black tails edged in white

Ventral (below)
red stripe

Male

Larva

Comments: As its name implies, the Dainty Sulphur is our smallest sulphur. Although it disperses northward from southern Texas and the desert Southwest to temporarily colonize much of the central U.S. each year, Florida populations are particularly sedentary. As a result, it is a rare vagrant or temporary colonist to Georgia. Fond of open, disturbed sites where its weedy larval host plants abound, it flies low among the vegetation and is easily overlooked. The butterfly produces distinct seasonal forms that vary considerably in ventral hindwing coloration.

Dainty Sulphur
Nathalis iole

Family/Subfamily: Whites and Sulphurs (Pieridae)/ Sulphurs (Coliadinae)

Wingspan: 0.75–1.25" (1.9–3.2 cm)

Above: lemon yellow with black forewing tip and black bar along trailing edge of forewing; female has orange-yellow hindwings with more extensive black markings

Below: hindwings yellow with greenish markings; seasonally variable; winter-form more heavily pigmented

Sexes: similar, although black markings more extensive on female

Egg: yellow, laid singly on host leaves

Larva: green with thin, lateral yellow and lavender stripes

Larval Host Plants: Spanish Needles and Green Carpetweed

Habitat: open, disturbed sites including roadsides, pastures, utility easements, vacant fields, agricultural land and canal banks

Broods: multiple generations

Abundance: rare

Compare: Barred Sulphur (pg. 383) is larger, has white to brown ventral hindwings and lacks orange along costal margin of the ventral forewing. Little Sulphur (pg. 381) lacks black bar along trailing edge of dorsal forewing.

Visitor Stray

Jan. Feb. Mar. Apr. May June July Aug. Sept. Oct. Nov. Dec.

male

Dorsal (above)
black apex
diffuse black bar

Ventral (below)
black spots
orange scaling
seasonally variable; yellow olive to heavily dusted with black

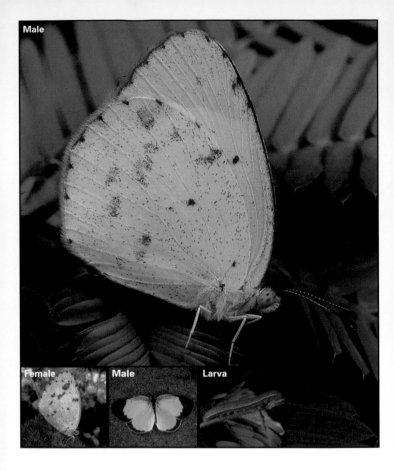

Male

Female   Male   Larva

Comments: The Little Sulphur is a small yellow butterfly
with a low, scurrying flight and an affinity for dry, open
habitats. A year-round resident of the Deep South and
a highly effective colonizer, it readily moves northward
with the onset of warm summer temperatures to
establish temporary breeding populations throughout
much of the eastern U.S., occasionally reaching the
Canadian border. It is particularly abundant in late summer and fall. Like other members of the genus, it
produces different seasonal forms that vary in coloration, behavior and reproductive activity.

Little Sulphur
Eurema lisa

Family/Subfamily: Whites and Sulphurs (Pieridae)/ Sulphurs (Coliadinae)

Wingspan: 1.0–1.6" (2.5–4.1 cm)

Above: bright yellow with black forewing tip, narrow black wing borders and often a faint cell spot; female pale yellow to near white with lighter black markings

Below: seasonally variable; hindwings yellow to near white with pinkish red spot on outer margin (often absent on male) and several small, subtle spots or patches; winter-form darker yellow with additional pattern elements and pink wing fringe

Sexes: similar, although markings and color paler on female

Egg: white, laid singly on host leaves

Larva: green with thin, lateral cream-white stripe

Larval Host Plants: Partridge Pea and Sensitive Pea

Habitat: open, disturbed sites including roadsides, pastures, utility easements, vacant fields, agricultural land and open sandhills

Abundance: occasional to common

Compare: Dainty Sulphur (pg. 379) and Barred Sulphur (pg. 383) both have black dorsal forewing bar. Dainty has black postmedian spots on ventral forewing.

Resident Visitor

Jan. Feb. Mar. Apr. May June July Aug. Sept. Oct. Nov. Dec.

Dorsal (above)
black apex
small black cell spot
black border
wing color variable (yellow to whitish)

Ventral (below)
black basal spots
pinkish red spot (often absent in male)
variable dark spots
seasonally variable

381

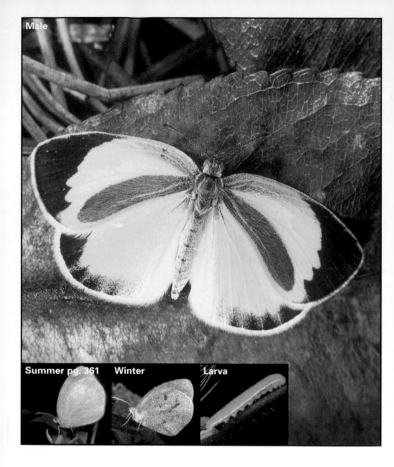

Male

Summer pg. 361   Winter   Larva

Comments: The Barred Sulphur is a common butterfly
of open, weedy sites throughout the Deep South,
where it is particularly abundant in the late summer
and early fall. Adults have a quick, dancing flight and
typically bob among low vegetation. It displays dramatic seasonal variation in color and behavior.
Individuals produced during the summer are short-
lived, reproductively active and almost pure white on
the ventral wings. Winter-forms have highly pigmented
and patterned ventral hindwings and overwinter in
reproductive diapause. It typically rests and feeds with
its wings closed.

Barred Sulphur
Eurema daira

Family/Subfamily: Whites and Sulphurs (Pieridae)/ Sulphurs (Coliadinae)

Wingspan: 1.0–1.8" (2.5–4.6 cm)

Above: seasonally variable; winter-form bright yellow; summer-form whitish; all have black wing tips and a black bar along the trailing edge of forewing; forewing bar is diffuse or absent in female; wide black hindwing border is reduced to a small patch in winter-form

Below: seasonally variable; hindwings light gray to pure white in summer-form; tan to reddish brown with numerous pattern elements in winter-form

Sexes: similar, although black markings paler and less extensive in female

Egg: white, laid singly on host leaves

Larva: green with thin, lateral cream stripe

Larval Host Plants: Joint Vetch and other Fabaceae

Habitat: open, disturbed sites including roadsides, pastures, utility easements, vacant fields, pond margins

Broods: multiple generations

Abundance: rare to common

Compare: Dainty Sulphur (pg. 379) is much smaller; lacks white ventral hindwings. Little Sulphur (pg. 381) lacks black dorsal forewing bar.

Resident Visitor Stray

Jan. Feb. Mar. Apr. May June July Aug. Sept. Oct. Nov. Dec.

male

Dorsal (above)
black apex
large black bar
irregular black marginal patch or continuous border

Ventral (below)
seasonally variable; immaculate white to patterned reddish brown

383

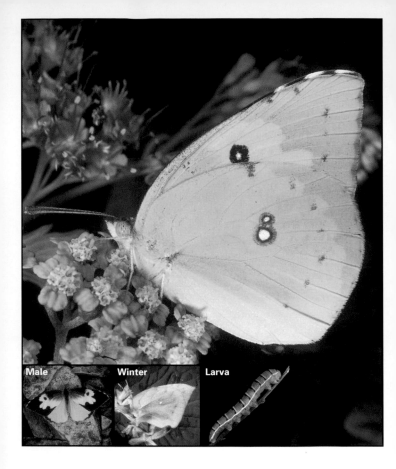

Male Winter Larva

Comments: The only Georgia sulphur with pointed forewings, the Dogface is named after the unique pattern formed by the irregular black and yellow markings on the dorsal surface of each forewing that resembles (with some imagination) the head of a dog in profile. Unfortunately, its distinctive namesake is visible only during flight, as the adults rest and feed with their wings tightly closed. Adults have a strong, rapid flight but frequently stop to nectar at available flowers. Both sexes may also be encountered sipping moisture at damp ground. The adults survive the winter months in reproductive diapause.

Southern Dogface
Zerene cesonia

Family/Subfamily: Whites and Sulphurs (Pieridae)/ Sulphurs (Coliadinae)

Wingspan: 1.9–2.5" (4.8–6.4 cm)

Above: yellow; forewing pointed with broad, black margin highly scalloped to form image of dog's head in profile, single back cell spot and increased black scaling on basal area; hindwing has narrow black margin

Below: hindwings seasonally variable; summer-form is yellow with two small silver spots; winter-form has increased rosy pink scaling

Sexes: similar, although black markings duller and less extensive on female

Egg: white, laid singly on host leaves

Larva: variable; plain green to green with orange lateral stripe and transverse black and yellow stripes

Larval Host Plants: False Indigo, Summer Farewell, White Prairie Clover, Alfalfa and clovers

Habitat: open, dry sites including pastures, pineland, oak scrub, old fields and roadsides

Broods: two or more generations

Abundance: rare to common

Compare: All other sulphurs in Georgia lack the pointed forewing apex.

Resident Visitor

Jan. Feb. Mar. Apr. May June July Aug. Sept. Oct. Nov. Dec.

male

Dorsal (above)
pointed apex

black cell spot

dog's head shaped
in yellow
surrounded by
black

Ventral (below)
seasonally variable;
yellow to heavily
dusted with pink
scales

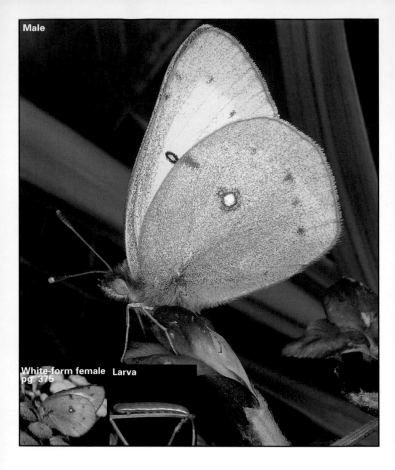

Male

White-form female pg. 375 Larva

Comments: Like its close relative the Orange Sulphur, this aggressive colonizer has likely benefitted from the spread of agriculture. Although often abundant northward, it tends to be an uncommon butterfly in the Deep South. The Clouded Sulphur is generally most abundant in commercial clover or alfalfa fields where it may occasionally become a serious economic pest. The species is sexually dimorphic and seasonally variable. Both yellow and white female forms are common and adults produced under cool, early spring or late fall conditions tend to be smaller and somewhat darker below than those of the summer generations.

Clouded Sulphur
Colias philodice

Family/Subfamily: Whites and Sulphurs (Pieridae)/ Sulphurs (Coliadinae)

Wingspan: 1.90–2.75" (4.8–7.0 cm)

Above: clear lemon yellow with bold, solid black wing borders and a prominent black forewing cell spot; hindwing has a central orange spot

Below: yellow to greenish yellow; row (often faint or occasionally absent) of dark submarginal spots; pink wing fringes; hindwing has central red-rimmed silvery spot and adjacent smaller satellite spot

Sexes: dissimilar; female is less vibrant, often has more black scaling and broader black borders enclosing yellow spots; also has a common white form

Egg: white, laid singly on host leaves

Larva: blue-green with a lateral cream stripe marked in black below and often containing faint red dashes

Larval Host Plants: various weedy herbaceous legumes including Alfalfa, Red Clover, White Clover and White Sweet Clover

Habitat: open, sunny sites including roadsides, fields, alfalfa fields, parks, vacant lots, pastures, gardens

Broods: multiple generations

Abundance: rare to occasional

Compare: Orange Sulphur (pg. 327) has at least some orange scaling above.

Resident

Jan. Feb. Mar. Apr. May June July Aug. Sept. Oct. Nov. Dec.

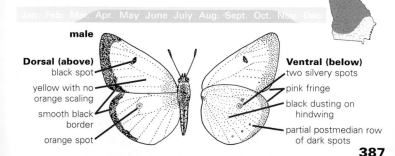

male

Dorsal (above)
black spot

yellow with no orange scaling

smooth black border

orange spot

Ventral (below)
two silvery spots

pink fringe

black dusting on hindwing

partial postmedian row of dark spots

387

Male

Female   Female   Larva

Comments: The Cloudless Sulphur is a large yellow butterfly with a fast, powerful flight. An abundant resident
of the Deep South, it regularly disperses northward to
temporarily colonize much of the eastern U.S. each
year, occasionally reaching the Canadian border. As fall
approaches, the species undergo a massive, southward
migration into the Florida peninsula. The annual event is
one of the Southeast's most impressive natural phe-
nomena. Adults have an extremely long proboscis and
can feed at many long, tubular flowers typically inaccessible to other butterflies.

Cloudless Sulphur
Phoebis sennae

Family/Subfamily: Whites and Sulphurs (Pieridae)/ Sulphurs (Coliadinae)

Wingspan: 2.2–2.8" (5.6–7.1 cm)

Above: unmarked bright lemon yellow; female has broken black wing borders and black forewing spot

Below: male is greenish yellow with virtually no markings; female is yellow with pinkish brown markings and several small silver spots in center of each wing; seasonally variable; winter-form adults more heavily marked

Sexes: similar, although female is more heavily marked

Egg: white, laid singly on host leaves or flower buds

Larva: green or yellow with broad lateral yellow stripe marked with blue spots or transverse bands

Larval Host Plants: various Cassia species including Partridge Pea, Sensitive Pea, Sicklepod Senna, Wild Senna, Maryland Senna and Christmas Senna

Habitat: open, disturbed sites including roadsides, vacant fields, agricultural land, parks and gardens

Broods: multiple generations

Abundance: occasional to abundant

Compare: Clouded Sulphur (pg. 387) and Orange Sulphur (pg. 327) are smaller, have a solid black cell spot on the forewing and broad, solid black wing margins.

Resident Visitor

Jan. Feb. Mar. Apr. May June July Aug. Sept. Oct. Nov. Dec.

Dorsal (above)
bright lemon yellow; female has irregular black margin and hollow round black spot

Ventral (below)
silvery discal cell spot or spots

spotting variable; male almost immaculate, female & winter forms more heavily marked

389

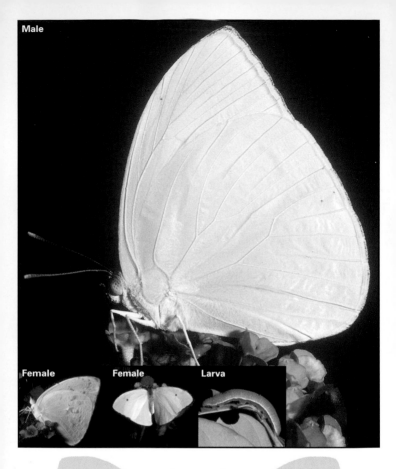

Male

Female   Female   Larva

Comments: The Statira Sulphur is a subtropical butterfly found throughout the year in south Florida. Although primarily limited to the sunshine state, it is a rare vagrant northward and has been recorded in south-eastern portions of Georgia. It is very similar in appearance to the more widespread and common Cloudless Sulphur and may be easily confused when in flight. The large adults have a strong, swift flight and are often found in close association with patches of their larval host. Both sexes readily visit available flowers. Males occasionally sip moisture at mud puddles.

Statira Sulphur
Phoebis statira

Family/Subfamily: Whites and Sulphurs (Pieridae)/ Sulphurs (Coliadinae)

Wingspan: 2.45–3.20" (6.2–8.1cm)

Above: male has two-toned appearance, lemon yellow basally and cream yellow toward outer margin; female is whitish yellow with a narrow black forewing border and round black cell spot

Below: pale yellow to greenish white

Sexes: dissimilar; female pale yellow to greenish white with narrow black forewing border and black cell spot

Egg: pale, laid singly on young host leaves

Larva: yellow green to blue green with a yellow lateral stripe and numerous small black tubercles

Larval Host Plants: Coinvine

Habitat: coastal marshes, mangroves, subtropical scrub, forest margins and gardens

Broods: multiple generations

Abundance: rare

Compare: Cloudless Sulphur (pg. 389) lacks two-toned yellow appearance and has black forewing cell spot with open center.

Stray

Jan. Feb. Mar. Apr. May June July Aug. Sept. Oct. Nov. Dec.

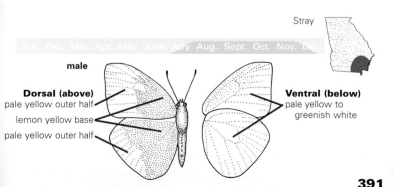

male

Dorsal (above)
pale yellow outer half

lemon yellow base

pale yellow outer half

Ventral (below)
pale yellow to greenish white

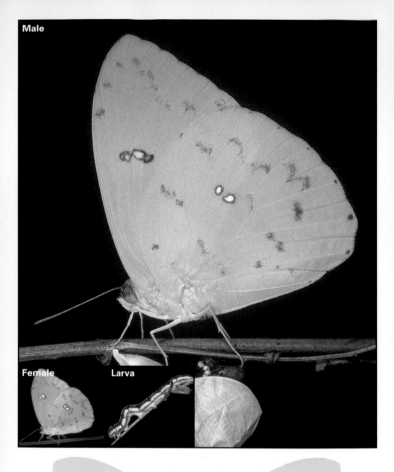

Male

Female   Larva

Comments: Named for its distinct orange forewing band in males, the Orange-barred Sulphur is a large yellow butterfly with a strong, swift flight. Found throughout the year in south Florida, it regularly moves northward each year to temporarily colonize additional portions of the peninsula but is unfortunately a rare stray across the border into Georgia. Most vagrants are encountered in late summer or fall. Unlike many butterflies, it is at home in more urban locations including home gardens, parks and even plant nurseries were its ornamental larval hosts commonly are found.

Orange-barred Sulphur
Phoebis philea

Family/Subfamily: Whites and Sulphurs (Pieridae)/ Sulphurs (Coliadinae)

Wingspan: 2.75–3.40" (7.0–8.6 cm)

Above: male is bright yellow with wide orange forewing bar and orange scaling along trailing edge of hindwing; female is seasonally variable with dark forewing borders and a broken diagonal spot band from the forewing apex

Below: male is bright yellow with small dark spots; summer-form female is orange yellow with fine dark mottling; winter-form female has increased markings

Sexes: dissimilar; female seasonally variable

Egg: white, laid singly on host leaves

Larva: green-yellow with a black lateral stripe and numerous black points

Larval Host Plants: various woody sennas including Candle Plant, Bahana Senna and Christmas Senna

Habitat: open, disturbed sites and urban areas

Broods: multiple generations

Abundance: rare

Compare: Cloudless Sulphur (pg. 389) is smaller and lighter yellow; males lack distinct dorsal orange bands and females lack the dark diagonal spots on forewing.

Stray

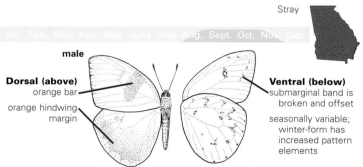

Jan. Feb. Mar. Apr. May June July Aug. Sept. Oct. Nov. Dec.

male

Dorsal (above)
orange bar

orange hindwing margin

Ventral (below)
submarginal band is broken and offset

seasonally variable; winter-form has increased pattern elements

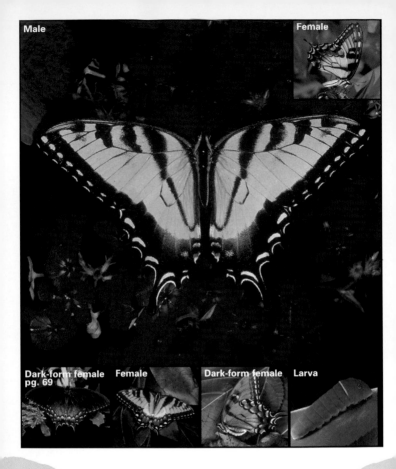

Comments: Easily recognized by its bold, black stripes and bright yellow wings, the Eastern Tiger Swallowtail is the state butterfly of Georgia. Adults have a strong, agile flight and often soar high in the treetops. Although fond of woodlands and waterways, it is equally at home in more urban areas. It is a common garden visitor favoring red, pink and purple flowers. Unlike many other swallowtails, it seldom flutters its wings while feeding. It instead rests on the blossom with wings open. Dark-form females mimic the toxic Pipevine Swallowtail to gain protection from predators. Females exhibit numerous intermediate-colored forms.

Eastern Tiger Swallowtail
Papilio glaucus

Family/Subfamily: Swallowtails (Papilionidae)/ Swallowtails (Papilioninae)

Wingspan: 3.5–5.5" (8.9–14.0 cm)

Above: yellow with black forewing stripes and broad black wing margins; single row of yellow spots along outer edge of each wing

Below: yellow with black stripes and black wing margins; hindwing margins have increased blue scaling and a single submarginal row of yellow-orange, crescent-shaped spots; abdomen yellow with black stripes

Sexes: dissimilar; male always yellow but females have two color forms; yellow female has increased blue scaling in black hindwing border; dark-form female is mostly black with extensive blue hindwing markings

Egg: green, laid singly on upper surface of host leaves

Larva: green; enlarged thorax and two small false eyespots

Larval Host Plants: Black Cherry, Wild Cherry, ash and Tulip Tree

Habitat: mixed forests, wooded swamps, forest edges, suburban gardens, old fields

Broods: multiple generations

Abundance: occasional to common

Compare: Yellow-form unique.

Resident

Jan. Feb. Mar. Apr. May June July Aug. Sept. Oct. Nov. Dec.

male

Dorsal (above)
yellow with black stripes

wide black border

yellow spots

long tail

Ventral (below)
yellow-orange spots

blue scaling

395

BUTTERFLY SOCIETIES

Butterfly societies are a great way to learn more about butterflies and moths in Georgia. They also provide resources to make valuable contacts, share your enthusiasm and get out into the field.

The Lepidopterists' Society
http://alpha.furman.edu/~snyder/snyder/lep/

North American Butterfly Association (NABA) www.naba.org

Southern Lepidopterists' Society www.southernlepsoc.org

PLANTS FOR YOUR BUTTERFLY GARDEN

The following are some recommended adult nectar sources and larval hosts for a Georgia butterfly garden. Most of the species are readily available at most retail garden centers or native plant nurseries. Before purchasing any landscape plant, always inquire with your local nursery personnel as to the specific soil, light, and care requirements needed for optimal growth and maintenance. Additionally, it is also a good idea to understand the plant's growth habit and eventual size at maturity before placing it in the ground. Visit a demonstration garden, a neighbor's yard or a nearby botanical garden to see how the plant looks after it has had a chance to grow a bit. Finally, remember that pesticides are not recommended for any butterfly garden as they can harm the very organisms you wish to attract. Consider using beneficial insects or insecticidal soap first before resorting to more extreme measures. If pesticides are required, always treat pest problems on a local level by applying treatment only to the infested plant and being careful of drift to neighboring vegetation.

Adult Nectar Sources
Herbaceous Perennials

Mexican Milkweed (Asclepias curassavica)

White Swamp Milkweed (Asclepias perennis)

Butterfly Weed (Asclepias tuberosa)

Carolina Aster (Aster caroliniana)

Spanish Needles (Bidens alba)

Florida Paint Brush (Carphephorus corymbosus)

Glorybower (Clerodendron bungei)

False Heather (Cuphea hyssopifolia)

Mist Flower (Eupatorium coelestinum)

Joe-pye Weed (Eupatorium fistulosum)

Indian Blanket (Gaillardia pulchella)

Moss Verbena (Glandularia pulchella)

Creeping Heliotrope (Heliotropium amplexicaule)

ironweed *(Vernonia spp.)*
Lantana *(Lantana camara)*
Purple Weeping Lantana *(Lantana montevidensis)*
blazing star *(Liatris spp.)*
Scarlet Beebalm *(Monarda didyma)*
Horse Mint *(Monarda punctata)*
Fire Spike *(Odontonema strictum)*
Drummond Phlox *(Phlox drummondii)*
Frogfruit *(Phylla nodiflora)*
Pickerelweed *(Pontederia cordata)*

mountain mint *(Pycnanthemum spp.)*
Autumn Sage *(Salvia gregii)*
Mexican Sage *(Salvia leucantha)*
sedum *(Sedum spp.)*
goldenrod *(Solidago spp.)*
Stokes Aster *(Stokesia laevis)*
Tall Verbena *(Verbena bonariensis)*

Shrubs and Trees
Glossy Abelia *(Abelia x grandiflora)*
Red Buckeye *(Aesculus pavia)*
Silktree *(Albizia julibrissin)*
False Indigo *(Amorpha fruticosa)*
Butterfly Bush *(Buddlea davidii)*
Pride of Barbados *(Caesalpina pulcherima)*
Bluebeard *(Caryopteris x chandonensis)*
New Jersey Tea *(Ceanothus americanus)*
Buttonbush *(Cephalanthus occidentalis)*
Redbud *(Cercis canadensis)*
Sweet Pepperbush *(Clethra alnifolia)*

Firebush *(Hamelia patens)*
hibiscus *(Hibiscus spp.)*
Dahoon Holly *(Ilex cassine)*
Yaupon Holly *(Ilex vomitoria)*
Virginia Willow *(Itea virginica)*
Chickasaw Plum *(Prunus angustifolia)*
Black Cherry *(Prunus serotina)*
Hog Plum *(Prunus umbellata)*
Wild Azalea *(Rhododendron canescens)*
Blue Porterweed *(Stachytarpheta urticifolia)*
Sweet Viburnum *(Viburnum odoratissimum)*
Chaste Tree *(Vitex agnus-castus)*

Vines
Coral Vine *(Antigon leptopus)*
Bougainvillea *(Bougainvillea glabra)*
morning glory *(Ipomoea spp.)*

Climbing Hempweed *(Mikania scandens)*
Maypop *(Passiflora incarnata)*
Flame Vine *(Senecio confuses)*

Annuals
Ageratum *(Ageratum houstonianum)*
Spider Plant *(Cleome hasslerana)*
Dianthus *(Dianthus chinensis)*
Globe Amaranth *(Gomphrena globosa)*
impatiens *(Impatiens spp.)*
Sweet Alyssum *(Lobularia maritima)*

Flowering Tobacco *(Nicotiana alata)*
Pentas *(Pentas lanceolata)*
Drummond Phlox *(Phlox drummondii)*
Tropical Sage *(Salvia coccinea)*
Mexican sunflower *(Tithonia spp.)*
Verbena *(Verbena X hybrida)*
Zinnia *(Zinnia elegans)*

Larval Host Plants

acanthus family *(Acanthaceae)*
Alfalfa *(Medicago sativa)*
Alligator Flag *(Thalia geniculata)*
Amaranth, Spiny *(Amaranthus spinosus)*
Arrowwood, Southern *(Viburnum dentatum)*
Ash, Prickly *(Zanthoxylum americanum)*
Ash, Wafer *(Ptelea trifoliata)*
ashes *(Fraxinus spp.)*
aspens *(Populus spp.)*
Aster, Bushy *(Aster dumosus)*
Aster, Frost *(Aster pilosus)*
Aster, Smooth Blue *(Aster laevis)*
Aster, Waxyleaf *(Aster undulatus)*
asters *(Aster spp.)*
Azalea, Flame *(Rhododendron calendulaceum)*
Azalea, Wild *(Rhododendron nudilforum)*
Barnyardgrass *(Echinochloa crus-galli)*
Bay, Red *(Persea borbonia)*
bean family *(Fabacea)*
beans *(Phaseolus spp.)*
Beech, American *(Fagus gandiflora)*
beggarweeds *(Desmodium spp.)*
bentgrass *(Agrostis spp.)*
Birch, Paper *(Betula papyrifera)*
birches *(Betula spp.)*
bittercress *(Cardamine spp.)*
Bitternut *(Juglans cinerea)*
Blackbead *(Pithecellobium keyense)*
blueberries *(Vaccinium spp.)*
Blueberry, Blue Ridge *(Vaccinium vacillans)*
Blueberry, Highbush *(Vaccinium corymbosum)*
bluegrass *(Poa spp.)*
Bluegrass, Kentucky *(Poa pratensis)*
Bluestem, Big *(Andropogon gerardii)*
Bluestem, Little *(Schizachyrium scoparium)*

bluestems *(Andropogon spp.)*
Bride's Feathers *(Aruncus dioicus)*
Bristlegrass, Hooked *(Setaria verticillata)*
Broomweed *(Sida acuta)*
Canarygrass, Reed *(Phalaris arundinacea)*
Candle Plant *(Cassia alata)*
Cane, Giant *(Arundinaria gigantea)*
Cane, Switch *(Arundinaria gigantea spp. tecta)*
cannas *(Canna spp.)*
Carpetgrass, Broadleaf *(Axonopus compressus)*
Carpetweed, Green *(Mollugo verticillata)*
carrot family *(Apiaceae)* includes dill, fennel and parsley
Cassia species *(Cassia spp.)*
Cedar, Atlantic White *(Chamaecyparis thyoides)*
Cedar, Southern Red *(Juniperus silicicola)*
Cherry, Black *(Prunus serotina)*
Cherry, Wild *(Prunus virginiana)*
Chestnut, American *(Castanea dentata)*
Citrus species *(Citrus spp.)*
Clover, Red *(Trifolium pratense)*
Clover, White *(Trifolium repens)*
Clover, White Prairie *(Dalea candida)*
Clover, White Sweet *(Melilotus alba)*
clovers *(Trifolium spp.)*
clovers, bush *(Lespedeza spp.)*
Cohosh, Black *(Cimicifuga racemosa)*
Coinvine *(Dalbergia ecastophyllum)*
composites *(Asteraceae)*
Coneflower, Cut-leaf *(Rudbecia lanciniata)*
Cordgrass, Smooth *(Spartina alterniflora var. glabra)*
cordgrass *(Spartina spp.)*
Crabgrass, Carolina *(Digitaria cognata)*

Crabgrass, Slender *(Digitaria filiformis)*

crabgrass *(Digitaria spp.)*

Croton, Silver *(Croton argyranthemus)*

Crownbeard, White *(Verbesina virginica)*

Cudweed, Purple *(Gnaphalium purpureum)*

Cudweed, Narrow-leaved *(Gnaphalium falcatum)*

Cudweed, Wandering *(Gnaphalium pensylvanicum)*

Cutgrass, Giant *(Zizaniopsis milacea)*

Cutgrass, Rice *(Leersia oryzoides)*

Cutgrass, Southern *(Leersia hexandra)*

Deertongue *(Dichanthelium clandestinum)*

Dock, Curly *(Rumex crispus)*

Dogwood, Flowering *(Cornus florida)*

dogwoods *(Cornus spp.)*

Dutchman's Pipe *(Aristolochia macrophylla)*

Elm, American *(Ulmus americana)*

Elm, Winged *(Ulmus alata)*

elms *(Ulmus spp.)*

Fabacea (Bean Family, includes clovers, vetches and many others)

Fescue, Red *(Festuca rubra)*

Foldwing, Branched *(Dicliptera brachiata)*

foxglove, false *(Agalinus spp.)*

Frogfruit *(Phyla nodiflora)*

Gammagrass, Eastern *(Tripsacum dactyloides)*

glasswort *(Salicornia spp.)*

Goatsbeard *(Aruncus dioicus)*

Goatweed *(Croton argyranthemus)*

gooseberries *(Ribes spp.)*

Gooseberry, Appalachian *(Ribes rotundifolium)*

Grass, Bermuda *(Cynodon dactylon)*

Grass, Indian *(Sorghastrum nutans)*

Grass, Purpletop *(Tridens flavus)*

Grass, Salt *(Distichlis spicata)*

Grass, St. Augustine *(Stenotaphrum secundatum)*

Grass, Stiff-leaved Bear *(Yucca filamentosa)*

Grass, Switch *(Panicum virgatum)*

Grass, Timothy *(Phleum pratense)*

grasses *(Poaceae)*

Gravelweed *(Verbesina helianthoides)*

Groundnut *(Apios americana)*

Hackberry, Common *(Celtis occidentalis)*

Hackberry, Dwarf *(Celtis tenuifolia)*

hackberries *(Celtis spp.)*

hawthorn *(Crataegus spp.)*

Hazelnut, Beaked *(Corylus cornuta)*

heath family *(Ericaceae)*

Hemp, Indian *(Sida rhombifolia)*

Hercules Club *(Zanthoxylum clava-hercules)*

Hickory, Bitternut *(Carya cordiformis)*

Hickory, Pignut *(Carya glabra)*

Hickory, Shagbark *(Carya ovata)*

hickories *(Carya spp.)*

Holly, American *(Ilex opaca)*

Holly, Dahoon *(Ilex cassine)*

Holly, Yaupon *(Ilex vomitoria)*

hollies *(Ilex spp.)*

Hollyhock *(Althaea rosea)*

Hop, Common *(Humulus lupulus)*

Horseflyweed *(Baptisia tinctoria)*

Huckleberry, Black *(Gaylussacia baccata)*

Hyssop, Water *(Bacopa monnieri)*

Indian Shot *(Canna indica)*

Indigo, Blue Wild *(Baptisia australis)*

Indigo, Carolina *(Indigofera caroliniana)*

Indigo, Creeping *(Indigofera spicata)*

Indigo, False *(Amorpha fruticosa)*

Indigo, Hairy *(Indigofera hirsuta)*

Indigo, White Wild *(Baptisia alba)*

Indigo, Wild *(Baptisia tinctoria)*

Kudzu *(Pueraria lobata)*

Lamb's Quarters (Chenopidium album)

Leadwort (Plumbago auriculata)

Leatherleaf (Chamaedaphne calyculata)

legumes (Fabaccae)

Locust, Black (Robinia pseudoacacia)

Lousewort, Canadian (Pedicularis canadensis)

lovegrass (Eragrostis spp.)

Lupine, Wild (Lupinus perennis)

lupin (Lupinus spp.)

mallow family (Malvaceae spp.)

Mallow, False (Malvasreum corchorifolium)

Mallow, Poppy (Callirhoe papaver)

Mango (Mangifera indica)

mannagrass (Glyceria spp.)

Mannagrass, Fowl (Glyceria striata)

Maypop (Passiflora incarnata –passionflower)

milk peas (Galactia spp.)

Milkbark (Drypetes diversifolia)

milkweed family (Asclepias spp.)

Milkweed, Common (Asclepias syriaca)

Milkweed, Mexican (Asclepias currasavica)

Milkweed, Sandhill (Asclepias humistrata)

Milkweed, Swamp (Asclepias incarnata)

Milkweed, White Swamp (Asclepias perennis)

Milkvetch, Canadian (Astragalus canadensis)

milkvetch (Astragalus spp.)

Mistletoe (Phoradendron serotinum)

mustard family (Brassicaceae)

Mustard, Garlic (Alliaria officinalis)

Mustard, Wild (Brassica campestris)

Myrtle, Wax (Myrica cerifera)

Nettle, Canadian Wood (Laportea canadensis)

Nettle, False (Boehmeria cylindrica)

Nettle, Stinging (Urtica dioica)

nettles (Urtica spp.)

Oak, Bear (Quercus ilicifolia)

Oak, Black (Quercus velutina)

Oak, Blackjack (Quercus marilandica)

Oak, Live (Quercus virginiana)

Oak, Myrtle (Quercus myrtifolia)

Oak, Northern Red (Quercus rubra)

Oak, Post (Quercus stellata)

Oak, Red (Quercus rubra)

Oak, Scrub (Quercus ilicifolia)

Oak, Southern Red (Quercus falcata)

Oak, Turkey (Quercus laevis)

Oak, Water (Quercus nigra)

Oak, White (Quercus alba)

oaks (Quercus spp.)

Oatgrass, Poverty (Danthonia spicata)

Orchardgrass (Dactylis glomerata)

Palmetto, Saw (Serenoa repens)

panic grasses (Panicum spp.)

Paspalum, Rustyseed (Paspalum langei)

Passion Flower, Corky-stemmed (Passiflora suberosa)

Passion-Flower, Incense (Passiflora "Incense")

Passion Flower, Yellow (Passiflora lutea)

passion flowers (Passiflora spp.)

pawpaws (Asimina spp.)

Pea, Butterfly (Clitoria mariana)

Pea, Partridge (Cassia fasciculata)

Pea, Sensitive (Cassia nictitans)

Pea, Veiny (Lathyrus venosus)

Peanut, Hog (Amphicarpa bracteata)

Pellitory (Parietaria floridana)

Peppergrass, Field (Lepidium campestre)

Peppergrass, Virginia (Lepidium virginicum)

Pepperweed, Common (Lepidium densiflorium)

Petunia, Carolina Wild (Ruellia caroliniensis)

petunia, wild (Ruellia spp.)

Pine, Eastern White *(Pinus strobus)*
Pine, Loblolly *(Pinus taeda)*
Pine, Pitch *(Pinus rigida)*
Pine, Shortleaf *(Pinus echinata)*
Pine, Virginia *(Pinus virginiana)*
Pipevine, Wooly *(Aristolochia tomentosa)*
pipevines *(Aristolochia spp.)*
Plantain, Narrowleaf *(Plantago lanceolata)*
plantains *(Plantago spp.)*
Plum, American *(Prunus americana)*
Plum, Chickasaw *(Prunus angustifolia)*
Plumbago, Wild *(Plumbago scandens)*
Plumegrass, Silver *(Erianthus alopecuroidum)*
poplars *(Populus spp.)*
pussy-toes *(Antennaria spp.)*
Radish, Wild *(Raphanus raphanistrum)*
Ragweed, Great *(Ambrosia trifida)*
Redbud *(Cercis canadensis)*
Redcedar, Eastern *(Juniperus virginiana)*
Reed, Common *(Phragmites australis)*
Rice, Annual Wild *(Zizania aquatica)*
rockcress *(Arabis spp.)*
rose family (Rosacea)
Saltwort *(Batis maritima)*
Sassafras *(Sassafras albidum)*
Sawgrass *(Cladium jamaicense)*
Sea Rocket *(Cakile lanceolata)*
sedge family *(Cyperaceae)*
Sedge, Shoreline *(Carex hyalinolepis)*
Sedge, Upright *(Carex stricta)*
sedges *(Carex spp.)*
Senna, Bahana *(Cassia chapmanii)*
Senna, Christmas *(Cassia bicapsularis)*
Senna, Coffee *(Cassia occidentalis)*
Senna, Maryland *(Cassia marilandica)*

Senna, Sicklepod *(Cassia obtusifolia)*
Senna, Wild *(Cassia hebecarpa)*
sennas *(Cassia spp.)*
serviceberry *(Amelanchier spp.)*
Shepherd's Purse *(Capsella bursa-pastoris)*
Shorthusk, Bearded *(Brachyelytrum erectum)*
Sida *(Sida acuta)*
snake-herb *(Dyschoriste spp.)*
Snakeroot, Virginia *(Aristolochia serpentaria)*
Sneezeweed *(Helenium autumnale)*
Sorrel, Sheep *(Rumex acetosella)*
Spanish Dagger *(Yucca aloifolia)*
Spanish Needles *(Bidens alba)*
Sparkleberry *(Vaccinium arboreum)*
Spicebush *(Lindera benzoin)*
Sugarberry *(Celtis laevigata)*
Sumac, Fragrant *(Rhus aromatica)*
Sumac, Staghorn *(Rhus typhina)*
Sumac, Winged *(Rhus copallina)*
sumacs *(Rhus spp.)*
Summer Farewell *(Dalea pinnata)*
sunflowers *(Helianthus spp.)*
Sweet Everlasting *(Gnaphalium obtusifolium)*
Sweetleaf, Common *(Symplocos tinctoria)*
Switchcane *(Arundinaria gigantea var.tecta)*
Switchgrass *(Panicum virgatum)*
Tamarind, Wild *(Lysiloma latisiliquum)*
Tea, Mexican *(Chenopidium ambrosiodes)*
Tea, New Jersey *(Ceanothus americana)*
Thistle, Yellow *(Cirsium horridulum)*
thistles *(Cirsium spp.)*
Threeawn, Arrowfeather *(Aristida purpurascens var. virgata)*
toadflax *(Linaria spp.)*
Toothwort, Cut-leaf *(Dentaria laciniata)*
toothworts *(Dentaria spp.)*

Tulip Tree *(Liriodendron tulipifera)*
Turtlehead *(Chelone glabra)*
twinflower *(Dyschoriste spp.)*
vegetables (broccoli, cabbage and others)
Velvetgrass, Common *(Holcus lanatus)*
Vetch, Carolina *(Vicia caroliniana)*
Vetch, Crown *(Coronilla varia)*
Vetch, Joint *(Aeschyomene americana)*
vetch, milk *(Astragalus spp.)*
vetches *(Vinca spp.)*
viburnum *(Viburnum spp.)*
Violet, Bird's-foot *(Viola pedata)*
violets *(Viola spp.)*
Walnut, Black *(Juglans nigra)*
walnuts *(Juglans spp.)*
Whitegrass *(Leersia virginica)*
Willow, Black *(Salix nigra)*
Willow, Carolina *(Salix caroliniana)*
Willow, Weeping *(Salix babylonica)*
willows *(Salix spp.)*
Wing-stem *(Verbesina alternifolia)*
Wisteria, American *(Wisteria frutescens)*
wisterias *(Wisteria spp.)*
Woodoats, Indian *(Chasmanthium latifolium)*
Woolgrass *(Scirpus cyperinus)*
Yellowrocket, Garden *(Barbarea vulgaris)*
yuccas *(Yucca spp.)*

CHECKLIST/INDEX

Use the boxes to check the butterflies you've seen.

ABOUT THE AUTHOR

Jaret C. Daniels, Ph.D., is a professional nature photographer and entomologist at the University of Florida specializing in the ecology and conservation biology of Lepidoptera. He has authored numerous scientific papers, popular articles and books on butterflies, insects, wildlife conservation and butterfly gardening. He currently lives in Gainesville, Florida, with his wife Stephanie.

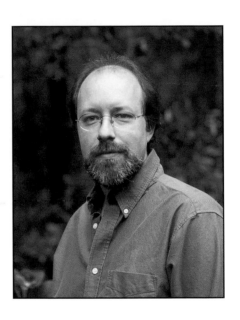